'Chantal Sicile-Kira's book is a clearly written, well-organised, carefully documented compilation of important information and useful advice. It will provide invaluable help and guidance to parents and professionals alike, especially those who are new to the world of autism. This book is not merely highly recommended – it is indispensable!'

Bernard Rimland, PhD
Director of the Autism Research Institute, Founder of the Autism Society of America, Editor of Autism Research Review International *and Chief Technical Advisor,* Rain Man

'Autism is one of those conditions about which much is said and written, but little is actually understood. Even when you speak with leading neurologists, they will often admit to having little knowledge, let alone comprehension of autism's manifold guises and complexities. More tellingly, the very word 'autism' is a profoundly loaded one. To be informed that your child is 'autistic' may be one of the most devastating to be visited on a parent – but as autism isn't a singular condition, but a spectrum of conditions (many of which can respond to treatment and assorted therapies), it is also frequently not the tragedy of a lifetime for either the child or the parents. Given autism's high profile now in the media, Chantal Sicile-Kira's book could not be more timely.

'This will be one of those smart, authoritative, user-friendly volumes which will not only demystify autism for the public, but will also be the essential book that both parents, health professionals, and a wide general readership will reach for in order to fathom this confounding condition. It has the potential to become a benchmark book – a true perennial, especially given that there is no such volume like this in the market now. Which makes this a book that's needed and one which should win a huge international audience.'

Douglas Kennedy
Bestselling author of The Big Picture, The Job *and* The Pursuit of Happiness

'Both parents and professionals will find a wealth of useful information in this user-friendly book, written by a parent who really knows about living with a child on the autistic spectrum.'

Cathy Mercer
Publications Department, The National Autistic Society

'Parents will find this book a huge help. It answers many of the questions we get asked on the Autism Helpline and, because Chantal is a parent herself, parents will find her approach very helpful. She packs a huge amount of information into this book without overwhelming the reader with facts.'

Sarah Benson
Autism Helpline

'This is the book we've all been waiting for. An essential source of information and advice in plain every day language that can help anyone who is affected by autism today, from the parent of a newly diagnosed child, to someone who has been in the trenches for years. Kudos to Chantal for providing us with this long overdue, user-friendly, how-to guide for dealing with autism.'

Portia Iverson
Co-founder and Scientific Liaison, Cure Autism Now Foundation (CAN)

'The word autism brings with it many fears, speculations and misunderstandings. Whether it is your own child or a friend or relative's who is diagnosed, this book will provide important information and insights to help you understand and participate in the child's development through having a better knowledge of this spectrum disorder. This reference guide is also invaluable for anyone in the community who comes across individuals with autism in their line of work.'

Anthony Edwards
ER's Dr. Mark Greene

'Chantal Sicile-Kira has written an encyclopaedic book with care and concern for those persons who must deal with autism. It reads clearly and provides answers to the important questions. I recommend it most highly.'

Joseph E. Morrow, PhD
Professor of Psychology, California State University, Sacramento and President, Applied Behaviour Consultants, Sacramento

Autism

Spectrum Disorders

The Complete Guide

by

Chantal Sicile-Kira

Vermilion
LONDON

9 10

Published in 2003 by Vermilion, an imprint of Ebury Publishing

Ebury Publishing is a Random House Group company

The Random House Group Limited Reg. No. 954009

Addresses for companies within the Random House Group can be found at
www.rbooks.co.uk

A CIP catalogue record for this book is available from the British Library

The Random House Group Limited supports The Forest Stewardship
Council (FSC), the leading international forest certification organisation.
All our titles that are printed on Greenpeace approved FSC certified paper
carry the FSC logo. Our paper procurement policy can be found at
www.rbooks.co.uk/environment

Mixed Sources
Product group from well-managed
forests and other controlled sources
www.fsc.org Cert no. TT-COC-2139
© 1996 Forest Stewardship Council
FSC

Printed and bound in the UK by CPI Mackays, Chatham ME5 8TD

ISBN 9780091891602

Copies are available at special rates for bulk orders. Contact the sales development
team on 020 7840 8487 or visit www.booksforpromotions.co.uk for more information.

To buy books by your favourite authors and register for offers, visit www.rbooks.co.uk

For Jeremy, Rebecca and Daniel
the stars of my universe

I know of nobody who is purely autistic or purely neurotypical. Even God had some autistic moments, which is why the planets all spin.

JERRY NEWPORT, *YOUR LIFE IS NOT A LABEL*

The history of man's progress is a chronicle of authority refuted.

AUTHOR UNKNOWN

Contents

Acknowledgements

Many people have contributed in different ways to this book. However, if it were not for two people in particular, the thought of writing a sort of 'guide for dummies' to autism would never had occurred to me. First of all my son, Jeremy, is the reason this book exists at all. His attempts to understand our world, coupled with his extraordinary (if a bit obsessive) attachment to very simple objects, never ceases to amaze me.

Secondly, my friend Debra Ginsberg (*Waiting, Raising Blaze, About My Sisters*) convinced me that I could – and should – write the book I always wished I could find in a bookshop. For this, and her constant support and pearls of wisdom, I am ever grateful.

If it were not for Douglas Kennedy, Charlie Viney, my agent and Amanda Hemmings, my editor, this book might still be a manuscript. Many thanks to them for sharing my vision.

A book of this sort could not have seen the light of day without the encouragement and support of some autism experts who gave generously of their time to read parts of the manuscript, and give me input: Bernard Rimland PhD (Director, Autism Research Institute), Portia Iverson (co-founder and Scientific Liaison for Cure Autism Now), Joseph Morrow PhD (founder, Applied Behavior Consultants), Jo Radford (Clinic Director, London Early Autism Project); Cathy Tissot, PhD (trustee, Parents' Autism Campaign for Education) and last, but not least, Temple Grandin PhD (Colorado State University). These amazing, driven people have given selflessly of their time and effort over the years to advance the cause of people with ASDs. They, and any non-profit organisation they may be affiliated with, deserve our support.

Leslie Macdonald is to be acknowledged for giving of her time and expertise on matters of education in the UK. For that, as well as her advice and support when I arrived as a new parent in Berkshire all those years ago, I am forever grateful.

Thank you to all those at The Berkshire Autism Society for their information-sharing. Their activism is to be admired and is a constant reminder that the power of a group of parents should never be underestimated.

Thanks to Soma and Tito Rajarshi Mukhopadhyay and others like them who have generously given of their time so that more may be known about ASDs. Thanks to Lenny Schafer for keeping us posted with the daily Schafer Autism Report.

The acknowledgements would not be complete without a heartfelt thank you to all the professionals, including tutors, who have taught my son or provided respite over the years. He wouldn't be who he is today if it weren't for your expertise and friendship.

Special thanks go to Candy and Alia for holding the fort so I could meet my deadlines.

Thanks to all my family and good friends on both sides of the Atlantic (you know who you are).

To Rebecca and Jeremy, thank you for understanding that you *are* more important than the book, but that I still needed the time to write it. Your patience (and snacks delivered with a hug) were much appreciated.

And lastly, to my husband Daniel, thank you for your unwavering loyalty and constant support on this journey called life.

Foreword

The autism/Asperger spectrum is very broad, ranging from a brilliant scientist to a person who remains non-verbal with a severe disability. There are many characteristics that are the same along the entire continuum. Two of the most important are problems with social situations and sensory sensitivities. Sensory problems are often overlooked. When I was a child, a loud school bell was like a dentist drill hitting a nerve. It hurt my ears.

Chantal Sicile-Kira originally contacted me to discuss sensory processing issues. She told me she was writing a general reference guide to autism spectrum disorders. This led to a series of phone calls and faxes. Finally, we met at an autism conference in San Diego, where I had been asked to speak, and Chantal handed me her manuscript, asking me if I would read it and tell her what I thought.

I read her book on my plane trip back home, calling Chantal from two different airports to tell her how impressed I was with the thoroughness of her manuscript, as well as her ability to take complex information and simplify it, rendering it understandable to everyone. This book gives the general public, professionals and parents a better understanding of the autism/Asperger spectrum, as well as providing lists of resources useful to those who are on the spectrum, and those who work and care for them.

I would like to give a word of advice to all people who work with children or adults on the spectrum: develop talents that can be turned into job skills or hobbies. Social interaction will develop through an interest that can be shared with other people. Special education teachers often put too much emphasis on deficits and not enough on building on areas of strength. As a visual thinker I was good at drawing, and my visual and drawing skills became the basis for my career as a designer of livestock facilities.

Skills tend to be uneven; an individual may be good at one thing and not another. I was good at drawing and building things, but algebra was incomprehensible because I could not visualise it. The minds of people on the spectrum are usually specialised. I have observed that there are three basic types of specialised minds: the visual thinking mind; the music and maths mind; and the non-visual numbers and language translator mind. Teachers and parents should work on utilising these strengths.

Individuals with autism often become fixated on a single thing, such as trains or aeroplanes. Use the strong motivation of the fixation to encourage activities. If a child likes trains, use trains in maths problems, read a train book to teach literacy, or invent a game involving trains that can be played with other children. A good teacher takes the fixation and broadens it out. Many great scientists pursued a childhood interest.

The autism/Asperger spectrum is a continuum from normal to abnormal. In my book *Thinking in Pictures*, I profiled former scientists such as Einstein who had childhood autistic traits. The British researcher Simon Baron-Cohen has also written on the appearance of autistic traits in scientists and physicists. When does 'computer nerd' become Asperger's? There is no black and white dividing line.

Individuals who remain non-verbal will often have something they are good at. Many of them have fantastic memories. They may be good at jobs such as reshelving books in the library or taking inventory of the stock at a shop. They would be good at a job that most people would find boring. Develop these skills so they can be useful.

People on the spectrum who have a fulfilling life now often had four important assets earlier in their life: early education and treatment; medication or other treatment for severe anxiety, depression or sensory sensitivities; development of their talents; and mentors and teachers to help them.

What I really like about Chantal's book are the many references to and quotes from people on the autism/Asperger spectrum. This information from personal experiences will give both parents and professionals much-needed insight into how autistic people perceive the world.

Temple Grandin, PhD
Author, *Thinking in Pictures*
Associate Professor of Animal Science at Colorado State University
Founder and President of Grandin Livestock Handling Systems, Inc.

Preface

Twenty-five years ago, in need of a full-time job to sustain me through college, I applied for a position at Fairview State Hospital for the Developmentally Disabled in Orange County in California, and was hired to teach adolescents self-help and social skills in preparation for community living. This was my first contact with the intriguing world of autism and some wonderfully unusual people (including the staff). I then worked for a short while as a case manager at Orange County Regional Center for the Developmentally Disabled, providing information and resources to families and their children. Twelve years later I had my son, Jeremy, who was eventually diagnosed with autism.

Nine years ago, unhappy with the educational provision my son was receiving in Berkshire, I removed him from school and became one of the first parents in the United Kingdom to start up a Lovaas-type home programme. Along with another parent, I hired college students and asked a Lovaas-trained professional to come to the UK to provide training workshops. Two of those students have since gone on to work as professionals in the field of autism spectrum disorders (ASDs).

Today Jeremy is fourteen, and I have this sense of déjà vu, just like Bill Murray's character in the movie *Groundhog Day* who wakes up every morning and lives the same day over and over again. For twenty-five years I've been getting up and researching for resources and new information in different countries, creating solutions 'outside the box', advocating, going on community outings and trying to teach appropriate behaviour in public, only now it's to and for my own son.

Living in three different countries and challenging the status quo in each one has developed my resourcefulness, creative thinking and negotiating skills to a level I never dreamed possible. Having a child with autism is challenging, but building all the family, educational, medical and community support systems needed is the real challenge. And everyone has a responsible part in this, not just the parents.

Thankfully, attitudes to autism have changed over the past years and people in general appear to be more tolerant, which is a good thing considering that ASDs have recently risen to epidemic proportions in certain parts of the world. Yet there still seems to be a lack of knowledge on this subject. That is why I have written this book, as a necessary general reference guide for a wide audience, including child-care workers, after-school programme leaders, scout masters, shopkeepers, bus drivers, as well as parents, teachers and other professionals.

I could have used a book such as this twenty-five years ago, when I tried to learn whatever I could to help my clients, and again after having my son. Since then, I have spent tens of thousands of hours learning about ASDs, how to navigate through the different systems and create what my son needs. It seems a waste to hoard it all for the benefit of a few people – thus I have written this book in the hope that it will inform and help many people. Knowledge is power, so use this guide to empower yourself.

Notes About the Book

I have used the term 'autism spectrum disorders' (ASDs) throughout this book to mean autism, pervasive developmental disorder (PDD) and Asperger's. If used, the word 'autism' means autism spectrum disorders. When speaking specifically about people with Asperger's syndrome I have used 'Asperger's'. As three out of four people with an ASD are male, I have most often used the pronoun 'he'.

Some resources are listed in the main text, and many more in the resources section in the back.

This book has been compiled to serve an informational purpose. None of the information is meant to be legal, medical or educational advice. Any treatments, therapies or interventions should be discussed with a competent professional. Please consult your GP before changing, stopping or starting any medical treatment. Laws and regulations change, and so the reader should get professional advice concerning matters of legal rights in terms of educational provision, health benefits and any other benefits. The author and publishers disclaim, as far as the law allows, any liability arising directly or indirectly from the use, or misuse, of the information contained in this book.

For more information about the author visit her website:

www.chantalsicile-kira.com

Autism
Spectrum Disorders

CHAPTER ONE

The Myths and History of Autism Spectrum Disorders

Beyond the world of what and why
Beyond the reasons and the concrete,
The 'abstract' lies with a richer glory
Somewhere in imaginations deep!

TITO RAJARSHI MUKHOPADHYAY, *BEYOND THE SILENCE*

Ten years ago, we were in the local doctor's office in a small village in Berkshire, where we had just moved. I was trying to explain to the receptionist why my three-year-old was obsessively walking around and around the waiting room, touching each chair he passed whether it was empty or not and obviously disturbing the other patients sitting in those chairs. We'd been waiting almost an hour to see the doctor. 'My son is autistic, he can't wait any longer,' I said. The receptionist replied, 'Well, if he is artistic, have him draw. Here are some crayons to keep him busy.' As she walked away, she mumbled under her breath about how badly behaved some children were, and how impatient the parents.

THE MYTHS ABOUT AUTISM SPECTRUM DISORDERS

Sad but true, this type of misunderstanding still occurs. However, as the number of people diagnosed escalates to epidemic proportions, most people today have come across autism spectrum disorders (ASDs). Still, as ASDs are mysterious and have attributes that can be strange, awe-inspiring and unexplainable, there are many myths that abound. Here are a few of them.

Myth number one:

the Rain Man myth – everyone with an ASD has a special, extraordinary talent

In the movie *Rain Man*, Dustin Hoffman plays Raymond, a young man who has autism. He goes on a road trip with his brother, played by Tom Cruise. Raymond has an incredible gift with numbers. His brother discovers this, and takes him off to Las Vegas so he can gamble and win some money.

There are certainly individuals with ASDs who have extraordinary talent, or more usually, an inconsistent profile where they excel or do well in one area, and have low performance in others. For example, years ago I worked with a young man who had a gift for memorising and was infatuated with sports. On my first day of work at Fairview State Hospital, he came up to me and said, 'I used be a sports newscaster. Ask me any question about sports and I'll fill you in.' He had memorised the pertinent statistics for the Olympic Games from the previous two decades. We talked sports and I did find him a bit odd. For a few minutes I entertained the thought that he was another employee, thinking what a dedicated person he must be to quit working for the media and join the staff at this hospital. Then I looked on my roster and realised he was one of my students for functional living skills. He definitely had a talent for sports statistics, but hadn't yet learned how to dress himself independently or tie his own shoes.

However, there are many more individuals with ASDs who have no particular special talent, any more than the rest of us do.

Myth number two:

everyone who has an ASD is a genius, a Thomas Jefferson in waiting

It is true that some people with ASDs are geniuses, but not everyone is. Thomas Jefferson, it appears, had characteristics of Asperger's, within the range of modern diagnostic criteria. Others such as Beethoven, Charles Mackintosh, Isaac Newton and Einstein have all been mentioned as famous people who could have been diagnosed as on the spectrum. However, for every person with an ASD who is a genius, there are many more who are mere mortals like ourselves.

Myth number three:
everyone who has an ASD is mentally retarded

First of all, because of the nature of ASDs, it is difficult to ascertain the cognitive level of people with these disorders. Many people with autism have communicated that they are sensory-overloaded. Some or all of their senses are 100 per cent more sensitive than in others, and therefore they process the environment differently from neuro-typicals (i.e. individuals considered to be 'normal'). People who are unable to speak, but have learned to type or write independently, express the difficulty they have in controlling their motor planning, i.e. sending signals to their muscles, much like people who have had strokes. In his book *Beyond the Silence*, Tito Rajarshi Mukhopadhyay explains, 'Of course from my knowledge of biology I knew that I had voluntary muscles and involuntary muscles. I also knew that my hands and legs were made of voluntary muscles. But I experimented with myself that when I ordered my hand to pick up a pencil, that I could not do it. I remember long back when I had ordered my lips to move I could not do it.'

Secondly, if you start with the perception that someone is mentally retarded, the expectations for that individual aren't going to be very high, and he will never be given the opportunity to reach as far as he can go. Better to hope he's a genius and be disappointed than never to have given a person the benefit of the doubt.

The reality is that the population of people with ASDs is much like the general population: some of us have special talents, some of us are geniuses and some of us are retarded. But most of us are just average earthlings.

Myth number four:
everyone who has a symptom of an ASD has an ASD

If a person has one or two characteristics of an ASD, it does not necessarily mean he has an ASD. As explained later, in Chapter Two, it is the number and severity of behavioural characteristics in the areas of social interaction, communication and repetitive stereo-typical behaviours that causes concern. That is why it is important to consult with a medical professional who is familiar with ASDs.

> FOOD FOR THOUGHT
> ## Even People With Autism Can Change
>
> Over the years, I have read enough to know that there are still many parents, and professionals, too, who believe that 'once autistic, always autistic'. This dictum has meant sad and sorry lives for many children diagnosed, as I was early in life, as autistic. To these people it is incomprehensible that the characteristics of autism can be modified and controlled. However, I feel strongly that I am living proof that they can . . .
>
> Temple Grandin and Margaret M. Scariano,
> *Emergence: Labeled Autistic*

Myth number five:
there is no cure for (or recovery from) ASDs

Tremendous advances have been made in the field of ASDs over the last decade. Granted, there is still no magic pill that cures everyone. However, there are cases of children who were diagnosed as clearly having ASDs, and who are now considered to be neurotypical or symptom-free by professionals (*Let Me Hear Your Voice* by Catherine Maurice; *The Sound of a Miracle* by Annabel Stehli). There are also accounts written by people who have recovered significantly from ASDs (*Nobody Nowhere* and *Somebody Somewhere* by Donna Williams; *Emergence: Labeled Autistic* by Temple Grandin and Margaret M. Scariano; *Thinking in Pictures* by Temple Grandin). Recovery means that they have overcome some of the symptoms they had that made it difficult for them to live full and successful lives in a world created by neurotypicals.

Myth number six:
people with ASDs have no emotions and do not get attached to other people

It is true that many people with an ASD show emotions in a different way from neurotypicals. However, just because a person does not show emotions in the way we are used to seeing them exhibited does not mean that they don't have feelings. One only has to read accounts by people with autism to realise that some individuals express emotions differently (*Nobody Nowhere* by Donna Williams) or are unable to show emotion at all because they are not in control of their muscles or motor planning (*Beyond the Silence* by Tito Rajarshi Mukhopadhyay).

It is very clear from reading books by people with autism (*Your Life is Not a Label*, by Jerry Newport; *Pretending to be Normal* by Liane Willey) that they are capable of forming attachments with other people, and do so. Some people with autism date, get married and have children, just as we do. Perhaps they are less expressive than others about their feelings, but that does not mean they are not attached to others.

Food for Thought
Does Autism Need to Be Cured?

Perhaps ethical consideration should be given to the concept of 'curing' autism. Saying that autism needs to be cured gives credence to the idea that everyone has to be 'normal', that there is something wrong with being different. Granted, many people would find life a lot easier if they did not have an ASD. But perhaps those who have extraordinary talents would not have those gifts, either. Would Beethoven have created his Ninth Symphony? Would Einstein have come up with his theory of relativity? Temple Grandin (who has designed one-third of all the livestock handling facilities in the United States) believes that her talent for solving concept problems is down to her 'ability to visualize and see the world in pictures', which can be attributed to having an ASD.

Gerald Newport is a 52-year-old author with Asperger's syndrome, and was a speaker at the 2001 National Conference on Autism put on by the Autism Society of America. His speech was entitled 'Every Child With Autism Must Become a Success', and was inspired by his concern about 'The unrealistic and divisive notion in our community that becoming normal is the only and optimal goal for our consumers. I will never be normal. I have become a success. I have acquired enough self-esteem to do my best in every endeavour. That is what former UCLA basketball coach John Woodon, calls success. I will focus on how we can teach all of our children to have self-esteem, make the most of who they are and lead full lives, normal or not.'

THE HISTORY OF AUTISM SPECTRUM DISORDERS

The labels 'autism' and 'autistic' come from the Greek work *autos*, meaning self, and were coined in 1911 by a psychiatrist, Eugen Bleuler. He used the terms to describe an aspect of schizophrenia, where an individual withdraws totally from the outside world into himself.

The early days – Kanner and Asperger

In the early 1940s both Leo Kanner and Hans Asperger, pioneers in the field of autism, used these terms in their publications (independently of each other), describing children with the characteristics we recognise today as being autistic; and hence the label autism was born. Kanner, an Austrian psychiatrist based at Johns Hopkins University in America, was the first to identify autism as a distinct neurological condition, in 1943, although he could not specify a cause. In 1944, Asperger, a Viennese paediatrician, published a doctoral thesis using the term autistic in his study of four boys. Both professionals described children who developed special interests, but also had deficits in the areas of communication and social interaction. Kanner's description was of children with severe autism, with the conclusion that it was a disastrous condition to have. Asperger's description was of more able children, and he felt that there might be some positive features to autism which could lead to great achievements as an adult. For thirty years, Kanner's description became the most widely recognised.

The term Asperger's syndrome was first used by Lorna Wing in a paper published in 1981, in which she described children much like the more able boys Asperger had described many years earlier. Unfortunately, Asperger died in 1980, and never knew that a few years later a condition named after him would become well known worldwide.

The 'refrigerator mother' days – Bettelheim

Meanwhile, Bruno Bettelheim, a Hungarian psychotherapist, reared his head in the mid to late 1940s, claiming that the source of autism was 'refrigerator mothers': cold, unfeeling parents who pushed their children into mental isolation. Bettelheim had spent 1943 and 1944 in concentration camps, and he likened the mental isolation of these children to that of the prisoners of war released from such camps after World War II. Bettelheim eventually moved to the United States and became director of the Sonia Shankman Orthogenic School in Chicago, where he was lauded for many years internationally. Sadly, his theories were widely accepted for two decades, though eventually his school fell into disrepute. Thanks to him, for many years autism was considered a mental illness (as opposed to a developmental disability), leading to limited treatment options for these children. Even as late as the early 1990s a few civilised nations (namely France and Switzerland) still considered autism a mental illness, offering psychoanalysis and psychiatric hospitals as the primary treatment.

In 1997, *The Creation of Dr B: A Biography of Bruno Bettelheim* by Richard Pollack was published. Pollack, whose younger brother attended the Orthogenic School where Bettelheim was director, conducted extensive research for his book. He discovered that before emigrating to the United States, Bettelheim had worked in the family lumber business and earned a degree in art history, and in fact did not have any qualifications to run a school or theorise about the causes of autism. Pollack also revealed that as director of the Orthogenic School, Bettelheim was known for his volatile, sadistic nature. He terrorised and beat the children, and treated the parents with disdain, blaming them for their children's problems and only allowing them infrequent visits.

A huge step forward – Rimland

We owe the dramatic change in psychiatry's perception of autism to Bernard Rimland, PhD, a psychologist and father of a son with an ASD. In 1964 Rimland wrote *Infantile Autism: The Syndrome and Its Implications for a Neural Theory of Behavior*, recognising autism as a biological disorder, not an emotional illness. This book influenced the choices that were made in treatment methods for autism. Rimland is the founder of the Autism Society of America (ASA) (www.autism-society.org), the first parent-driven organisation to provide information and support to parents and professionals. He also founded the

---

FOOD FOR THOUGHT
Shades of Bettelheim

My son was born in Paris. Having worked with individuals with ASDs in the United States, I recognised early on that he had this disability. We sought help and guidance, and although the professionals denied he had autism, they sent us to a psychoanalyst. The psychoanalyst had plenty of Bettelheim books on her shelves, yet was quick to explain that she did not subscribe to Bettelheim's 'refrigerator mother' theory. However, after a few sessions it was decided that my son had suffered separation issues from breast-feeding. This the analyst gleaned from watching him spin round objects (which reminded him of his mother's breasts) and chase after one that he had 'lost' when it fell and rolled under a piece of furniture.

Autism Research Institute (ARI) (www.autismresearchinstitute.com), in 1967, creating a worldwide network of parents and professionals concerned with autism, which is still going strong. (Note of interest: Rimland was technical adviser for the movie *Rain Man*.)

The present – it's a spectrum disorder, and it's on the rise

In the not too distant past, professionals used terms including autism, Asperger's, pervasive developmental disorder (PDD), PDD Not Otherwise Specified (PDD-NOS), high-functioning, low-functioning and others when discussing ASDs. Most recently these syndromes, and others that share some of the same symptoms, have been placed under the umbrella term autism spectrum disorders. Some professionals still do not include Asperger's syndrome under the term ASDs. However, because they share some of the same symptoms and therefore the same treatments, in this book the term ASDs is considered to include Asperger's syndrome.

Though the different ASDs may vary in the number and intensity of the behavioural symptoms they share, it is still the same three characteristics that are impaired: social relationships, social communication and imaginative thought. These characteristics can be present in a wide variety of combinations. Two people, both diagnosed with the same label, can have varying skills, deficits and aptitudes. One of them could be severely incapacitated, the other might appear only to be a bit odd and lacking in social graces. What it all boils down to is that there is no standard type or typical person with an ASD, just as there is no standard type of non-autistic or neurotypical individual. Thus, people with ASDs present a wide spectrum of abilities.

Another important development is the increase in the number of books written and websites created by those who have ASDs. Some books are about what it was like growing up with an ASD (*Pretending to be Normal* by Liane Willey; *Nobody Nowhere* by Donna Williams; *Beyond the Wall* by Stephen Shore; *Emergence: Labeled Autistic* by Temple Grandin and Margaret M. Scariano). Others give advice based on experience and knowledge about what is helpful for someone with an ASD (*Freaks, Geeks and Asperger Syndrome* by Luke Jackson; *Autism: An Inside-Out Approach* by Donna Williams; *Thinking in Pictures* by Temple Grandin; *Your Life is Not a Label* by Jerry Newport). The insights the authors share about what sensations they are feeling, why they act the way they do and what has helped them in their struggles give us a glimpse of what it can be like to have an ASD. Such accounts and suggestions are invaluable in helping those trying to understand the behaviours of individuals unable to communicate about themselves, though it must be borne in mind that these experiences are personal and may not be true for everyone with an ASD.

Another change in recent years is the dramatic rise in the number of individuals diagnosed with ASDs, now said to be reaching epidemic proportions in the UK, the US and other countries. In 1979, it was estimated that in the UK 35 children in 10,000 would be diagnosed with autism; by 1993 the figure had risen to 91 in 10,000 (the National Autistic Society), and it is estimated that there are now approximately 500,000 people somewhere on the spectrum. Studies in the US, Iceland and Japan have all recorded incidence rates of autism much higher than previously assumed, some worse than in the UK. A US Department of

Education study from 1992 to 1997 reported a 173 per cent increase in the number of children with autism in public schools, compared with a growth of all non-autism disabilities in the same population of only 16.7 per cent. It is interesting to note that the growth of autism in the US is significantly greater than the growth of the population as a whole, which, according to the Census Bureau, was 13.1 per cent over the last decade.

Though some of the unprecedented rise in numbers can be attributed to changing definitions and better diagnosing, ASDs are clearly becoming the fastest-growing disability of this decade.

The future

We are at the dawn of a new era. The last decade was encouraging in the wealth of knowledge that has been acquired, and in this next decade we are sure to discover the causes of ASDs. Since the mid-1990s there have been tremendous advances in the field of medical science. The growth of parent- and professional-driven ASDs organisations, coupled with the ease of access to the internet, has ensured a strong lobbying force aimed at encouraging scientists and politicians alike to devote resources to research into the causes of ASDs and how to help those with these conditions. There are many notable scientists and professionals in the UK who have done much to advance our knowledge of ASDs, and continue to do so. These include Professor Sir Michael Rutter; Doctors Lorna Wing, Francesca Happé, Tony Charman, Patrick Bolton, John Swettenham, Rita Jordan, Gillian Baird; Professors Simon Baron-Cohen, Anthony Bailey, Uta Frith, Pat Howlin, Stuart Powell, Dorothy Bishop, Digby Tantam, James Russell; Mr Paul Shattock OBE, Mr Phil Christine, Ms Maureen Aarons and Ms Tessa Gittens.

Since its inception in 1962 with little funding and a handful of members, the National Autistic Society (NAS) has grown into the UK's foremost organisation for people with autism and those who care for them. Thanks to organisations such as NAS, the All Party Parliamentary Group on Autism (APPGA), Parents Autism Campaign for Education (PACE), Cure Autism Now (CAN), National Alliance for Autism Research (NAAR), Families for Early Autism Treatment

(FEAT), the Autism Research Institute (ARI), Defeat Autism Now (DAN), the Autism Society of America (ASA) and The Schafer Autism Report, research is being funded, findings being shared and information disseminated.

CHAPTER TWO

What Autism Spectrum Disorders Are and How to Know if a Person Has One

All people like to put things into categories. I do so with my buttons, ribbons, and bits of colored glass. As for people, I had only ever truly felt there were two categories: 'us' and 'them'. Most people see things in these terms, too, but with different and more value-laden definitions.

DONNA WILLIAMS, *NOBODY NOWHERE*

The day my son's diagnosis was confirmed is indelibly etched on my mind. I was in the TV studio producing a soap opera when the operator announced that I had a call waiting from the hospital. Although I felt sure that my son was not developing properly, the medical professionals had up until now refused to listen to my concerns.

Somehow I held it together while the dramatic love scene was being taped, gave my nod of approval to the director and headed for my office to take the call. When I was given the news about my son, I felt stunned, shocked, unable to breathe. Even though I had felt there was something amiss, I had wanted to be proven wrong. Now it was acknowledged and I had to deal with that reality.

I went back down to the studio floor to finish taping the day's show. Somehow I got through it. Over the next few days, it was a relief to go to work and throw myself into the make-believe drama, which now seemed quite ordinary compared to the real-life emotional drama I was living. After many weeks and many tears of frustration and sadness I thought that perhaps now, with a diagnosis, we could move forward .

Why Seek a Diagnosis?

If you have any concerns about your child, it is important that you consult with a medical professional who is experienced in ASDs. Hopefully, you will have worried needlessly. But if not, it is important that you have a diagnosis as early as possible, in order to access services. Research shows that early and intensive treatment works best in helping these children make sense of their world. However, research also shows that our brains have neuroplasticity, which means that they continue to reorganise themselves by forming new neural connections throughout life. So, no matter the age, learning can still take place.

If you are an adult and think you may have an ASD, just knowing there are others like you can bring an extra dimension to your life. Perhaps exchanging information on skills you have developed to handle situations that are hard for you can be helpful.

People in the past were hesitant about applying a label because they felt that the label of autism was permanent and signified that there was no hope for that person. This should no longer be the case. In fact, since 1994, ASDs are now classified as pervasive developmental disorders, reflecting the medical profession's belief that intervention can lead to improvement and sometimes recovery.

Your label to use or not

Having an ASD diagnosed can open doors for you that would otherwise be closed. Your child may be eligible for early intervention services and therapies from local agencies and treatment under medical insurance. It will also allow the parent and professional to search out more knowledge on what to do, using the label as a starting point to gather information. However, you must remember that you, as the parent, or the person with an ASD, own the label. It is up to you to use it or disclose it when it is helpful, or not to use it if you are uncomfortable doing so, or if you feel it is not helpful or necessary. It is your information and your choice. Be aware also that over time, the diagnostic criteria change, and the opinion of the experts as to what those criteria should be differs as well. So although a diagnosis is helpful and necessary to access services, as a parent you would do better to focus on the behavioural characteristics that tell you more about the child and how to help him, than to get hung up on the diagnosis and what it means.

Sometimes it may take a long while for an official diagnosis to be reached. You will need the diagnosis to access services from government agencies; however, as a parent there are things you can be doing to help your child while you are waiting. Read Chapter Six on family life for suggestions in this area. This is also a good time to be doing your own research; see Chapters Four and Five.

Keep in mind that each person is unique, whether he or she has an ASD or not, as Jerry Newport (an adult with Asperger's) reminds us with the title of his book: *Your Life is Not a Label.*

CHARACTERISTICS OF AUTISM SPECTRUM DISORDERS

If the last decade has been encouraging in terms of treatments and research findings, in the next decade we are sure to find the causes of these disorders and invent medical tests to diagnose them. Meanwhile, the definition and diagnostic processes of ASDs are in a state of flux and constantly being improved as discoveries are made. What you have here is a road map of what is currently known and used.

The statistics

Autism spectrum disorders are considered to be the result of a neurological disorder that affects the functioning of the brain. They are four times more prevalent in males than females and typically appear during the first three years of life. ASDs are some of the most common developmental disabilities.

The concerns

At this point in time, there is no medical test to diagnose for ASDs. Any diagnosis is based on observable characteristics, that is, the behaviour that a person is exhibiting.

Because of the nature of the symptoms, ASDs are difficult to diagnose at a very early age. If the child is their first, the parents have no experiences with which to compare. Seeing other toddlers and

FOOD FOR THOUGHT
Getting Diagnosed

'All the insecurities and frustrations I had carried for so many years were beginning to slip away. I had not imagined a thing. I was different. So was my little girl. Different, challenged even, but not bad or unable or incorrect. I understood my husband's tears and his fear for our daughter's future, but I did not relate to them. I knew my innate understanding of what the world of AS is like would help my daughter make her way through life. Together, we would find every answer either of us ever needed.

'I had finally reached the end of my race to be normal. And that was exactly what I needed. A finish – an end to the pretending that had kept me running in circles for most of my life.'

Liane Willey, *Pretending to be Normal:
Living with Asperger's Syndrome*

children develop differently, they may start to worry. When voicing these concerns to relatives, friends or neighbours, the parent will often hear things like 'She'll grow out of it.' Sometimes parents will talk to their GP about their concerns regarding the child's lack of verbal communication and eye contact, his failure to respond to his name, and his obsessive attachment to certain objects.

In many cases, a baby will develop normally and then start to regress at around eighteen months. These children are usually easier to diagnose because of the obvious difference in past and present behaviours which parents and professionals can attest from looking at photos, watching videos and comparing observations.

Often the parents may be concerned because their child is a walking encyclopedia on a particular topic such as trains, plays obsessively in the same way with the same toy or will eat only certain foods. Perhaps it is the kindergarten teacher who notices that he does not appear to engage in conversation with his classmates and has a difficult time with any change in routine. Or a child may be considered 'naughty' at school because of certain behaviours, and perhaps the parents haven't noticed anything amiss because he is an

FOOD FOR THOUGHT
How I Got the Doctor's Attention

When my son was a baby, I worried because he would sit rather floppily, content to play with the same toy in the same spot for hours, enabling me to get a lot of my pre-production work done. When I shared my fears with family and friends, they inevitably replied, 'So he takes after his dad! Not everyone has to be as energetic as you. He's a calm baby. Just be happy you can get your work done.' The paediatrician was not very supportive of my concerns, so I invited him to my son's first birthday party. Seeing the contrast between my son and a room full of healthy babies, he was forced to face the fact that some tests might be in order.

only child, or they think that boys mature less quickly than girls. This may be true, but it is better to be sure and investigate your concerns.

The doctor may be hesitant to jump to any conclusions, because not all reported observations are necessarily objective and they can be interpreted in different ways. Everyone knows someone who was a late talker. On the other hand, a parent may not listen to concerns voiced by a child-care worker, a teacher or a neighbour. This is unfortunate because the earlier the diagnosis, the sooner the intervention, the better the prognosis.

Some people with an ASD may reach adulthood without ever having been diagnosed. They may have always felt as if they were not on the same wavelength as others socially, emotionally or sensorially. Perhaps they exhibit some of the characteristics listed in the box on pages 18–19. In such a case, having a diagnosis would be useful in putting them in touch with information and organisations that may be able to help them.

Three areas that characterise autism spectrum disorders
There are basically three areas of observable symptoms that characterise ASDs. Some of the symptoms may be mild, others more obvious. It is the number and severity of these symptoms that leads

Does This Person Have Autism?

Advice to parents: Follow your instincts. You are the expert on your child. If you have any concerns, voice them to your family doctor. Take notes on whatever behaviours (see pp. 18–19) are of concern by keeping a notebook, listing the behaviours and their frequency. Find out which medical professional in your area is knowledgeable about autism and consult with them. It is better to have your child checked out than to lose precious time waiting for him to 'grow out of it'. You can obtain a list of professionals by contacting the National Autistic Society at www.nas.org.uk Another good resource is the diagnostic checklist provided by the Autism Research Institute (ARI). To obtain this checklist, go to ARI's website (www.autismresearch institute.com) and fill out the request form.

Advice to general practitioners and other professionals: Take care how you voice your concerns, but voice them! Better to be proved wrong than to say nothing. If you are unsure about what constitutes an ASD, the National Autistic Society has a section just for you on their website (www.nas.org.uk). You can also consult the Checklist for Autism in Toddlers (CHAT) on the same website. In Britain, this screening tool, which takes under five minutes to administer, has been shown to be highly effective in predicting which children tested will develop autism, PDD, Asperger's or other developmental syndromes You may also wish to obtain the diagnostic checklist provided by the Autism Research Institute (ARI) by going to www.autismresearchinstitute.com and filling out the request form.

Advice to adults who might have an ASD: Again, the National Autistic Society can help you. Their website address is www.nas.org.uk

to concerns on the part of the parent or the professional. Examples of behaviours that portray these characteristics are listed in the box on pages 18–19. Lorna Wing, MD, FRCPsych, a founding member of the National Autistic Society, consultant psychiatrist at the NAS's Centre for Social and Communication Disorders, and author of *The Autistic Spectrum*, refers to a triad of impairments:

Behavioural Characteristics of Autism Spectrum Disorders

A word of caution: this list is not meant to be a diagnostic checklist, but is intended to give you some ideas of the types of behaviours someone with an ASD may exhibit. Remember, it is the number and severity of these behaviours that may lead to talks with a professional about performing a diagnostic assessment (see 'Diagnostic Criteria', page 20).

Some of these behaviours are seen on one end of the spectrum (i.e. classic autism); others on the opposite end (i.e. high-functioning autism, Asperger's syndrome).

Impairment of social relationships
As a baby, does not reach out to be held by mother or seek cuddling
Does not imitate others
Uses adult as a means to get wanted object, without interacting with adult as a person
Does not develop age-appropriate peer relationships
Lack of spontaneous sharing of interests with others
Difficulty in mixing with others
Prefers to be alone
Has an aloof manner
Little or no eye contact *not always!*
Detached from feelings of others

Impairment of social communication
Does not develop speech, or develop an alternative method of communication such as pointing and gesturing
Has speech, then loses it
Repeats words or phrases instead of using normal language (echolalia)
Speaks on very narrowly focused topics
Difficulty in talking about abstract concepts
Lack or impairment of conversational skills

Impairment of imaginative thought

Inappropriate attachment to objects

Obsessive odd play with toys or objects (lines up or spins continually)

Does not like change in routine or environment (going to a different place, furniture moved in house)

Will eat only certain foods

Will use only the same object (same plate, cup, same clothes)

Repetitive motor movements (rocking, hand flapping)

Others (may accompany other characteristics)

Peculiar voice characteristics (flat monotone or high pitch)

Does not reach developmental milestones in neurotypical timeframe or sequence

Low muscle tone

Uneven fine and gross motor skills

Covers ears

Does not respond to noise or name, acts deaf

Does not react to pain

Becomes stiff when held, does not like to be touched

Becomes hyperactive or totally non-responsive in noisy or very bright environments

Eats or chews on unusual things

Puts objects to nose to smell them

Removes clothes often

Hits or bites self (hits head or slaps thighs or chest)

Whirls himself like a top

Has temper tantrums for no apparent reason and is difficult to calm down

Hits or bites others

Lacks common sense

Does not appear to understand simple requests

Frequent diarrhoea, upset stomach or constipation

- **Impairment of social relationships**: An individual may not use or understand non-verbal behaviour or develop peer relationships that are appropriate to his developmental level, or may appear aloof and indifferent to other people.

- **Impairment of social communication** : There may be a total lack of or delay in the development of speech (with no attempts to communicate by gestures). The individual does not sustain or initiate conversation, or uses language in a stereotyped and repetitive manner.

- **Impairment of imaginative thought**: An individual may have an all-encompassing, intense preoccupation with one interest or topic; or have inflexible, nonfunctional rituals or routines. Repetitive motor mannerisms such as hand flapping or spinning of objects maybe observed. Often there is a lack of make-believe or social imitative play.

Other characteristics

Although difficulties in one or more of the areas listed above are required for a diagnosis of an ASD, there are different observable behaviours that do not necessarily fit into any of the three. These other characteristics are often associated with ASDs, although on their own they do not call for a diagnosis of an ASD, and are important when evaluating and assessing for the purpose of putting together a treatment plan.

Diagnostic Criteria

Unfortunately, at this point in time there is no objective or medical test that can be given to an individual to diagnose an ASD. Rather it is a process of elimination based on checking on any areas of concern (i.e. perhaps the child is deaf or hard of hearing and that is why he does not respond to his name) and observations based on the individual's development, as well as social and communication skills.

Medical tests

The following are suggested medical tests for the purpose of eliminating other possible reasons for the person's behaviour, or to see if other specific disorders and developmental disabilities exist. The doctor you consult may suggest other tests as well. Keep in mind that after a diagnosis, other evaluations and assessments will be necessary to give you the information you need to form a plan of treatment.

Hearing: Tests such as audiograms and tympanograms can indicate if a child has a hearing impairment. Audiologists can test the hearing of individuals by measuring responses such as blinking or staring or turning the head when a light is presented.

Genetic testing: Blood tests can show abnormalities in the genes that could cause a developmental disability.

Electroencephalogram (EEG): An EEG can detect tumours or other brain abnormalities. It also measures brain waves that can show seizure disorders.

Metabolic screening: Blood and urine lab tests measure how a child metabolises food and its impact on growth and development.

Magnetic resonance imaging (MRI): Magnetic sensing equipment creates, in extremely fine detail, an image of the brain.

Computer-assisted axial tomography (CAT scan): CAT scans are useful in diagnosing structural problems in the brain by taking thousands of exposures which are then reconstructed in great detail.

Behavioural checklists
Since there is no medical test that can be given to diagnose autism, professionals are dependent on observing the behaviours of the person in question as well as the medical and developmental history. There are behavioural checklists available that are used to determine if the person has the specific number of characteristics as defined in the *Diagnostic and Statistical Manual of Mental Disorders (DSM-IV)*, which is the standard reference for the definition of autism. A good diagnostic checklist is available through the Autism Research Institute at <u>www.autism.com/ari</u>

Diagnostic and Statistical Manual of Mental Disorders (DSM-IV)
This medical diagnostic handbook, currently in its fourth edition, is internationally used and recognised. When the *DSM* was revised in 1994, some changes were made. Previously, the category of pervasive developmental disorders (PDD), which includes autism, was coded or classified with other long-term stable disorders that have a poor prognosis. Now PDD has been classified with more transient, temporary and episodic clinical disorders. This is a positive move that reflects what current research is now showing: that there is a possibility of improvement with intervention, and that symptoms can vary in intensity.

The diagnostic criteria for autism have changed slightly as well. In order for a person to be diagnosed with autism, they still need to show deficits in the broad areas of social interaction, communication and stereotyped patterns. However, the number of symptoms which fall under these categories has been reduced from 16 to 12, making this diagnostic category more homogenous. A third change made was the addition of three new autism-related disorders: Rett's disorder, childhood disintegrative disorder and Asperger's syndrome.

All individuals who fall under the PDD category in the *DSM-IV* have some communication and social deficits, but the levels of severity are different. Here are the differences between specific diagnoses that are used:

Autistic disorder (or classic autism): A child with this disorder shows impairments in imaginative play, social interaction and communication, with an onset before the age of three. The child exhibits stereotyped behaviours, activities and interests.

Childhood disintegrative disorder: The child develops normally and has age-appropriate verbal and non-verbal communication skills, social relationships, play, and adaptive behaviours, for at least the first two years and then shows a significant loss of previously acquired skills.

Rett's disorder: So far, only girls have had this progressive disorder. There is a period of normal development through the first five months and then a loss of previously acquired skills. The girl loses the purposeful use of her hands, which is replaced with hand wringing.

There is severe psychomotor delay and a poorly coordinated gait. (It is now possible, thanks to the recent development of a new genetic blood test, to test for this disorder.)

Asperger's syndrome: A child with Asperger's tests in the range of average to above average intelligence and has no clinically significant general delay in language. However, the child will show impairments in social interactions including difficulty in using social cues such as body language, and has a restricted range of interests and activities.

Pervasive developmental disorder Not Otherwise Specified (atypical autism): A diagnosis of PDD-NOS may be made when a child does not meet the criteria for a specific diagnosis, but there is a severe and pervasive impairment in specified behaviours.

You may wish to consult the diagnostic criteria from *DSM-IV* at www.psychologynet.org/autism.html or at www.pediatricneurology.com

---

FOOD FOR THOUGHT

Is It High-Functioning Autism , PDD-NOS or Asperger's Syndrome?

It appears that the terms high-functioning autism and Asperger's syndrome are sometimes used interchangeably by certain professionals and authors. Although Tony Attwood (a world-renowned clinical psychologist who specialises in the field of Asperger's syndrome) considers that technically Asperger's syndrome is part of the autistic spectrum, he feels it is important to recognise that the child with Asperger's does not simply have a mild form of autism, but a different expression of the condition. He is concerned with the past negative connotations of the word autism. However, while in the old days the word put fear into everyone's heart, today we are on a different playing field. The word autism, as in autism spectrum disorders, does not imply a bleak and meaningless life in isolation, separated from the rest of society. What is important is that the person gets the help they need, and that their treatment is based on the behaviours they are exhibiting, not on the label.

CHAPTER THREE

What Causes Autism Spectrum Disorders and Why Do People With ASDs Act the Way They Do?

Men and women are puzzled by everything I do. My parents and those who love me are embarrassed and worried. Doctors use different terminologies to describe me. I just wonder. The thoughts are bigger than my expressions to get a shape. Every move that I make interprets my helpless way to show how trapped I feel in the continuous flow of happenings. The happenings occur in a way that show the continuity of cause and effect. The effect of a cause becomes the cause of another effect. And I wonder . . .

TITO RAJARSHI MUKHOPADHYAY, *BEYOND THE SILENCE*

It used to be that autism was pretty rare. Seven or eight years ago if I mentioned the word autism, people would have heard of it, but nobody had ever encountered it except at the cinema by watching *Rain Man*. Now it seems everyone is related to or lives next door to someone with an ASD. Recently I had to take my son to the casualty department at the local hospital. While we were sitting in the waiting room one woman looked at us and turned to her companion, saying, 'Seeing that boy over there reminds me, how is your friend's nephew doing, the one with autism?' Then we got called in for X-rays and the technician looked at Jeremy and said, 'So, what school district do you live in? Are you happy with his programme? My son's ten and we finally got what he needed at school for him.' When we got home, I called the airline to confirm reservations for a summer family visit.

When I told the reservation clerk I would be travelling with someone with autism and needed to make special seating arrangements, she said, 'Don't say another word. I know just what you need. My cousin's son has autism . . .'

IT'S AN EPIDEMIC

There has been much discussion over the past few years about the reason for the rise in the numbers of those diagnosed with autism spectrum disorders in the UK, the US and other parts of the world. Some would argue that ASDs are diagnosed better and earlier, resulting in higher figures than before. Others argue that there is a true increase in the number of children with autism. In order to have a better understanding of what is actually occurring, a close look at some official numbers and reports is in order.

Numbers in the UK

In 1993 the prevalence of ASDs in the UK was estimated by the National Autistic Society at 91 in 10,000 children of all ages, compared with 35 per 10,000 in 1979. In 2001, the Medical Research Council, commissioned by the Department of Health to look at how many children had been recognised as having an ASD, estimated that 1 in 166 children under the age of eight was affected. However, teachers reported much higher numbers of children with ASDs than any of these estimates: an NAS survey of seven local education authorities found that 1 in 152 children had a formal ASD diagnosis, while 1 in 86 had an ASD-related special educational need.

Elsewhere in the world

In the UK as in many other places worldwide, it is difficult to make comparisons of numbers of children diagnosed over the years because of the lack of a central record-keeping system for ASDs.

Figures from the California Department of Developmental Disabilities are often quoted because of the strict record-keeping necessitated by state laws. California is required under the Lanterman Developmental Disabilities Act to provide services to persons with developmental disabilities. These services are provided through regional centres which must keep accurate data on the number and type of clients they serve. The criteria for diagnosing cases are strictly adhered to, and not changed over time.

The Department of Developmental Services is required (for budgetary reasons) to report to the legislature the incidence of autism and pervasive developmental disorders compared with other developmental disabilities. In March of 1999, the department reported to the legislature that the numbers of persons entering the system and receiving services had jumped 210 per cent between 1987 and 1998 (*Changes in the Population of Persons with Autism and Pervasive Developmental Disorders in California's Developmental Services System: 1987–1998*). The California legislature was surprised and concerned by these findings.

Debate immediately started between autism experts, government officials and parent-driven charity organisations on why such high figures were being recorded in California, as well as in the UK and other parts of the world. Some discounted the increasing rates of ASDs, attributing the rise to better and earlier diagnosis, a change in definition that now encompassed the more able and those with Asperger's, and a migration to certain areas for better services.

The legislature therefore commissioned the University of California's Medical Investigation of Neurodevelopmental Disorders (MIND) Institute to investigate these findings. In October 2002 Dr Robert S. Byrd and his colleagues reported back with results that made headlines all around the world.

Byrd and his colleagues found that the huge jump in autism rates from 2,778 in 1987 to 10,360 in 1998 could not be explained by changes in the criteria used to diagnose autism, or by an increased migration to California of children with autism. Nor could it be explained by statistical anomalies. The report also found that the parent reports of regression at an early age did not differ between the two different age groups studied; however, more parents of the younger group reported gastrointestinal symptoms in the child's first fifteen months of life.

Dr Byrd's study clearly showed a tremendous increase in autism in California for some unknown, unexplainable reason. Meanwhile, in early January 2003, figures released by the California Department of Developmental Services showed an increase of 31 per cent from the previous year of children diagnosed with level one autism, the most severe kind (these figures do not include persons with PDD-NOS, Asperger's or any other ASD).

Other studies are showing increases as well. For example, a study by Yeargin-Allsopp, M et al., published by the *Journal of the American Medical Association* in January of 2003 on rates of autism in the metropolitan area of Atlanta, Georgia, compared to the 1980s and 1990s, confirmed that the apparent increase is real. It is certain that we are in the throes of a huge increase in autism. What no one knows is why.

What Causes Autism Spectrum Disorders?

In response to the question 'What causes ASDs?' the writer is sorely tempted to reply, 'We don't know,' and move on to the next chapter. However, no guide to ASDs would be complete without an attempt at explaining the causes of the most recent epidemic to hit our planet.

What does not cause ASDs
It is infinitely easier to talk about what we know does not cause ASDs. It is known for a fact that ASDs cannot be caught through osmosis, dirty doorknobs or bad parenting. Other than that, nothing can be said for sure.

Where to get updates on the latest research
What follows is by no means an exhaustive look at the science behind the causes of autism. The interested reader can follow on a regular basis the latest discoveries and ongoing research. Be aware that it is best to read the actual study or report than to read summaries and news releases, as the edited versions may only tell half the story. Also, the reader needs to be aware that in autism and science there are politics, and each organisation has its own inter-pretation of research studies and what they mean. In order to gain an

understanding of this highly controversial topic, the reader is advised to consult a wide variety of websites and journals such as those listed below and form his own opinion:

- **National Autistic Society**: Check the website or write to get names of reputable science and research publications as well as the NAS's stand on certain issues after their careful review of research.

- **Medical Research Council**: Information on current research funded by the MRC is listed on their website. The MRC published the *MRC Review of Autism Research: Epidemiology and Causes* in December 2001.

- **Autism Research Institute International Newsletter**: Dr Bernard Rimland publishes a quarterly newsletter with summaries of current research. The ARI website has information on many research studies (www.autismresearchinstitute.com)

- **Cure Autism Now SCIENCEWATCH**: Maintains a database of all research abstracts related to autism found on PubMed since January 2001.

- **The National Library of Medicine Pubmed**: To locate any research articles concerning autism, visit the National Library of Medicine Pubmed at: www.ncbi.nih.gov/entrez/query.fcgi Use the search engine to find abstracts of articles you are interested in reading. There are tutorials on the site with instructions for more advanced search techniques. Some abstracts will link you to the full article on the website of the journal where it is published. Some journals will provide full text for free while others require a subscription or fee.

- **The Autism Research Unit** at University of Sunderland, UK, **The Medical Investigation of Neurodevelopmental (MIND) Institute**, USA, and **The National Alliance For Autism Research (NAAR)**, USA, all list current research funded by them on their respective websites.

- **The Lenny Schafer Report** is the largest daily (almost) newspaper on ASDs; edited by Lenny Schafer and available free through the internet. To subscribe http://www.freewebz. com/schafer/SARHome.htm

What is known about the causes of ASDs?

There is strong evidence for a genetic component and a biological basis. Most researchers believe that ASDs have different causes that may be affecting the same brain systems or hindering development by disrupting the different abilities needed for communicative and social development. Here is what is known:

- There is a genetic predisposition to autism. Regions of interest, sometimes called 'hot spots', have been found on certain chromosomes, the most important so far on chromosome 7q, although others are involved. If one identical twin has autism there is a 60–95 per cent chance of the other having it as well. However, identical twins with the same genetic make-up and the same physical environment may have different expressions of ASDs – one may be very able, the other very disabled.

- There have been a number of findings in regard to differences in brain activity, not all in agreement with each other. However, most scientists who study autism would agree that some brain circuits are different in a person with an ASD.

- Serotonin, a neurotransmitter important for normal brain functioning and behaviour, has been found elevated in a subgroup of people with autism and in some first degree relatives who are unaffected. This is the only key biochemical finding since the 1960s that has held up to be true over time.

- There is a large body of anecdotal findings reported by parents and medical professionals, that some children with ASDs appear to have biochemical and immunological problems. Some possible causes being mentioned are: mercury toxicity, yeast problems, casein and gluten sensitivity and viral infections.

● In some studies, much greater levels of environmental toxins such as lead, antimony (a flame-retardant chemical present in many household items) and aluminium have been found in hair and blood samples of children with autism when compared with non-autistic children. This leads to the hypothesis that some children with ASDs cannot detoxicate, and thus accumulate toxins in their bodies.

For a long time, the favoured theory was that autism was all about the genes. It is true that genes come into play. However, the dramatic rise in recent years in ASDs cannot be attributed to a rise in genetic anomalies.

Perhaps we are seeing different disorders, each caused by a different problem, but with symptoms resembling one another. Perhaps the differences are all being caused by a yet unknown single underlying cause.

It appears most likely that there is a genetic predisposition to autism spectrum disorders, interacting with environmental factors that may play a key role in affecting the gastrointestinal tract, the immune system, the sensory nervous system and the brain.

FOOD FOR THOUGHT
Autism – a Hit and Run Epidemic

Lenny Schafer is the publisher and editor of the world's largest daily publication about autism. More than 20,000 people subscribe to *The Schafer Autism Report*, which is free of charge. A Danish study published in the *New England Journal of Medicine* in November 2002 concluded that there was no basis for the belief that the MMR vaccine was responsible for the increase in autism. This created quite a stir in the autism community. Some applauded the study, others criticised it. Lenny had this comment to make:

'The autism epidemic is like an epidemic of out-of-control hit-and-run accidents. Something big and dangerous collides with your child and leaves him or her devastated from the assault. We don't know the offending vehicle nor the driver nor the time of the collision. But these cars don't wreak the same damage on everyone they hit. It seems some more than others, and most not at all. Our public health detectives arrive on the scene long after the perpetrators have fled and announce that they have no idea what caused all the damage, but decide that the main problem is that the bodies of those presenting the most damage are too weak to sustain the blows like the others because of their genes. 'We do know that it's probably not a single gene behind hit-and-run-ism, but rather a few of them acting together,' pronounces the chief detective.

Some noisy parents of the victims say that their kids got hit right after they saw a police car in the neighbourhood. A lot of them are saying the same thing. 'Go investigate police cars!' scream the parents. 'My son was fine until a police car came around. You are supposed to protect, not hurt our children!'

'Hysterical mothers being driven by greedy lawyers and useless anecdotes,' smirks one detective to another. 'We're looking into this,' assures the detective, 'and we will spend some resources on research and find those bad genes. By the time your other children grow up and are ready to have children of their own,' they continue, 'we'll know which of them ought to consider adopting, by their genes. Problem solved.'

In the meantime, the detectives assure them, 'We've looked over some traffic reports and there really isn't any increase in hit-and-run accidents. It's just more pedestrian accidents being reclassified as hit-and-run because we're spotting them better.'

Like with hit-and-run research, almost all the money that goes into autism research today, both public and privately raised funding, is used for finding the faulty genes and/or faulty body parts, not the perpetrators of the assault. Almost nothing comparatively goes into treatment research for our kids already afflicted. Even the familiar parent-run autism research fundraising groups like CAN, NAAR and the parent-influenced MIND Institute spend the bulk, if not all, of their funds on genetic-related, or like research.

(The exception here is the Autism Research Institute, which spends all of its research dollars on treatment-related issues. The ARI is somewhat of a maverick within the research community, willing to help parents experiment with anecdote-mostly-tested treatments at first, if necessary, and often with good results. This is risky stuff; few others are ready to help parents willing to go this course. But the ARI does not spend its resources researching the cause of autism, either.)

The problem here is that if vaccines do play a role in autism – and this Danish study doesn't eliminate a reasonable possibility for a genetic subset of the population – relying on the promoters of the same vaccines, such as government public health agencies, to find the 'real' or even the 'other' environmental factors causing this large upswing in autism and other immune disorders is akin to asking O.J. Simpson to find the 'real' killers of his ex-wife and her friend.

Inherent to public health is politics. And the political reality of the autism epidemic is that the watchdogs, and the vaccine pharmaceutical companies and their agent researchers, have too many conflicts of interests for the issue to be settled by epidemiologic research alone. This research only looks at the results of pathology upon a population, and does not easily prove or disprove cause. This allows too much wiggle room for self-serving spin (and counter-spin). A growing number of citizen public health advocates find vaccines to be poorly tested, and sometimes dirty with toxins like mercury. Vaccine-strain measles virus is showing up in the cerebral spinal fluid of autistic children and nobody can tell us how it got there, if not via the MMR vaccine.

Genetic and epidemiological research are not the primary tools for finding the cause of autism. The final answers will come from biomedical and clinical research. Someone had better start examining these kids, and soon. Until we start seeing efforts and money spent to pay for the clinics to do this research (and also, along the way, to treat our children), all other research serves as little more than alibi research.

The murky vaccine–autism connection has been effective leverage by some autism research advocates for getting the public health watchdogs and the media to sit up and pay attention to autism. Soon this leveraging won't be necessary as the prevalence rates will reveal more and more autism-victimized sons and daughters and grandsons and granddaughters of congress-people, movie and sports celebrities, investors in pharmaceuticals, etc., people not so readily dismissed as anecdotal hysterics – and who in ever growing numbers will demand answers, not alibis. Not everyone is as willing as some autism research fundraisers to let vaccines off the hook just yet.'

THE MMR JAB AND AUTISM – IS THERE A CONNECTION?

The possibility of a vaccination–autism connection has become highly controversial; there is intense debate going on among scientists. On the one hand, there is a growing tendency to blame vaccinations for all the cases of regressive autism in the past ten years (regressive autism is autism that appears in a child at around the age of eighteen months, after a normal development, causing the child to regress). However, vaccinations in themselves do not cause autism, or millions more children would be autistic. Neither does Thiomersal, an organic compound present in some vaccinations. But perhaps these are triggers for children who are genetically predisposed to have autism, and who have immune systems that are not functioning properly.

On the other hand are the government and the vaccine manufacturers stating that vaccines are safe, and that those refusing to vaccinate their children are putting the public's health at risk.

In reality, no one knows for sure. It is difficult for the average person to form an educated opinion just from reading the newspaper headlines. Many headlines in the UK and the US over the past few years have stated that expert groups and panels have found no link between childhood vaccination and autism. In reality, a careful review of the different government and experts' reports actually show the following:

- In response to Petition PE 145, calling for an inquiry into issues surrounding the alleged relationship between the combined measles, mumps and rubella vaccine (MMR) and autism, the Health and Community Care Committee reported to the Scottish Parliament in 2001 that 'What is clear to the committee is that while there is an absence of any scientific data of a causal link between the MMR vaccine and the onset of autism, it remains impossible to prove conclusively the absence of a link.' The committee also called for further research.

● The Centers for Disease Control and Prevention and the National Institutes of Health in the US asked the Institute of Medicine (IOM), a branch of the National Academy of Science Report, to establish an independent expert committee to review immunisation safety concerns. *The Immunization Safety Review: Measles-Mumps-Rubella Vaccine and Autism*, issued on 23 April 2001, stated that 'Although the committee has concluded that the evidence favors rejection of the causal relationship on the population level between MMR vaccine and ASD, the committee recommends that this issue receive continued attention . . . Its conclusion does not exclude the possibility that MMR vaccine could contribute to ASD in a small number of children . . .'

● The Medical Research Council in the UK published a *Review of Autism Research: Epidemiology and Causes* in December 2001. It states: 'It is important to recognise that epidemiological studies cannot prove that vaccines are safe but can only exclude specified adverse reactions with a certain degree of confidence,' before going on to state that: '. . . Currently there are no epidemiological studies that provide reliable evidence to support the hypothesis that there might be an association between MMR and ASD.'

So all we know is that, so far, no connection has been proved for the vast majority, but nor has any connection been disproved for a subset of children who may be at risk. It is also difficult for the average person to know what the research studies we read about in the news really prove or disprove. As soon as the results of a study are published, another expert issues a statement questioning their validity or unveils a connection between the researcher and a drug company that produces vaccines. For example, the largest study to date, a review of medical records of half a million Danish children born from 1991 to 1998, by scientists at the Danish Epidemiology Science Center, was published in the *New England Journal of Medicine* in November 2002. The report concluded that there was no basis for the belief that the MMR vaccine was responsible for the increase of autism. This led to newspaper headlines such as 'Study finds no sign that child vaccine causes autism' (*The Boston Globe*, Saturday November 9, 2002). However, the Danish study raised several legitimate criticisms from other researchers and autism experts (including Dr. Wakefield and Dr. Bernard Rimland). For example, the authors of the Danish study failed to mention that the mercury-containing Thiomersal is not included in the paediatric vaccines used in Denmark, meaning that their findings are not applicable to the US or the UK populations. Another is that the medical records reviewed were selected from psychiatric clinics and hospitals, and contained no data in regard to immune system dysfunction or inflammatory bowel disease.

What is real is the growing number of parents who have seen differences in their children before and after the MMR vaccine, and have photographs and videos that clearly document regression. This is a fact for those families that no government report will erase. Although it is true that this represents a small number of the total of children vaccinated, it should be of great concern to the medical community.

Everyone agrees on one point: that more valid, unbiased research is clearly needed. Some areas that are of concern in regard to vaccinations are:

● Thiomersal (Thimerosal in the United States), a preservative containing mercury, is currently used in vaccines such as the diphtheria and tetanus pre-school boosters in the UK. The MMR vaccine (triple or single) currently used in the UK does not have thiomersal as a preservative. One of the theories in the US is that the rise in ASDs matches the increased exposure of young children to thiomersal as the number of vaccinations required has increased over time from 8 to 22. In the United States there is a much more aggressive vaccination schedule than in the UK. During most of the 1990s many American six-month-olds were exposed to a total of 187.5 micrograms of ethyl mercury through vaccination. At that time, the Environmental Protection Agency's (EPA) daily 'safe' dose for methyl mercury was 0.1 micrograms per kilo. In July 1999, the American Academy of Pediatrics (AAP) chaired by Dr Neal Halsey MD, the Public Health Service (PHS) agencies and vaccine manufacturers agreed to reduce or remove thiomersal from most vaccines. This decision was based on the assumption that the health risks from methyl and ethyl mercury were the same. It is now possible to get the recommended schedule of vaccinations in the US without thiomersal. In the autumn of 2002, the Department of Health in Britain backed the continued use of thiomersal-containing vaccines, stating that the alternative vaccines without the mercury preservative were less effective.

● It has been suggested by expert panels that when the MMR triple vaccine was first introduced, not enough testing was carried out to ensure its long-term safety in regard to the interaction between multiple vaccinations and potentially fragile immune systems.

● There is valid concern about the serious risk to public safety if children are not immunised. Until recently, mumps and measles were practically non-existent, and these diseases pose serious threats to children. The number of cases of measles has been climbing in the UK and the disease has been responsible for the deaths of some children. Rates of immunisation in the UK are said to have fallen below the World Health Organisation's recommended level.

● There is debate about medical professionals and what information they should divulge to families in their care about a possible ASD–vaccine connection. Government and health officials say there is no connection between MMR and ASDs, so that is usually the message passed on to the health consumer. Should doctors tell parents that a connection between the two has not been proved, but has not been disproved either? What constitutes an 'informed consent'? If a physician suggests that a child should not be vaccinated, and that child then contracts measles or mumps, he would open himself up to the risk of litigation.

● In rare cases, the measles virus has been found in the fluid that bathes the brain and in cerebrospinal fluid. In some children, measles viruses have been found in the gut. It is theorised that these viruses cause inflammatory bowel disease, which in turn allows the peptides to cross the blood–brain barrier and affect neurotransmission, leading to some of the behaviours associated with ASDs. DNA analysis has shown that the strain of measles found in autistic children is from the vaccine, and not a wild virus.

● Currently, single vaccines are not licensed by the Medicines Control Agency in the UK and are not available on the NHS. However, some doctors are making them available to their patients on a private basis.

Conclusion

Obviously, there is an urgent need for more research into vaccinations and the MMR connection. Meanwhile, parents need to educate themselves by going to the sources and reading for themselves. For some information about scheduling of vaccinations and possible adverse reactions, as well as conditions of non-use for the vaccine, go to the Autism Research Unit at the University of Sunderland website (hhtp://osiris.sunderland.ac.uk/autism/). However, any decisions regarding vaccination should be discussed and taken with your general practitioner. Another good source of information about vaccinations is *What Your Doctor May Not Tell You About Children's Vaccinations* by Stephanie Cave and D. Mitchell. Although this book is written with the US vaccinations in mind, there is information in here that will be helpful to every concerned parent. The author discusses clearly the pros and cons of the different vaccines, and offers a risk-benefit analysis, as well as an alternative vaccination schedule that may minimise exposure to any possible risks.

Another source of information is the National Vaccine Information Center (NVIC), a non-profit educational organisation founded in 1982. Located in Virginia, NVIC is the oldest and largest US parent-led organisation advocating reformation of the mass vaccination system and is responsible for launching the vaccine safety movement in America in the early 1980s. Contact:

National Vaccine Information Center
421-E Church Street
Vienna, VA 22180
Phone: 703-938-DPT3
Fax: 703-938-5768
Web: http://www.909shot.com/

FOOD FOR THOUGHT

Calling Michael Moore

As the MMR vaccination debate continues, the eye of the storm is the existing conflict between private health policy – what is best for the individual – and public health policy – what is best for the herd. Some parents feel there is a risk in having the MMR vaccination and do not wish to vaccinate their child. Although this is a private decision, it has a direct bearing on the public. As more and more parents refuse to vaccinate, the number of children catching serious life-threatening diseases such as measles and mumps, that were once practically eradicated, is rising.

And although the message from most government panels of experts is that vaccinations are safe, the public is being sent mixed messages by the powers that be.

Perhaps what is needed, in addition to more valid research, is for the documentary film-maker Michael Moore (*Roger and Me, Bowling for Columbine*) to take an in-depth look at this controversial subject. His interviewing techniques could come in handy. He could get the answers to questions the rest of us on both sides of the Atlantic wish we could ask.

For example, did the Prime Minister, Tony Blair, have his youngest son vaccinated? And if he did, was it a single or triple vaccine? Did the DTP or DT vaccine contain thiomersal? Did he get it on the National Health?

And perhaps Moore could find out the real story behind Dr Andrew Wakefield's resignation from his position at the Royal Free Hospital. Was he forced to resign because the powers that be did not like the fact that he went public with his controversial report in 1998 on a possible connection between the MMR vaccination, serious intestinal inflammation and ASDs? (Dr Wakefield is currently Director of Research for the International Child Development Resource Center in Florida.)

Moore can surely ferret out the mysterious author of the rider that was attached to the Homeland Security Act which was presented to Congress in November 2002. The rider had been slipped in to limit the amount of compensation that families of vaccine-injured children could receive from drug companies supplying vaccines. The author was brave enough to slip it in, but not to come forward to claim authorship.

Maybe Michael can find out why, soon after, the attorneys for the Bush Administration asked a federal court to seal MMR vaccine records, blocking access to documents of hundreds of cases of autism allegedly caused by childhood vaccines, in order to keep them from the public. Because of public outcry, the Bush Administration withdrew its motion.

Perhaps Michael can tell us, are we ordinary citizens suffering from paranoia, or do we have reason to be concerned?

WHY PEOPLE WITH ASDS ACT THE WAY THEY DO

As mentioned in the previous chapter, a diagnosis of an ASD is based on observable behavioural characteristics. We are beginning to have an understanding of why people have those observable characteristics, that is to say, why they behave the way they do.

From observation and written accounts by people with ASD, we can understand what some of the behaviours mean. This is helpful information for the general public so they can develop an understanding of why people with ASDs might act a certain way, and understanding is a near neighbour of tolerance! It is invaluable knowledge for parents, carers, teachers and other professionals who are trying to decide what therapies, treatments and interventions could help a person with an ASD.

Behaviours are a form of communication

For the very young, and those who are non-verbal, behaviours can be the only way for them to communicate with us and the only way for us to understand what is going on with them. Many of these behaviours are avoidance behaviours. The brain structure of many people with ASDs is unlike ours, with some processing circuits wired differently, and it is important to realise that they cannot help what they are doing; they are not just 'being difficult'.

Parents, caregivers and teachers can observe a person's behaviours and try to analyse the reason behind them. There is a certain amount of guesswork involved, but by systematically picking one behaviour and writing down your observations, you will probably find a pattern.

For example, if a child keeps taking his clothes off, he is probably sensitive to the feel of fabrics on the skin. It would be helpful to observe and take notes on this particular behaviour, such as whether he is doing it when he is wearing a certain type of fabric, or a certain fit or cut of clothing. Identifying what he can wear will make it easier for him to be comfortable. Perhaps he can be desensitised by a sensory integration technique of 'brushing' the skin with a soft plastic brush specifically made for that purpose.

Striking a balance between changing the environment and changing the behaviour

As parents and caregivers, we need to find the balance between trying to change the environment and changing the individual. Usually a bit of both will be in order. For example, if behaviours indicate possible food allergies, and tests indicate that that is so, a change in diet (the environment) is in order. However, the person may need to learn to tolerate (slowly, through desensitisation) eating certain foods recommended by the diet that perhaps he would not eat before.

If a person has auditory and visual sensory processing difficulties, perhaps he will undergo auditory training or vision therapy, and will avoid spending too much time in noisy, bright environments. Classrooms should not be lit with fluorescent lighting, but the child also needs to learn an alternative appropriate behaviour, such as requesting a break or permission to go for a walk, rather than have a temper tantrum (p.44).

Listed below are some behaviours and what they can mean. Keep in mind that these are generalisations and that everyone is different, so they may not be true for everyone. Nonetheless, this is a good place to start trying to analyse a person's behaviours. Then, when looking at treatments and therapies, you will already have an idea of areas in which you can help this person. Remember too that some behaviours can be indicative of different causes, so you need to look at the total person.

FOOD FOR THOUGHT

'From as far back as I can remember, I always hated to be hugged. I wanted to experience the good feeling of being hugged, but it was just too overwhelming . . . Being touched triggered flight, it flipped my circuit breaker. I was overloaded and would have to escape, often by jerking away suddenly.'

Temple Grandin, *Thinking in Pictures*

SOME OBSERVABLE CHARACTERISTICS AND WHAT THEY COULD MEAN

Finicky eating

● Eating only from certain food groups can be indicative of food allergies. Sometimes the discomfort created by food allergies can cause other behavioural symptoms similar to sensory processing issues. Often, frequent diarrhoea or constipation accompanies eating problems due to allergies.

- Eating only foods of the same texture, smelling the food before eating it, and not eating foods that produce a crunching sound can indicate sensory processing issues, as can chewing or eating unusual non-food items.

- Eating only exactly the same foods, if accompanied by other examples of insistence on sameness, can show high sensory sensitivities or apprehension of the unknown.

Avoidance of auditory stimulation

- Covering the ears or appearing deaf (i.e. not responding when name is called) indicates auditory processing difficulties and a high sensitivity to sound. A person may cover their ears to try and block out the sound, or tune out completely.

- Leaving a room when people enter may be a way of avoiding too much auditory stimulation.

- Listening to and repeating TV commercials or songs could indicate that the person has got used to hearing those sounds, i.e. has desensitised himself to them. Listening to people talk is more difficult because people don't usually say the same thing twice, and no two people speak the same way.

- People with autism often have a monotone or peculiar intonations because they don't understand the concept of nuance, and that *how* you say something conveys an additional meaning to *what* you say.

No reaction, or else a strong reaction to touch

- Some babies become stiff when you pick them up, some children will fall and cut themselves and not cry. Usually this indicates that their tactile sense is out of whack. Perhaps a child's tactile sensors are overly sensitive and he does not like to be touched, or they are very dull and he doesn't feel sensations the way most people do.

Removes clothes or shoes often

- A person may not like the feel of particular textures on their skin. Certain fabrics and shoes can make people with extremely sensitive tactile sensors uncomfortable.

Lack of eye contact

- People with visual processing problems find it hard to look at people straight on; usually they look from the side of their eyes.

Unusual body movements

- Rocking in chair, or back and forth from one foot to the other, could be a stress release from too much stimulation, or not enough.

- Flicking of fingers could also be a release from stress, but if doing it in front of the eyes, it could be a visual processing stimulation.

- Awkward movements and running into furniture can be a symptom of poor body mapping, not knowing where one is in space, or poor fine and gross motor skills.

Does not play with or imitate others

- People with autism are often lacking in the social skills, interests and understanding which the rest of us find so important. Also, a child with sensory processing issues will have difficulty being near other children who are, in his eyes noisy and unpredictable, and who have texture and smells associated with them that the child with an ASD cannot tolerate.

Lines up objects

- This can show a need for sameness. Usually children who line up toys are also the ones who do not like change in their routine, may have repetitive speech, and do not like to see the furniture moved into a different pattern in their home.

- They may have a hard time making sense of their world, and so the sameness in certain areas provides a predictability and security missing from an existence which they are having a hard time comprehending.

Temper tantrums, hyperactivity and aggression towards self or others

- Temper tantrums or meltdowns in children can be a result of sensory overload, or change in the sameness which provides security.

- Places with a lot of light and noise, such as supermarkets and waiting rooms with fluorescent lighting, are really hard on people with sensory processing issues.

- Aggression towards others could be for any number of reasons, such as sensory overload (i.e. sudden loud noises near someone's ear could cause them to jump up and strike out at the person provoking the noise as it can be very painful).

- Self-aggression could be due to seeking sensory stimulation, feeling pain or frustration.

CHAPTER FOUR

Newly Diagnosed Adults and Parents of Children With Autism Spectrum Disorders: After the Diagnosis

The book was finished and now I had a word for the problems I had fought to overcome and understand. The label would have been useless except that it helped me to forgive myself and my family for the way I was . . . I wanted to meet the other autistic people I'd been told about and were surprised to find out that they were few and far between, scattered across the country and across the world. I was even in a smaller category. I had become 'high functioning'. Nevertheless, I needed to meet others.

DONNA WILLIAMS, *NOBODY NOWHERE*

When you are a parent of a child who is developing more slowly than typical children, you may feel alone, but you are not. Knowing that you are not alone is a big part of the cure for the worry and pain. Parents whose children are not developing typically can greatly benefit from understanding the similarities between themselves and others. A lot of healing occurs when you exchange stories with others in similar circumstances . . .

ROBERT A. NASEEF, *SPECIAL CHILDREN CHALLENGED PARENTS*

It was hard for me to go to my first Berkshire Autistic Society meeting. I was taking another step towards acknowledging that my child had a disability and that it wasn't just going to go away. It felt as if I was becoming a member of a club that I didn't really want join. The only thing I had in common with the roomful of people was the label our children shared, but even so our children were so different from each other. But we helped one another. We shared resources, information, anger, tears and advice. We gave each other energy and the courage to do what was needed. We shared stories about our children that were too embarrassing to tell anyone else, and we laughed at the absurdity of our situation. And most importantly, the group developed resources that were non-existent. We created change in the status quo.

YOU ARE NOT ALONE

Because of the epidemic rise in the numbers of individuals diagnosed with autism spectrum disorders, you are not alone. Whether you are a parent, or an adult with autism, having access to others like yourselves is necessary, not only for the sharing of information but also for your mental health.

FOOD FOR THOUGHT
Why Parents Need to Gather Their Own Information

In 1999, the National Autistic Society surveyed parents of people with ASDs, people with ASDs and partners of people with ASDs concerning the diagnosis and assessment of the condition. Out of 294 respondents, 49 per cent reported that the overall help they received at the time of diagnosis was inadequate. When asked what kind of support they would have liked, 45 people mentioned practical advice on how to help a child, 38 would have liked contact with other parents and 35 mentioned educational help or help choosing a school.

(*Opening the Door: A report on diagnosis and assessment of autism and Asperger syndrome based on personal experiences*, The National Autistic Society, 1999.)

There is power and comfort in numbers
In this chapter, suggestions and resources will be provided for the parents of children with ASDs, and for the recently diagnosed individual. Professionals can also learn much by accessing the same sources. It is true that you are not alone: there are many organisations, associations, books and websites ready to help you. Remember too that there is comfort to be had in meeting others experiencing the same situation as you. There is also power in numbers: the more people who get together, the more useful ideas float around.

FOOD FOR THOUGHT
Tips to Keep in Mind on Your Quest for Knowledge

● Make sure you are seeking information from reliable sources. Just because you read something on a website or in a magazine does not mean it is accurate.

● Take it one step at a time and seek only what you are ready to assimilate. Focus on the present. Learn what you can that will help you today, or over the next six months. At this early stage, if you try to think too far ahead, you may feel overwhelmed. Do only what you feel capable of doing, and read only what you are ready to digest.

● Learn the jargon. If someone uses a word you don't understand, look it up, or ask for an explanation.

● Ask questions if you don't understand. Ignorance is not bliss, and life will become a lot easier if you get used to asking questions. Before going to any meetings or appointments, write questions down. Ask and ye shall receive.

● What works for one may not necessarily work for yours. Everyone is different, you need to find what is right for your child.

● Do not be intimidated by others. Some parents feel overawed by medical or educational professionals. There is no need to feel this way. They may be an expert in their field, yet you are the expert on your child. ASDs are very complex and even educational and medical experts do not know everything. Together you can be a team.

Adults who have a diagnosis of an ASD may find support through the NAS or local chapters. There are online resources and websites available to you that are run by people with Asperger's. They are listed in the resources section at the end of this book.

Professionals who are new to the field of autism spectrum disorders would do well to read about the experiences of parents and consult the resources available to parents in order to learn more about this disorder.

Parents and professionals alike would benefit and gain a greater understanding of autism and Asperger's by reading accounts by people with ASDs, either in books or on websites.

EMPOWER THYSELF – SEEK KNOWLEDGE

The first step in gaining an understanding about ASDs is to gather knowledge. Here are some places to start.

Make contact with charities or societies dedicated to ASDs. The first step should be to make contact with other people in the same situation, i.e. others who have an ASD, or other parents. The first place to start is the National Autistic Society. They have an excellent website (http://www.nas.org.uk/) with valuable information for parents, professionals and adults with ASDs. The NAS also has local chapters, and you can find them at http://www.nas.org.uk/groups.html.

Local chapters may be able to give you more localised information and organise meetings with speakers. The national office can supplement any information your local chapter may not be able to give you. You may not feel ready to attend a chapter meeting or a coffee morning, but if you do, find out when they are taking place. Ask local chapters or organisations if they have a lending library of books you can borrow. This is a good way of filtering through the different books, and only buying the ones you really will use over and over.

Make contact with other families or adults diagnosed with an ASD: Through your local association or websites, make contact with others in your situation. If you are an adult who has just been diagnosed, you might find it helpful to contact another adult who has an ASD. This can be done on the telephone or online. Parents will find it helpful to talk to others who have been in the same situation or are going through it now.

Contact the Autism Research Institute (ARI): For over 35 years, Dr Bernard Rimland's non-profit organisation has been a clearing house for all kinds information about the diagnosis and treatment of ASDs. Dr Rimland's 1964 book *Infantile Autism: the Syndrome and its Implications for a Neural Theory of Behaviour* dramatically changed the accepted perception of autism. He is also the founder of the Autism Society of America, and initiated the Defeat Autism Now! project. Dr Rimland collects and encourages as well as conducts research on the causes, diagnoses and treatments of ASDs. Not only does he analyse the research studies conducted all over the world, he compiles anecdotal information from parents and caregivers. He has amassed detailed case histories of over 30,000 children with ASDs from more than 60 countries. This makes for an enormous body of information on ASDs, the only one of its kind.

Dr Rimland also publishes the quarterly *Autism Research Review International,* and his institute provides information packets, books and videotapes charging only the cost of the postage and materials. Contact details for the ARI can be found in the resources section at the end of this book.

Read accounts written by adults with autism spectrum disorders: For everyone, reading books by people with ASDs gives an insight into what was helpful to them and explains some of their feelings and behaviours. For newly diagnosed adults, this may help you to understand that there are others out there with similar challenges, and perhaps their stories will hold tips to helping you live in a neurotypical world. See the resource section for some recommendations.

Read books written by parents of children with an ASD: If you read only one book, make it *Facing Autism* by Lynn Hamilton. It is a particularly good book, full of valuable information about the latest methods shown to be effective with children with ASDs. Parents can take comfort from reading books by others who have been there, knowing that all have the same struggles and fears. The information that other parents have shared about their experiences can save new parents a lot of time and energy, and give you tips on all sorts of different aspects. See the resource section for other recommendations.

Learn about any funding and services for which you may be eligible: If you are not already, you and your child will soon be consumers of the various wonderful systems that are there to help you: your local educational authority, the NHS, the benefits system. This gives you certain rights as well as responsibilities (see p. 71).Your local chapter and the national offices of the NAS can provide you with the information you need. Educate yourself by talking to other parents who have been there before. Start the application process for anything you feel you are eligible for. Things take time.

Get on waiting lists: It is important that you get your name on any lists for services you feel you may need to access at some point. Who knows what the future holds? You may need to get on lists for speech evaluations, respite care, an assessment of special education needs, or other services. If you are investigating applied behaviour analysis (ABA), it's best to call the few providers in the UK and get on their lists (see Chapter Five). You may not want or need it in the end, but remember, it is easier to get off a list than to get a service when you haven't been on one in the first place.

Start keeping good records: Start keeping a record of all medical visits and professional appointments. Keep track of telephone conversations as well. Filing papers in a three-ring binder in chronological order is the best way to organise information. Do not separate papers by profession (i.e. speech assessment, psychological assessment), as a chronological order of all papers makes it easier to see a complete picture of the child at different ages.

Videotape your child: This is a good way of seeing how a child develops and progresses. Our memories may fade, but videos don't lie. Also, if ever you need to prove a point on how a particular method is working, a video can illustrate the points you are making and can make a strong visual impression about the difference in your child.

Do whatever you can to interact with and teach your child: You may be waiting on lists for some time. Do what you can to connect with your child: read to him, sing to him, play with him. Don't wait for someone else to do it. Connecting with this child may not be the same as connecting with his siblings (if any), but you will connect.

Take care of yourself: Most importantly, stay healthy. Remember that you still have a life outside this child. Take time for yourself and for your partner as well as any other children. There is a whole world out there, and you need to recharge your batteries to keep things in perspective.

Seek out positive people: Stay away from negative people who sap your energy. Later in this chapter, we will discuss the grief cycle and how it affects people. Sometimes you will meet individuals in organisations who are constantly depressed or relatives who are handling the diagnosis worse than you are. Everyone is entitled to a bad day here and there where they feel as if they have hit rock bottom. However, the whole point of having a good cry or a moan is to get it out of your system, and then get on with your day. You need to save your energy to help your child, your own family and yourself; don't let others drain it from you.

Who said what? Buyer beware

You will meet people at support groups, visit many websites, read books, get advice from professionals. All these sources of information are helpful, but you must be able to sift through the information and analyse what is valid for you:

Information from other parents: Parents will say that a particular treatment worked or didn't work for their child. They may say a certain therapy is the best thing on the market since sliced bread. Remember, they are talking from their point of view, based on their child. Your child may share a common diagnosis or label, but that does not mean the children have the same treatment needs. You need to evaluate the information from the parent based on what you know about your child. Keep in mind that just as people have certain political or religious beliefs, they also have particular beliefs when it comes to autism and treatment.

Information from websites: The great thing about the internet is the accessibility to information and the ease of researching particular topics. The down side is that any Tom, Dick or Harry can put up a website, and many of them have. The result is that while many websites are valid, informative and based on fact, others simply put out information based on the particular bias of the individual or company who has set them up. You need to read everything with a grain of salt and learn to develop analytical skills if you don't have them already. I liken getting information from the internet to talking to strangers in a bar. You never know who you are talking to until you investigate and ask a few questions. Would you take advice from a stranger in a bar? You would probably want to know more about him before you believed and acted on anything he said.

Information from books: Books are generally good sources of information, though again you need to bear in mind who is writing the book and what perspective they are writing from. Also, look at when the book was published. If you are preparing for a meeting with your local educational authority, you want to make sure you are consulting a recent publication that takes into account changes in the Education Act, and not something written five years ago.

Information from professionals: Professionals are very knowledge-able people and can be experts in their field, but that does not mean that they are knowledgeable about the latest treatments and therapies for ASDs. Neither are they experts on your child; you are. Again, you need to know more about a professional's experience and training, and what biases they have. It does not mean that what they have to say is not valid, but like everyone, they are shaped by their experiences. Perhaps they have not yet worked hands-on with a child of your age or functioning level. If they have, did the children they worked with progress?

Information from autism organisations: ASDs organisations are wonderful sources of information. Just be aware that they have opinions, just like people do. Sometimes there can be the appearance of a conflict of interest. It is hard for an organisation to support one type of approach if they are using another in schools that they run. Unfortunately, autism is not free of politics. But remember that all organisations are doing their best to help people with ASDs; you just have to be able to gather information and make your own decisions about what is best for your child and your family.

FOR PARENTS: THE EMOTIONS

Life is a series of choices. Granted, as a parent you did not choose for your child to have an autism spectrum disorder. However, you can choose how to react to it and what you are going to do about it. The first place to start is to learn about the emotions you are feeling, and to understand that they are real and unavoidable, and that all parents will go through them at some time or another. These emotions need to be addressed. A good place to start is to acknowledge them and accept that it is normal to have them.

The moment your life changes for ever

There are certain events that change the course of world history; dramatic events that are indelibly etched in all our memories. And along with the memory of the actual event, there is the memory of where you were or what you were doing when you got the news. September the 11th and the terrorist attack on the Twin Towers; the day that John F. Kennedy was assassinated; Princess Diana dying in a car crash in Paris; *Challenger* exploding on take-off: all these are events that we as members of the human race shared collectively.

> ### FOOD FOR THOUGHT
>
> What it comes down to is that you expected something that was tremendously important to you, and you looked forward to it with great joy and excitement, and maybe for a while you thought you actually had it – and then, perhaps gradually, perhaps abruptly, you had to recognize that the thing you looked forward to hasn't happened. It isn't going to happen. No matter how many other, normal children you have, nothing will change the fact that this time, the child you waited and hoped and planned and dreamed for didn't arrive.
>
> Jim Sinclair, 'Don't Mourn For Us'

After disastrous events, all of society grieves together; and though we are all different, we can mourn together and acknowledge the feelings the event has provoked.

The day a parent learns that his or her child has a disability is like one of those dramatic event days. For some, it feels as if they have just been hit in the stomach and had the wind knocked out of them. Even if the parent suspected that there was something wrong with the child, they can't believe this is happening. For every parent of a child with a disability, this moment is forever etched on their mind.

The difference is that no one else is sharing your pain. When the parent leaves wherever it is that he got the news and walks into the street or car park, his whole world has changed, but there is no comfort to be had, no collective reaching out to one another. The other people in the street or the other cars have the same life they had an hour earlier. Only the parent's has changed for ever.

The grief cycle

In her book *On Death and Dying*, psychiatrist Elisabeth Kubler Ross introduced her famous 'stages of dying' or 'stages of grief' model, in which she lists the five stages a dying person goes through when they are told about their terminal illness as denial and isolation; anger; depression; bargaining; and finally acceptance.

The emotions that a parent goes through when raising a child with a chronic health need or disability, including ASD, have been likened to Kubler Ross's five stages of grief. The difference is that instead of going through each stage chronologically, parents are on a continual cycle, going through different stages at different times. They never graduate completely out of the grief cycle but do eventually learn to spend more time in the acceptance phase.

FOOD FOR THOUGHT
You Never Get Over It, You Just Learn to Deal With It

It was one of those beautiful Parisian spring days that makes you feel that all is right with the world. I decided to stop at the café after a walk with my four-year-old son.

At the next table, a mother and her ten-year-old boy were laughing at a joke he had just told her. She asked him about his school day and he talked about the games he played at recess. When the waiter came to take their order, the boy grinned impishly at his mother and asked imploringly, 'Maman, can I please have a pain au chocolat and a hot chocolate?' 'It's going to ruin your appetite for dinner, but go ahead,' she replied, ruffling his hair.

When the waiter came to take our order, I asked my son what he wanted, as he stared at the speckles of dust in the air reflected by the light, his head cocked to one side, while spinning the spoon he had found on the table. He appeared not to hear me; it was as if I had not even spoken. I looked with envy at the other table, at that mother sharing an everyday ordinary moment with her child. And that now-all-too-familiar ache descended as I realised once again that I would never have a moment like that with my son; I would never just sit and share a joke and have a conversation with him. I wondered if he would even ever look at me with the same interest he showed the spoon.

I reached for the spoon and started fidgeting with it. My son looked at the movement of the spoon. I picked it up and twirled it in front of my face. For an instant he looked into my eyes and smiled before fixating back on the spoon, melting my heart in the process. Perhaps, I thought, I will never be able to have a conversation with him about recess, but I know we will connect somehow; we will find a way, our way.

Why do parents go through the grief cycle?

First of all, parents are mourning the death of the child they never had, the death of the future they had envisaged sharing with their child. They have not actually lost their child, but they have lost their fantasy child, the one they had hoped for and dreamed about. As Jim Sinclair so rightly puts it in his article 'Don't Mourn For Us', 'Much of the grieving parents do is over the non-occurrence of the expected relationship with an expected normal child. This grief is very real, and it needs to be expected and worked through so people can get on with their lives – but it has *nothing* to do with autism . . . It isn't about autism, it's about shattered expectations.'

Secondly, parents go through this grief process because until recently autism was considered incurable, and parents were told to go home and accept that there was no hope for their child, and to plan on institutionalising their child in the future when life with autism got to be too much. The medical professionals had nothing to offer but condolences.

Thirdly, parents who have children with regressive autism (a child who developed normally and then started regressing at around eighteen months) may feel the very real loss of the child they did have, of seeing their child slip away into autism.

However, a diagnosis of autism is no longer a diagnosis of despair and hopelessness. There is a chance of recovery and even cure for some individuals. And for the rest, there is much that can be done to help them reach their potential. There are so many new treatments, therapies and educational strategies out there. Dedicated parents and professionals have fought hard (and are still fighting) to get research funded, discoveries made, services provided, laws enacted and information shared so that all individuals with ASDs can have a future. The grief cycle is still here, but the future looks brighter for all of us.

The positive aspects of the grief cycle

An important part of this grieving process is to realise that to grieve is normal and necessary. It is important for the well-being of the family that the parents recognise and acknowledge this grief as well as the emotions that will continually resurface.

Each emotion on the grief cycle, if recognised, can be fuel for positive action. If you are at the anger stage, for example, you might use that anger to refuse to accept a third-rate educational programme for your child and to request an appropriate placement.

Parents need to learn to recognise where they are on the cycle, and how to use that emotion to gain knowledge and empower themselves. Then, on the days that they feel strong and capable, they will be ready for action.

Remember, when it comes to autism spectrum disorders, early intervention is the best intervention. The sooner you can use these emotions to help yourself, your child and your family, the better off you all will be.

The different stages of the ASD grief cycle

Shock and disbelief: The first reaction a parent usually has when hearing the diagnosis, even if they suspected something was wrong, is disbelief. 'There must be some mistake.' 'This can't be happening.' At this point, the parent usually does not process exactly what has happened or the enormity of what has just been said. They often go into automatic-pilot mode and sit through the motions of the rest of the meeting without really taking in any more information. Some parents may even feel physical pain, as if someone has torn them open. They may feel as if they have been smothered in a dark heavy blanket and are unable to see or hear or breathe.

Tip for parents: Leave the meeting and allow yourself time to react to what you have heard. React however you want to react. Don't do anything or make any decisions until your body stops reacting. Make an appointment to come back another time, when you have had a few days to process the initial shock. Make a list of questions to ask. You may find it helpful to talk to close family and friends; you may wish to isolate yourself. Take time for yourself.

Denial: At this stage, parents think there is some mistake which will eventually be cleared up. Even though they may see the obvious and it has been confirmed by a professional, they still think, 'There is nothing wrong with my child. They must have mixed up the test results.' In denial, parents often seek second or third opinions, or some magical treatment that will 'cure' their child.

Tip for parents: Use your denial positively: gather information and learn more about autism. Some parents start 'shopping' for services, looking for that one treatment that will cure their child. Now, you know there really is not a magic pill out there, but denial can fuel you to get informed and learn all you can.

Anger or rage: Once a parent has got through the denial stage after the initial diagnosis, they will often be angry. 'Why me?' 'How come there are people out there with perfectly healthy children who don't appear to care about them, and our poor child has the disability after all the planning we did?' Often, the professional who gave them the initial diagnosis bears the brunt of their rage. They may feel anger towards their spouse, towards God, if they believe in one, towards the child, maybe even towards a sibling for being healthy and normal (which leads to feelings of guilt . . .). They will feel anger at the disability. At sensitive times, such as when seeking educational provision, this anger may flare up and be misdirected at representatives of the local educational authority.

Tip for parents: Feel angry! You have a right to be. But don't misdirect your anger at the people who are trying to help you. Anger carries a lot of energy with it that can be focused to enable you to be an advocate for your child. Learn to refocus your anger and do something positive with it: perhaps write those letters asking for services or more assessments; just wait a few days and reread them once you have calmed down, then tone down the inappropriate bits before sending them off.

Confusion and powerlessness: You are now entering a world you know nothing about, hearing new words that sound foreign. You are confused: 'What does this really mean about my child?' 'I don't understand what the doctor is talking about.' And this confusion leaves you feeling powerless. Powerlessness results from feeling that now you have to rely on the advice and expertise of others, people you don't even know that well and have no reason to trust: 'The specialist says this is the best method.'

Tip for parents: Of course you are confused and feel powerless; you have entered a territory you know nothing about. There is a solution: start learning the terminology and the subject, and little by little you will become knowledgeable. And knowledge is power. You will feel less and less confused and more in control once you have the knowledge to make informed decisions. It will take time but you will get there.

Depression: Sometimes everything seems like a struggle. The inability to cure or change the disability leads to feelings of despair. The idea that this is not the life the parent had dreamed of, that this is not the family they had hoped for is more than can be borne. They realise that autism is 24/7, and that they are on a train they never wanted to board and there is no getting off. The lack of sleep does not help, either.

Tip for parents: This is when you need to take some time away from autism, even if it is only a few hours. Have a good cry and then pamper yourself. Call a friend and do something you really enjoy: go to the pub, play some golf, go shopping. If talking to friends, family or other parents is not helping you get out of your depression, contact a counselling service or ask your doctor to recommend a therapist, perhaps even a bereavement counsellor.

Guilt: Parents feel guilt about having a child with a disability. After the diagnosis, the guilt is about 'What did I do to cause this to happen?' 'Was it the glass of red wine I had at my birthday party when I was pregnant?' 'I shouldn't have allowed the doctors to give him those vaccinations.' 'Am I being punished for something I have done?' Later on, when they revisit the guilt stage on the cycle, it will be about 'I'm not doing enough for my child.' ' I should have taken a second mortgage on the house so he could have more therapy and alternative treatments.'

Tip for parents: Don't beat yourself up over this. All parents do what they think is best at the time. Take the time to sit back and think about all the positive things you have done for your child. Pat yourself on the back for what you have done. Nobody's perfect.

Shame or embarrassment: At some point parents will feel shame about not having a perfect child. 'What will people think?' Later, as the child gets older, they are nervous about people's reactions to the child's behaviour in public. They catch someone staring at their child. They think, 'Gosh, I wish he wouldn't flap his hand while he is walking.' 'His lack of eating skills and his disruptive behaviour is ruining everyone else's dinner at this restaurant.' 'People must think I'm a terrible parent when he acts this way.' And then, of course, they feel guilty about feeling shame, which puts them on another part of the cycle.

Tip for parents: Get over it. Do not worry about what others are thinking. In the big picture, it doesn't matter. Think of it this way: your child is different and interesting and your life with him will not be boring. Develop a sense of humour. Stand straight and tall, look confident. Just think about making this a positive experience for your child, not about the others. When people see that you are at ease with your child in public, or see that you are trying to cope with a difficult situation, they will respect you.

FOOD FOR THOUGHT
Shame and Embarrassment

My son is 14 now, and sometimes he finds it difficult to be in certain environments, and will start flapping one of his hands or will rock slightly on the spot. I am so used to being stared at that I forget that they are looking at me because of my son's behaviour and I start thinking, 'Is there food on my face?' 'Are my buttons undone?'

My son is usually good about keeping his hands to himself, but every once in a while he will get attracted to a pattern or a colour or a shiny object and will touch someone's bag or sweater while we are queuing at the supermarket. Obviously we work hard at teaching him that this is inappropriate, but sometimes he sees something that is just too tempting. Of course I immediately stop him, reprimand him and apologise to the person in question. I often get them laughing by saying something like, 'He knows quality when he sees it, he only goes for the top designers.' Humour helps to put us all at ease.

Fear and panic: Parents will inevitably feel fear and panic: 'What will happen to my child?' Times of transition can bring about these panic attacks. 'How will he adjust to the new school?' 'Another new teacher! Is she going to understand his learning style?' 'What will he do after high school?' and of course the biggest panic attack comes from the dreaded 'What will happen to him and who will look out for him when we are dead and buried?' or 'I want him to live with us at home but we can't handle it any more. Is there a good safe place for my child?'

Tip for parents: Pour yourself a stiff drink and then acknowledge that what you are feeling is fear of the unknown. Use the fear and panic to propel you towards gathering knowledge about the choices you have in regard to whatever issue you are feeling fear about. Write down everything you think the new teacher should know about your child and give her the letter with a smile, telling her you hope it is helpful information. Find out about his options after high school. Visit group homes or residential schools to see what they are really like. Just having the knowledge about the options will make you feel better. If you are not happy with the options, perhaps you will find yourself at the anger stage and that will propel you to organise with other parents and advocate for better choices.

Bargaining: After a while parents start to bargain with whatever higher intelligence or God they believe in. 'If the forty hours of behavioural therapy per week for two years cures my son, I will adopt a poor family to send money to every week for the rest of my life.' 'If it is only autism, I can accept it, but if it's mental retardation as well . . .' If he can learn to communicate in some way . . .' The process of bargaining is a way for the parent to accept a part of the problem without taking on the whole problem.

Tip for parents: As time goes on, you will find that you are bargaining less and less as you start to have more acceptance of your situation and get to know your child, his potential and the options out there.

Hope: Parents have moments when they feel hopeful. 'We may make it through this.' 'This diet/therapy/medication seems to be helping our child.' 'He is getting this concept.' 'He's keeping his behaviours under control.' Just like any parents, there are times when we are encouraged by the accomplishments of our child or we meet professionals or treatments that are having a positive impact on him.

Tip for parents: Celebrate and cherish each and every one of these moments. Tuck them away and pull them out on the days when you feel bleak and could use some hope. These are the moments that make you feel that life is good. Treasure them, share them with those who have shared your sorrows so they can also share in your joy.

Isolation: Sometimes parents feel isolated: 'My child is the only one who is not acting appropriately.' Or they seek isolation because they do not want to see the reminders that they have a different child or a different life from everyone else's, or because they feel that they must protect their child.

Tip for parents: Sometimes you feel an overwhelming need to isolate yourself from others because the pain of seeing other parents interacting normally with neurotypical kids is too great. It is not a good idea to stay isolated, however. To get through this, use local associations to find other families who have children with ASDs or other disabilities. You will feel more comfortable with them, as you will understand each other's concerns. Eventually, over time, you will come to feel more comfortable spending time with other families who are not in the same situation as you.

Acceptance: Parents will feel acceptance of their child's disability only after having experienced and worked through some of the other emotions discussed above. Acceptance means that they are feeling some control over the situation. The problem may not be solved to the level that they wish, but they see that they are able to cope and live with the hand they have been dealt. Acceptance also means that they realise that there will be days filled with anger or grief, and days that they will have strength. On any given day you will be in one spot on the grief cycle or another, but it's OK. The parent is learning to cope and knows it's all right to have those emotions. Also, accomplishments that may seem ordinary and small to others will be moments you savour and cherish.

Don't Mourn for Us

This in an excerpt from an article published in the Autism Network International newsletter, *Our Voice*, Volume 1, Number 3, 1993. It is an outline of the presentation Jim Sinclair gave at the 1993 International Conference on Autism in Toronto, and is addressed primarily to parents. Jim has autism.

'Autism is not death. Granted, autism isn't what most parents expect or look forward to when they anticipate the arrival of a child. What they expect is a child who will be like them, who will share their world and relate to them without requiring intensive on-the-job training in alien contact. Even if their child has some disability other than autism, parents expect to be able to relate to that child on the terms that seem normal to them; and in most cases, even allowing for the limitations of various disabilities, it is possible to form the kind of bond the parents had been looking forward to.

But not when the child is autistic. Much of the grieving parents do is over the non-occurrence of the expected relationship with an expected normal child. This grief is very real, and it needs to be expected and worked through so people can get on with their lives – but it has *nothing* to do with autism . . . It isn't about autism, it's about shattered expectations.

I suggest that the best place to address these issues is not in organizations devoted to autism, but in parental bereavement counseling and support groups. In those settings parents learn to come to terms with their loss – not to forget about it, but to let it be in the past, where the grief doesn't hit them in the face every waking moment of their lives. They learn to accept that their child is gone, forever, and won't be coming back. Most importantly, they learn not to take out their grief for the lost child on their surviving children. This is of critical importance when one of those surviving children arrived at the time the child being mourned for died . . .

. . . That isn't the fault of the autistic child who does exist, and it shouldn't be our burden. We need and deserve families who can see us and value us for ourselves, not families whose vision of us is obscured by the ghosts of children who never lived. Grieve if you must, for your own lost dreams. But don't mourn for us. We are alive. We are real. And we're here waiting for you . . .'

FOR ADULTS WITH ASDs:
GETTING DIAGNOSED LATER IN LIFE

In the past, many individuals with ASDs on the very able end, or with Asperger's syndrome, who were able to function pretty well, did not get diagnosed until later in life. However, many felt that they were in some way different and, once diagnosed, report feeling relieved at knowing that there are others out there like them and that there is a reason why they never fitted in.

Knowing that there is a name or label for what you have gives you the option of looking up information and seeing what strategies are out there to help with some of the challenges you may face. Being diagnosed allows you access to support groups and information you did not know existed. You may wish to read books by people with ASDs who give suggestions on how they cope with some of the challenges, or look up information on the internet. These resources are listed at the end of the book.

The next section may be helpful to you as well as to parents of children with ASDs.

FOOD FOR THOUGHT

Liane Holliday Willey recognised that she had Asperger's syndrome at the time her daughter was diagnosed. In her book *Pretending to be Normal*, this is what she has to say about realising she had Asperger's as well:

'Yet, no matter the hardships, I do not wish for a cure for Asperger's syndrome. What I wish for is a cure for the common ill that pervades too many lives; the ill that makes people compare themselves to a normal that is measured in terms of perfect and absolute standards, most of which are impossible for anyone to reach. I think it would be far more productive and so much more satisfying to live according to a new set of ideals that are anchored in far more subjective criteria, the fluid and the affective domains of life, the stuff of wonder . . . curiosity . . . creativity . . . invention . . . originality. Perhaps then, we will all find peace and joy in one another.'

How to Develop the Survival Skills You Need

Most parents or adults with ASDs will need at one time or another to ask for support or advice. In this section, developing survival skills will be discussed, followed by some basic information on where to start to develop the supports you need.

The survival skills

Working through the educational systems in three different countries has provided me with untold opportunities for observing and learning about how systems work and don't work, the politics involved, and how to ask the right questions. This has been helpful in developing strong survival skills and enabled me to become an effective advocate for my son.

Think of the work you do, and about what skills you used to get and keep your job. Think of the skills used by other people working in the same company. All these skills are the kind you will need either as a parent of a child with an ASD or as an adult with the condition. Applying the skills used every day in work situations is what you will need to obtain the services you or your child need and keep good relationships with all the people involved.

For example, the skills I developed while producing TV shows are the same skills I used to obtain my son's educational needs: gathering information, analysing data, listening to consultants' and other team members' expertise, using good clear communication, learning to negotiate, preparing for meetings, deciding what was worth fighting for, working as part of a team, expecting professional behaviour, monitoring progress, forgiving honest mistakes and rewarding a job well done. Sometimes people had to be kicked off the team or there were major disagreements, but at the end of the day, there was a show in the can.

Communicating: Every job involves communicating, whether it is with the public, clients or fellow workers and the boss. Even if you work the graveyard shift as a security officer, at some point you need to be ready to communicate in case of an emergency. Communication is the major building block of all relationships, and relationships are what you need to develop in order to get the help you need, or the educational programme that is appropriate. Being effective at communicating means being able to listen as well as to talk. It means being polite and respectful, and clear about what you are talking about.

Planning: Every company has a business plan, and every worker has a plan of action for what they will do that day, whether it is putting hamburgers together or marketing software. Whether you are dealing with the NHS, the local council or your local education authority, planning should now be a part of your life. Planning means looking at what your needs are today, in six months, next year, five years from now and so on. What do you envision for your child or for yourself? How are you going to make that happen? How can the services on offer help you reach your goals? All the decisions you make are about getting towards the dream or vision you have for the future.

Researching and analysing: Before making major decisions at work you have to research your options and then analyse the information. If you are a chef, you may research where to buy the supplies you need to prepare certain meals, and then analyse the information you have uncovered to come up with the place that best suits your needs and your customers' requirements. If your company needs a photocopy machine, you research the different suppliers and analyse the various options. As a parent, or an adult with an ASD, you need to research the different treatments and diets, education and work opportunities available. You also need to research what funding options are open to you. Then, analysing the information will help you decide what plan of action is best for you.

Marketing: If you have a new product to sell, you have to convince your clients that it is the best thing on the market since sliced bread. At work, when someone has a plan of action they want adopted, the whole team has to be convinced to jump on the bandwagon, or the plan will not fly. To sell the idea to colleagues, marketing needs to take place. The person with the idea goes around to his colleagues and persuades them of the benefits of his plan. The same needs to be done once you have developed a plan of action; you need to convince the other team members (i.e. the local education authority, your GP) on the merits of your plan. In getting what you need, you will need to market your ideas (using those effective communication strategies) and present the information and analysis as to how you came up with this plan and why.

Negotiating: At work, you may have to negotiate time off with your boss. With clients, you may negotiate different prices or marketing plans. Either way, you have to be prepared to discuss your needs, and to know how far you are willing to go to get what you feel you need. When it comes to services, you may not have as much room for negotiation, but in some cases you may. With the local educational authority, for example, you may be able to negotiate for an educational provision they are hesitant to provide due to cost or lack of experienced personnel. Keep in mind that doing this is not easy, but it is possible.

Rewarding and acknowledging: Once you have obtained what you wanted at work, or at least been given the opportunity to present your point of view, you need to reward the people involved by acknowledging the time they spent considering your proposal. The same holds true if you have negotiated and signed a deal with a client, or even if you didn't come to any agreement. A simple 'Thanks for taking the time to listen to me' or 'I appreciate your support', whichever the case may be. This applies to the people you, as a parent, or an adult with an ASD, have been 'negotiating' with, even if you don't agree with the results.

Perhaps, as an adult, you didn't get the results from the community care assessment you had hoped: remember, you may be asking that person for help again down the line. If you are a parent, you will be in touch with your local educational authority for many years, so it is better even in disagreement to acknowledge their efforts. 'It looks as if someone took a lot of time out of their schedule to do this assessment and I appreciate the effort' is a good way of acknowledging the effort made before announcing that, unfortunately, the assessment did not address the real issue.

Monitoring: Every business has to have some form of monitoring put in place. The person frying chips has to monitor the amount of chips needed, the temperature of the oil and how long the chips have been in the fryer. A doctor has to monitor the health of his patients post-operation. Even after your child has an individual education plan (IEP) and everyone leaves feeling satisfied that he is going to receive the support service he needs, monitoring must take place. This is where good communication skills are really necessary, as sometimes it is a gentle nudge to get a service started. For example, perhaps as an adult with an ASD you have been assured a promised service or source of funding is to begin at a certain date. If it does not, you may need to make a few phone calls to find out what the status is, and what can be done to get the support in place.

FOOD FOR THOUGHT

'When my daughter was diagnosed with Asperger's syndrome, her doctors gave me one outstanding piece of counsel. They told me that my husband and I would now become the experts on AS. We, in effect, would stand as her greatest advocates. The truth of their prophecy has been shown virtually every day. The general public is largely uneducated in AS. I have grown to believe that this is the single most damaging element to the AS cause, that is, understanding and acceptance. Without knowledge of the symptoms, outcomes and even confounding attributes, it is nearly impossible for others to recognize and support AS individuals.'

Liane Willey, *Pretending to be Normal*

HOW TO GET THE INFORMATION YOU NEED

In an earlier section, we talked about the need to find out about funding possibilities and start the paperwork, as well as getting on waiting lists for services. Here are some other tips.

Find out what is available: All therapies cost money. Adults may need funds to supplement their wages. If you are not independently wealthy, someone in the family will need to become the designated expert on 'how to get the treatment without it coming out of the family budget'. This person will need to learn about their rights in terms of education, social services and the National Health Service. If you have private insurance, find out what it will cover. Find out all you can about any financial support you may be eligible for.

Learn to ask questions: Do not suppose that private insurers, the local council, the local educational authority, social services or the National Health Service will automatically tell you what you have a right to. Dare to ask questions. They have budgetary concerns. Sometimes they will tell you only what they are offering on a regular basis, what they wish to provide, not what you are entitled to. Most people have not been taught to think 'outside the box'. You will need to learn to ask the right question to get the right answer. Think of it as playing detective. Often a case is cracked when the detective asks a question that brings out information that people did not volunteer, as they felt it was unimportant or did not concern the case. The same can be true when looking for funding, employment support or an appropriate education. As a parent, or an adult with an ASD, you will need to be proactive, and learn to communicate in an assertive, non-aggressive manner. Always be polite. The people on the other end of the phone or the other side of the counter are only doing their job as they have been taught.

Talk to others in the same situation: Ask other parents or adults with ASDs in your area for some ideas about what they have been able to obtain. There are many options for help out there. Each agency has a brochure explaining clients' rights and some even have advocates to help you. To learn more about what you or your child may be entitled to, obtain a copy of the *Disability Rights Handbook* (tel. 020 7247 8776).

Learn to ask for and accept help: When you are used to being self-reliant, it is difficult to ask for help or to accept help that is offered. My advice to you is: get over it! Remember the times you have helped others and keep in mind that you will help others in the future. Now is not the time to have a stiff upper lip and be too proud to accept help.

Learn how to answer questions in a way that fully explains your situation: For example, with the Disability Living Allowance, you may be eligible for 'help in getting around'. Somewhere on the form you will be asked if your child can walk. Most people would reply 'yes' if the child is not physically handicapped. However, some children with autism do not follow instructions and are not safety-conscious; some will run into the street, others may tantrum. The real question in your mind should be: is my child capable of getting somewhere independently without adult prompting of any sort? If the answer is no, the correct response to 'Can your child walk?' is 'My child needs help to move from one place to another.'

WHERE TO START TO LOOK FOR FUNDING

Having an ASD or having a child with an ASD can be expensive. Knowing what the options are financially and what is available to you, should you need it, is a great source of comfort and frees your mind to focusing on the other important stuff. The first thing to do is to obtain a copy of the *Disability Rights Handbook* (see page 69). Here are some places to start your search.

Insurance

The National Autistic Society has negotiated an insurance policy which offers reasonable cover at about £15 per year per family or carer. This insurance policy is backed by Ecclesiastical Insurance and has the advantage of being ASD-specific. Contact: The Company Secretary, National Autistic Society, 393 City Road, London, EC1V 1NE.

Financial support

Disability Living Allowance for children and adults: You may be able to claim for this if the person needs more help than others of the same age. You can claim for personal care, and in some instances for help in getting around. Call your local chapter of the National Autistic Society and ask someone who has claimed successfully to answer any questions you may have. Forms for the DLA can be obtained from your local Benefits Agency office.

Invalid Care Allowance: This weekly cash benefit is paid to people who are caring for a severely disabled person. You may claim if you are unable to work full time because you are providing for a child or an adult who receives a higher or middle rate of the Disability Living Allowance. There are some restrictions. Forms for ICA may be obtained from your local Benefits Agency office.

Incapacity Benefit / Income Support: When a person reaches their sixteenth birthday, they may be eligible for one of these supports. It is best to start setting this up six months in advance. There are some restrictions, and Child Benefit will cease if either one is claimed. Look at the *Disability Rights Handbook* to find out more.

The Family Fund Trust: The Trust's purpose is to provide grants and information relating to care of children, in order to alleviate some of the stress on families. Families caring for a severely disabled child living in the UK may apply, by contacting The Family Fund Trust, PO Box 50, York Y01 9ZJ (tel: 01904 621115; website: www.familyfundtrust.org.uk).

Grant-Making Trusts: Families can apply for trusts for help and support. RADAR (The Disability Network) can tell you how to obtain a copy of the most recent information (RADAR, 12 City Forum, 250 City Road, London EC1V 8AF; tel: 020 7250 3222; email: radar@radar.org.uk).

MISCELLANEOUS INFORMATION

Useful telephone numbers
Benefit Inquiry Line : 0800 882 200
Rights Advice Line: 020 7247 8763

Local authority care services
Contact your local authority and see what services are available that you may not be aware of.

Useful concessions: unisex toilets
Unisex toilets are practical, as you can avoid long queues and parents can supervise children of the opposite sex who need the facilities. There are approximately 4,259 unisex toilets accessible to the disabled in the UK that are fitted with a National Scheme lock. The list of those toilets is published by RADAR and is available for £5. Keys cost £3.50 and are available from your local district council or RADAR upon declaration of disability.

Respite care: for children and adults
Different forms of respite care are available for children and adults with special needs, depending on the local authority in your area. For information with regard to children, contact the Disabled Children's team in your area. For adults, contact the Community Teams for Adults with a Learning Disability. Your local autism society chapter may be able to give you more information and names of people to contact.

Diagnosis: for children
Referral for diagnosis can be made by your GP to an appropriate professional. If you would like a second opinion, you may have to fund this yourself. Some professionals have long waiting lists. Check with the local NAS chapter or national office for information about what is available in your area.

Diagnosis: for adults

Adults who may have Asperger's syndrome or high-functioning autism can obtain a free diagnostic assessment from Cambridge Lifespan Asperger Syndrome Service (CLASS). A formal diagnosis is useful for accessing resources and support such as disability benefits, social skills training and supported or sheltered employment. See your GP and ask him to write to CLASS to request a referral. Contact: Mrs J. Hannah, CLASS Coordinator, Department of Psychology, Downing Street, Cambridge CB2 3EB (tel: 01223 333936; fax: 01223 333561; email: jh373@cam.ac.uk).

There are more resources specific to adults in Chapter Nine, as well as in the resources section at the end of the book.

CHAPTER FIVE

Treatments, Therapies and Interventions

'Therapies', 'techniques', and 'treatments' used with people with 'autism' present themselves like shops along the High Street; they have little relationship to one another and each shop will encourage you to shop at their store and tell you why their product is THE product.

But each of these shops sells something quite different from the next. Some deal with behaviours, some with brain development, some with biochemistry, some with cognition or with the mind and some with the soul – and some don't deal with anything but make a good job of appearing to.

The problem with services behaving like High Street shops is that people with 'autism' don't just have problems with behaviour or communication or perception or their senses or with brain development or with biochemistry, or with stress levels or with troubled souls. Because people with autism are whole beings, most of them have trouble with the whole lot, which all interconnect and feed into each other at some point.

To get any all-round service, people with autism don't need a High Street of competing shops, they need a department store where each department is aware of what the others offer and points people in the direction of other services which complement their own.

DONNA WILLIAMS, *AUTISM: AN INSIDE-OUT APPROACH*

When Jeremy first stood up and walked on his own, his first steps were not towards me. He got up and followed the patterns in the rug. We were living in Paris at the time, and psychoanalysis was the treatment on offer to cure Jeremy's autism. When my husband was offered the opportunity to work on Legoland in Berkshire, we jumped at the chance to move to England, where at least Jeremy could attend a special needs school.

Soon after arriving in England, I read *Let Me Hear Your Voice* by Catherine Maurice, and I also met Cathy Tissot, whose autistic son attended the same school as mine. We discussed the book a few times, saying how we would like to try the Lovaas programme (a home-based applied behaviour analysis programme), but we felt it was a lot to take on. Frankly, we were both overwhelmed with our respective situations; not only were we mothers of children with severe autism, we were also foreigners, far from family and friends, with no close circle of support to rely upon.

Meanwhile, Jeremy did not progress at school. While helping out in his class, I witnessed what I considered to be physically abusive and unsafe treatment of a child. That, coupled with the headmaster's seeming indifference and refusal to look into the situation when confronted, did it for me. I knew I had to remove my son from school and try to teach him myself. At the time, practically no one was doing the Lovaas programme in England, but Cathy and I decided we would give it a try. I remember going to her house one evening, trying to get the nerve up to call the the Life Institute, Lovaas' centre in California, to find out if there was a consultant who could come and put on a workshop to train us and students to work with our children.

Making that phone call changed my life. That was the moment when I stopped being a victim of the systems in place, took control and realised I was not powerless to help my son. I was lacking in knowledge, but I would learn whatever I had to. I knew my son was severely autistic, but I also knew he could learn, and that he should be given the opportunity to reach his potential, whatever that would be. Now, I was going to learn strategies to teach my son and help him make sense of the world.

HOW TO KNOW WHAT WILL HELP

In the past, there were practically no options for people with ASDs in terms of treatments, therapies and interventions, and this was the source of much anguish and stress. Nowadays options abound, and the challenge is more about getting information about them and trying to decide what best fits the needs of the person with the ASD, before figuring out how you can access that treatment or therapy.

In Chapter Four, where and how to get information was discussed. In this chapter, you'll learn more about how to know what can help a particular person with an ASD, and about many of the different treatment and therapy options that are available.

Where to start

The first thing to do is to look at the person with an ASD. Here are some things to consider:

The age of the person: A person who is diagnosed at age 10 or 16 or 25 or even 45 will have different therapy and treatment needs from a child diagnosed at two or at five. For example, a very young child may need to learn to speak or develop a system of communication. An older child may have language skills but no social skills. Adults may have sensory processing issues that could be helped through physiologically oriented therapies. Remember that although for a long time people have been talking about the early years as the 'window of opportunity' for learning, recent research has shown that brains have neuroplasticity, which means that they continue to reorganise themselves by forming new neural connections throughout life. As more is discovered about the brain, we are finding out that you *can* teach an old dog new tricks.

What the person is like in terms of functioning level or ability: ASDs cover a wide range of functioning in terms of behavioural characteristics, communication and social awareness, and sensory integration issues. If a formal diagnosis has been made, any assessments made at that time may give you more information about the person. There are many different assessments that are used depending on the age and ability of the person: speech and language, occupational therapy, functional behaviour analysis, neuropsychiatric tests, developmental, intelligence and academic tests. A parent of a child with an ASD has a good knowledge base of what their child is able or unable to do just from living with him and observing his capabilities and deficits.

The person's behaviours: A diagnosis of autism is based on observable characteristics, and it is important to look at a child's behaviours and try to understand what they indicate. Is the child covering his ears frequently when there is a lot of activity in the room? Does he often have diarrhoea? Does he have tantrums when you change his routine? Is he always trying to remove all his clothes? Does he appear clumsy and uncoordinated?

Whether the person is a visual or an auditory learner: Many people assume that all people with ASDs are visual learners and therefore that visual strategies will work with everyone. This is not the case, as some people are auditory learners. It is helpful to establish which sense your child uses best.

What the person's strengths and weaknesses are: Every person has strengths, and if you can identify them, you can build on them to fortify the weaknesses.

What goals this person has, or you have for your child: Each person needs to think about what their overall goal is. Perhaps it is a general goal of 'recovering' a child from autism; perhaps it is to have the child reach his potential. Perhaps it is addressing one particular area of a person's life or skill area where he needs to learn practical or coping skills.

What treatments the person has already had (if any): Looking at what has been helpful and what has not can be useful at times in analysing whether or not a particular treatment is worth pursuing.

Whether it is time to reevaluate: Is the person changing, growing? Perhaps a treatment appropriate at one time is no longer the case.

Every once in a while it's a good idea to step back and decide whether the current treatments are still useful or appropriate. It may be time to change or 'tweak' a current treatment.

As Donna Williams suggests at the beginning of this chapter, in the quote taken from her book *Autism: An Inside-Out Approach*, all these therapies, treatments and interventions truly need to be looked at with a department-store mentality, rather than a high-street approach. ASDs are all-invasive, and rarely does one therapy alone provide all the help a person needs. Therapies or treatments are not exclusive of others, and a visit to different departments or types of therapies is often needed.

What to consider when looking at treatment options

After looking at the needs of the person with an ASD, there are other factors to consider before deciding on what treatments and therapies to pursue at this particular time. Some of these are:

- The potential risk to the individual. Does the therapy have side effects? Is it risky to mental or physical health? Do the possible risks outweigh the possible gains? Does it use any form of punishment?

- The family. ASDs are a family thing, as they affect everyone in the household either directly or indirectly. But so does the treatment. The parents have to think about how the treatment or therapy fits into the family. What kind of involvement is expected from others? How will this treatment affect any siblings? Is the family going to be able to follow through with whatever the professional deems necessary (i.e. giving supplements on a regular basis, sticking to a diet, generalising skills learned)? Can the family commit to the prescribed treatment or therapy for whatever time it takes or is recommended? Are all responsible adults in the household in agreement about the particular treatment and supportive of seeing it through? If the treatment fails, how will it affect the family?

FOOD FOR THOUGHT

If I were the parent of a very young child, and this were a perfect world, I would do the following:

● Start an applied behaviour analysis programme with trained therapists and proper supervision for 30–40 hours a week, with a parent doing at least six hours. Research has shown that this method of teaching is effective. It is not a 'cure' for all children, but every child can learn and progress. A parent who is involved and keenly aware of the programme will be able to help the child generalise skills, and get to know the child's strengths and weaknesses.

● Start a sensory integration programme tailored to the child's needs, overseen by a professional who is trained and experienced in sensory integration. Almost everyone with an ASD has sensory integration difficulties in one area or another. This can make it difficult for a child to focus and learn.

● Follow the Sunderland Protocol or the three-step plan developed by DAN! medical practitioner Jeff Bradstreet. If a child is having allergic reactions or intolerance to some foods, if he is not metabolising enough of the nutrients his body needs, if he has toxins in his system: all or any of these could affect his health, his brain functioning, his sensory processing and his ability to learn.

● Try supplements such as vitamin B6, magnesium and DMG. Data based on thousands of cases and twenty published studies show that these supplements have helped 50 per cent of the children who have tried them. If following the Sunderland Protocol or the three-step plan, supplements are in the treatment at some point.

● Engage the child in fun activities, such as music or singing or horse-riding.

● Involve the child in physical therapy or exercise. If my young child were behind in his developmental levels for gross motor skills, I would find a physical therapist to show me what I could do to help strengthen his muscles. If that were not an issue I would make sure my child got plenty of exercise, doing something he enjoys.

The reality is, this is not a perfect world, and each family must decide what the needs of the child are, what the needs of the family are, and what they feel capable of taking on.

- The financial cost of the therapy. Money does not grow on trees. Do you have to sell your home to provide this therapy or intervention? Is insurance going to cover it? Are you asking for the local educational authority or National Health Service to fund the treatment? If yes, do you have the tenacity to advocate effectively to obtain the appropriate type of service?

- Can the treatment be integrated into whatever existing programme the child already has, and if so, how? For example, in the case of a special diet, can it be carried over to all of the child's environments? Will the treatment's inclusion be at the expense of other equally important aspects of the child's programme?

- What evidence exists to validate this method of treatment? Is the therapy being touted as a miracle cure for everyone? Is there scientific validation of this treatment? What does the anecdotal evidence have to say?

- Is this treatment or therapy autism-specific, and if not, has it proved effective with individuals with ASDs? Some treatments may not be specifically created with ASDs in mind, but can be very beneficial. However, it is important to verify how others with an ASD have done with this treatment. For example, early intervention is a great concept. However, some programmes do not work well with all children with autism, because most children with ASDs do not imitate or tune into social cues the way other developmentally delayed children do, and therefore need first to be taught how to imitate or understand those social cues.

- How is the effectiveness of the therapy going to be measured? With any treatment or therapy, there should be record-keeping in order to track effectiveness. Parents need to ask who is responsible for taking data, how data is taken, how often it is recorded and how often is it reviewed.

FOOD FOR THOUGHT

She Had Experience, Just Not the Right Kind

My son is very challenged by sensory integration issues and has many fine and gross motor problems. One year he came home from school with rug burns on his chest and back, the result of an inexperienced occupational therapist's attempts to perform sensory integration on him. After a few phone calls (and I must say no apology from the therapist or the school district in question), two Individual Educational Plan team meetings, a sensory integration (SI) and occupational therapy (OT) assessment, another occupational therapist was brought into the picture. At this point, concerned not only about the quality of my son's educational experience but also for his safety and comfort level, I asked specific questions of the therapist they were proposing about her experience. The therapist said she had a few years of experience with sensory integration, as well as working with adolescents with autism. All seemed well with the world.

After a few months, I received reports from school that the therapist was concerned about the occupational therapy goals for my son. She felt the goals were unrealistic, and that he was not progressing on any of them. The goals the IEP team had identified were doing up his trousers and learning to cut with a knife. I met the therapist to ask how I could help. After chatting with her, I realised that though she had worked with adolescents with ASDs, they had been able students who could follow instructions and did not have the same level of motor difficulties as my son. The therapist had not needed to teach these skills before and was unable, in spite of her professional training, to figure out a way to teach my son these basic tasks. I had not thought before to ask about the ability level of the children she had worked with, thinking that as a professional she could figure things out for varying levels of ability.

The therapist was at a loss about how to teach my son, even though he had a well-trained school aide who was more than willing to help. Needless to say, my son learned to do up his trousers after the aide analysed the different steps and which ones were creating difficulty for him and then wrote up a task analysis, and worked on teaching him this skill in a systematic manner.

So, the moral of the story is, ask the right questions. No matter how long my son has been in the system, I am always learning a few more questions that I should have asked.

● What is the track record of the treatment provider of the therapy or treatment? How long have the practitioners been doing this therapy and with what age group? What level of ability has this person worked with? If it is dietary supplements, is it a reputable company that is making them?

● Does the person prescribing the treatment or supervising the course of treatment have all pertinent information about the person being treated? Make sure the person knows as much about the individual in question as possible. It's a good idea to write down anything you think the provider should know, especially if he is dealing with a young child, or someone who is unable to communicate independently about himself. Information that is helpful includes other treatments that may have been tried, the person's likes or dislikes, and particular behaviours the practitioner should know about. Any allergies to food or medication, phobias, chances of seizures, special diets, etc., are all valuable information.

TREATMENTS, THERAPIES AND INTERVENTIONS

This is not meant to be an in-depth overview of all the treatment options, but rather a brief explanation about the most well-known or currently popular ones. Resources are included for those who want more information. Therapies or interventions are listed here for informational purposes only and does not mean that they are endorsed by the author or that they are prescribed for any particular person. The reader should investigate further the treatments that interest them and make an informed decision with professionals and others who may be concerned.

SKILL-BASED TREATMENTS

Listed here are programmes that look at what the person is able to do, and work on specific skills to improve their level of functioning.

Relationships and emotions are considered important, but the basic premise is to start working on specific skills the person needs to acquire in order to be able to learn and live in society.

Applied behaviour analysis (ABA)

This has been proved to be the most effective way to teach young children with ASDs. Specific skills are taught by breaking them into small steps, teaching each step one at a time, building on the previous one. Different methods are used to help the child learn, such as prompting (helping the child by guiding him through the desired response), shaping, and rewarding (for correct responses). ABA has been used for many years to successfully teach individuals of varying abilities, and can be used to teach in all skill areas, including academic, self-help skills, speech and language, and socially appropriate behaviour.

B.F. Skinner is the grandfather of ABA, thanks to his study of 'operant conditioning' and his book *The Behavior of Organisms* published in 1938. ABA is based on the theory that all learned behaviours have an antecedent (what happened before the behaviour was exhibited) and a consequence (what happened after the behaviour was exhibited) and that all such behaviour is shaped by the consequences of our actions, meaning that we are motivated by the consequence to repeat that behaviour. For example, most adults work because they are rewarded by a wage or salary. If they stopped receiving that wage, they would stop working.

Some of the terms used in ABA include:

Task Analysis: This consists of analysing a skill or task that needs to be taught, by identifying each step of the skill, and which steps the person needs to learn. For example, if teaching someone at home how to set the table, you would analyse the whole sequence, from walking to the cupboard, opening the cupboard with the right hand, picking up a plate with the left hand, closing the cupboard with the right hand, walking to the table, and so on.

Discrete Trial Teaching (DTT): This is a method of teaching that is very systematic and consists of the teacher's presentation or request, the child's response, and the consequence to that response (i.e. a reward if correct); a short pause, and then the next trial. Each trial is 'discrete' that is to say separate, so it is clear what is being requested of the child, and what is being rewarded.

The Lovaas Method: This is an intensive ABA programme developed by Dr O. I. Lovaas at the UCLA Young Autism Project and aimed at pre-school children. In 1987 Lovaas published a study that showed dramatic results on 19 children with autism who had received intensive ABA therapy: the average gain in IQ was 20 points, and 47 per cent of the children (nine of them) completed first grade in a mainstream class. In 1993, eight of the nine were still enrolled in mainstream classes and had lost none of their skills.

Verbal Behaviour Therapy: This is ABA therapy as it pertains to language behaviour and is based on Skinner's behavioural analysis of language.

ABA Providers, workshops and supervisors

Parents for the Early Intervention of Autism in Children (PEACH) is a parent-run charity that provides information and training on ABA.

The Brackens
London Road
Ascot
Berkshire SL5 8BE
Tel: 01344 882248
Fax: 01344 882391
Email: info@peach.org.uk
Website www.peach.org.uk

The London Early Autism Project (LEAP) is a clinic and programme for the treatment of pre-school children throughout the UK based on the work of Dr Ivar Lovaas.

LEAP House
699 Fulham Road
London SW6 5UJ
Tel: 020 7736 6688
Fax: 020 7736 8242
Email: info@londonearlyautism.com
Website: www.londonearlyautism.com

Applied Behavior Consultants (ABC) is a 15-year-old ABA firm specialising in autism treatment, with three day-schools and numerous in-home programmes in California.

Dr Joseph Morrow PhD, BCBA
Applied Behavior Consultants (ABC)
4540 Harlin Drive
Sacramento
CA 95826, USA
Tel: (1) 916 364 7800
Fax: (1) 916 364 7888
Website: http://www.abcreal.com/

Center for Autism and Related Disorders (CARD)
CARD develops ABA programmes designed around each child's strengths.

Olivia Wilson, Managing Consultant
Acorn House
Moorefield Road
Orpington
Kent BR6 0HG
Phone: 01689 837373
Fax: 01689 896656
Email: o.wilson@centerforautism.com
Website: www.centerforautism.com

Autism Partnership
Ron Leaf PhD and John McEachin PhD
Provide intense behaviour treatment for children.

PO Box 3389
Sheffield S10 5WR
Tel: 0114 263 1087
Email: info@autismpartnership.com
Website: www.autismpartnership.com/uk

UK Young Autism Project is affiliated to the UCLA Multi-Site Young Autism Project.
Directors: Svein Eikeseth PhD, Diane Hayward BSc, Catherine Gale BSc

Room 18
20 Mortlake High Street
London SW14 8JN
Tel: 020 8392 3931 (client services and careers); 0121 459 5810 (all other enquiries)
Website: www.ukyap.org

ABA websites and internet discussion groups: This discussion list is for all parents using ABA and Lovaas in the UK for the sharing of information about home-based ABA programmes, mainstreaming, combining ABA with special schools and sharing information about Consultants: http://groups.yahoo.com/group/ABA-UK/

Behavioral Intervention Association: This website includes a list of questions that help parents analyse different providers of behavioural therapies as well as think about all that a home programme entails: www.bia4autism.org/questions.php

Life Institute: Dr Lovaas' official website: www.lovaas.com

Website by Christina Burk: This has good explanations about various aspects of ABA: http://www.christinaburkaba.com/index.htm

The ME-List: A Lovaas therapy discussion list on the internet. To sign up: http://php.iupui.edu/~rallen/me_list.html

ABA-UK Discussion Group: For parents in the UK who use ABA: www.egroups.com/group/aba-uk

ABA books

Teaching Developmentally Disabled Children: The ME Book by O. Ivar Lovaas
Facing Autism by Lynn M. Hamilton
Let Me Hear Your Voice by Catherine Maurice
Behavioral Intervention for Young Children with Autism edited by Catherine Maurice, co-edited by Gina Green and Stephen C. Luce
A Work In Progress: Behavior Management Strategies and a Curriculum for Intensive Behavioral Treatment of Autism by Ron Leaf and John McEachin

Picture exchange communication system (PECS)

This is a practical communication system that allows a person to express his needs and desires without being prompted by another person, by using pictures or a series of pictures to form a sentence. The child first learns to communicate by handing someone a picture of the object he wants, then sentence strips and so on. Not only does this facilitate communication, it motivates the child to interact with others. PECS is easy to incorporate into any existing programme, and does not require expensive materials. Behaviourally based instructional techniques are used to implement the programme (such as prompting, shaping, fading, etc). Basic concepts such as numbers, colours and reading can be taught using PECS, and the picture icons can be used for visual schedules to help the child. Co-developed by Andy Bondy and Lori Frost, this method helps relieve the frustration of those unable to speak and does not inhibit a child's ability to acquire and use speech. Many children who began with PECS went on to develop verbal language.

Contact
Pyramid Educational Consultants UK Ltd
17 Prince Albert Street
Brighton BN1 1HF
Tel: 01273 728888
Website: www.pecs-uk.com

Book
A Picture's Worth: PECS and Other Visual Communication Strategies in Autism by Andy Bondy and Lori Frost.

Facilitated communication (FC)

This is a type of communication that was originally developed for use with individuals who had problems controlling or using their muscles (such as cerebral palsy sufferers), and therefore were unable to communicate independently. A facilitator holds the communicator's hand or arm in a certain manner, thus allowing the communicator to point to letters on a letter board or keyboard. In Australia, Rosemary Crossley tried using this method with people with autism. By the early 1990s the use of facilitated communication became widespread in other places in the world. Many non-verbal people with autism were soon able to communicate with a facilitator.

However, this method became controversial because of the lack of research proving that it was the individuals who were communicating and not the facilitators. There have been about 50 studies carried out on FC, but none of them has been able to prove scientifically that it works.

Recriminations continue. Critics of FC say there is no research backing up the claims of its supporters and the supporters criticise the research methods used to explain the failure of the studies to prove the authenticity of the communicator's response.

The goal of facilitated communication was for the individual to eventually be able to communicate independently, without the use of a facilitator. However, it is rare to find the individual who has become independent. Whether this is due to the facilitator not working towards independence by withdrawing support over time, or the inability of the person to communicate on his own, is unclear.

Website:
Facts About Facilitated Communication by Douglas Bilken:
http://soeweb.syr.edu/thefci/fcfacts.htm

Social Stories
This method promotes desired social behaviour by describing
(through the written word) social situations and appropriate social
responses. Developed by Carol Gray, social stories may be applied to
a wide variety of social situations and are created with the learner who
takes an active role in developing the story.

Research has shown that many people with autism have mindblindness. That is to say they do not understand that people think
differently than they do, have their own plans and points of reference.

FOOD FOR THOUGHT
Facilitated Communication: Its Rise and Fall

Can some autistic children who cannot speak communicate
meaningfully in writing?

By Dr Bernard Rimland, founder Autism Research Institute

I was probably the first person to discuss this question publicly, in
my lectures and writings, starting in the early 1970s. I reported that
a very small percentage of autistic individuals are able to express
their own thoughts in writing, but not speech. I referred to these
individuals as 'autistic-crypto-savants': crypto meaning the ability
was hidden, waiting to be discovered. I discussed and described
several such rare individuals whom I had encountered during a
period of several decades and urged that efforts be made to identify
and encourage them.

In the mid-1980s I began to hear from colleagues in Australia
about Rosemary Crossley, the Director of the DEAL Center in
Melbourne, who was using a technique she called 'Facilitated
Communication' to elicit writing – usually very sophisticated and
highly literate – from severely handicapped, non-speaking autistic
and mentally retarded clients. Facilitated Communication (F/C) was

based on the assumption that these autistic or mentally retarded individuals had very little control of their hand and finger movements, and therefore needed the help of trained 'facilitators' to support their hands, while they used their fingers to spell words on a keyboard or a letterboard.

Crossley's work also attracted the attention of Douglas Biklen, a professor at Syracuse University in New York, who spent a month at the DEAL Center in 1989, and returned to the U.S. with bombshell news: virtually all autistic and mentally retarded persons were very capable of expressing themselves fluently, usually immediately, if they were provided with a skilled facilitator. The media were ecstatic. The major magazines and all the television networks featured Douglas Biklen and the miraculous breakthrough he had brought with him from Australia. Many parents were also ecstatic – their beloved non-speaking children were able not only to communicate, but to communicate eloquently. Academia joined the celebration. Conferences held at major universities and elsewhere were attended by standing-room-only crowds.

But things were not very rosy in Australia. The government-sponsored Intellectual Disability Review Panel investigated Crossley's methods and claims and was not impressed, noting that intellectually-disabled individuals are 'extremely susceptible to influence by people who may be unaware of the extent to which they may be influencing decisions'.

I began receiving clippings of newspaper articles from Australia saying a number of parents had been charged, by their own children using facilitated communication, with physical and sexual abuse. In one such widely-publicised case, a 29-year-old mentally handicapped woman, Carla, had been forcibly removed from her home by the police after she had allegedly accused her parents of sexually abusing her. After more than a year of the parents fighting these charges, the court awarded them full guardianship of Carla, concluding that the allegations made through F/C were untrue. During the trial the facilitator demonstrated to the court how skillfully Carla could answer various questions. She was able to give an anatomically correct description of sexual intercourse, for example. However, when the defense asked Carla 'What is the name of your dog?' there was no answer.

There were a number of such alleged abuse cases in Australia, then very quickly the same phenomenon began in the U.S., where parents, teachers and others were being accused via F/C of sexual and physical abuse.

The courts were confronted with a number of questions: 'Is F/C a valid technique? How can we be sure that the communication is coming from the handicapped individual, rather than from the facilitator?'

The controversy over F/C raged on for a number of years. Numerous experimental studies were undertaken to determine its validity; many of which by the facilitators themselves, who wanted to prove, under carefully controlled circumstances, that the messages they believed they were eliciting from their clients were in fact coming from their clients, and not from themselves.

To date, approximately 70 such studies have been published, involving some 500 mentally-handicapped individuals. The major outcome of all this research is very clear: it shows overwhelmingly that if the facilitator does not know the answer to a question, the client cannot respond correctly. Further, the more carefully the study was done, the more likely F/C was to be found invalid. The few studies which the authors claimed to support the value of F/C tend to be poorly designed and poorly executed. Even the results that are said by F/C proponents to show that F/C is valid are very weak. (For example, the client might be able to point to the letters C-A-T when shown a picture of a cat. This is a far cry from the ability to 'express his own thoughts in his own words,' as originally claimed by Crossley and Biklen.)

The consistently negative findings from the research studies, as well as the consistently anti-F/C decisions of the courts, have led most major organisations that advocate for the developmentally disabled to condemn F/C as being an invalid method of communicating. These include the American Academy of Child and Adolescent Psychiatry, the American Academy of Pediatrics, the American Psychological Association, the American Speech and Hearing Association and the American Association on Mental Retardation.

But a few non-speaking autistic persons *can* write. I am aware of at least three books that were written by autistic individuals who could write but not speak. The autistic author of one of these books learned to write via facilitated communication. The other two authors emphatically deny that their writing is the result of their having been exposed to facilitated communication.

Howard Shane has been directing a clinic for non-speaking children at the Boston Children's Hospital (Harvard University Medical School) for 25 years. He is considered to be an expert on the use of augmentive means of communication for non-speaking children, including autistic children, having worked with hundreds of autistic children during this time. I asked him how many non-speaking children were able to write meaningfully. He replied that perhaps three or four of the hundreds of children he had seen, or approximately 1 percent could do that. But if the question were very simple, such as 'What is this?' ('D-O-G') or 'What colour is this?' ('R-E-D'), the number might be 5–10 percent. However, he said, F/C was quite unnecessary in teaching such children, since if they are interested in words or letters, they tend to learn on their own, or with encouragement from their parents or teachers.

Let us now consider the specific question: how can you tell if it is your child or the facilitator who is communicating by F/C? Use the same method that many of the courts have used: send the facilitator to another room so he cannot hear what is being said. Select several objects that you can show and describe to the child, for example, a comb, a $5 bill, and perhaps a picture of a horse. Invite the facilitator back into the room and ask him/her 'What did we discuss while you were gone?'

An even simpler method: the facilitator helps the child name objects on flash cards visible to both him and the child. Then move the cards to where only the child can see them.

In one case in Massachusetts, a man who had been in jail for eight months because of allegations made via F/C that he had sexually molested his girlfriend's child, was immediately released when the facilitator was totally unable to assist the child in spelling the names of any of the several objects that had been discussed during the facilitator's absence from the room.

The bottom line: be careful!

This may be why they are unable to anticipate what others may say or do, which creates problems in social behaviour and communication.

Social stories usually have descriptive sentences about the setting, characters, and their feelings and thoughts, and give direction in regard to the appropriate responses and behaviours. Comic strip conversations are illustrations of conversations that show what people say and do, as well as emphasise what people may be thinking. Social stories and comic strip conversations can be adapted to many levels and situations, and anyone can learn to create them. They are particularly useful for learning how to deal with unstructured time such as lunchtime.

Books

Comic Strip Conversations: Colorful Illustrated Interactions with Students with Autism and Related Disorders by Carol Gray

The New Social Story Book by Carol Gray

The Original Social Story Book by Carol Gray

Teaching Children with Autism to Mindread: A Practical Guide for Teachers and Parents by Patricia Howlin and Simon Baron-Cohen

Social skills groups

These teach specific social skills by breaking them down and providing practice in a 'safe' environment. Depending on the age or grade level, different social skills are emphasised, including making conversation, turn-taking, joining a group, dealing with bullying, friendship and understanding facial expressions. Social skills training usually takes place in groups of four to six children and is usually beneficial for the more able person with an ASD. Social skill development is one of the biggest challenges children with ASDs face, and a well-structured social skills group can be beneficial.

Books

Autism/Asperger's: Solving the Relationship Puzzle by Steven E. Gutstein

Autism: A Social Skills Approach for Children and Adolescents by M. Aarons and T. Gittens

An Integrated Approach to Social Communication Problems by M. Aarons and T. Gittens

The Social Use of Language Programme (SULP)

This programme is a multi-sensory programme useful in developing interpersonal and social abilities from a thinking skills and communication perspective. SULP has been shown to be effective in students with various and mixed abilities. No research has been done to date to prove its effectiveness with students who have ASDs; however, anecdotal evidence indicates that SULP could be beneficial for those on the higher end of the spectrum. This programme is structured, yet flexible, and uses strong visual and action activities such as games, modelling and video feedback.

Contact

ICAN

4 Dyers Building

Holborn

London EC1N 2QP

Tel: 0870 010 4066

Email: info@ican.org.uk

Website: http://www.ican.org.uk/

PHYSIOLOGICALLY ORIENTED INTERVENTIONS

Effective teaching methods are extremely important, but so is the child's physical and neurological health. If an individual's body and/or brain is not working properly, learning will be that much more difficult, and for some, close to impossible. Scientists are hard at work discovering all the secrets the brain has to offer, and much is still unknown. However, as there is a definite connection between the body and the brain, a healthy body is a priority.

This category of treatments, including therapies that address sensory issues as well as dietary and biomedical interventions, holds many possibilities. Bear in mind that this list is not exhaustive. Some of these treatments have no side effects and some do. Some are expensive, some are cheap. Some have empirical research to back them up, some of them have only anecdotal reports.

Before starting any of these interventions, data should be taken over at least a two-week period on all of the person's negative (tantrums, hyperactivity, bedwetting) and positive (communication, staying on task, eye contact) behaviours. This will give a baseline of the behaviours before treatment. During and after treatment, the same types of notes should be taken. This will enable you to judge whether or not the treatment is having an effect.

THERAPIES THAT ADDRESS SENSORY ISSUES

Jean Ayres, an occupational therapist, first described sensory integration dysfunction as a result of inefficient neurological dysfunction. The auditory, visual, tactile, taste and smell senses are what give us information about the world around us. Individuals with sensory disorders have senses that are inaccurate and send false messages. Children and adults with hypersensitivity overreact to stimuli, while others have hypo-sensitivity, which prevents them from picking up information through their senses. Sensory malfunction can also be an inability to understand and organise sensory information when it is received.

Sensory integration dysfunction symptoms are many and varied depending on which sense or senses are perturbed. When he has auditory sensitivities a child may cover his ears, overreact or underreact to noise, or try to escape from groups. Tactile sensitivities can be indicated by a seemingly high tolerance for pain, refusal to keep socks and shoes and sometimes clothes on, difficulty in brushing teeth and hair, dislike of having hair washed. Visual issues may be apparent if a child is sensitive to light, likes to watch things spin or move (tops, hands on a clock), spins himself or other things or turns lights on and off. These are a few examples of behaviours that display sensitivities in certain areas; however, you may wish to consult Lynn Hamilton's book *Facing Autism* for a more complete list.

Sensory issues are not autism-specific, and therefore the methods below were not specifically developed for people with autism. Many children and adults who have sensory disorders do not have an ASD. However, all books that I have read written by adults with an ASD describe sensory impairment of one kind or another, and all the children with autism that I know appear to have some sort of sensory issue. It is important that you choose therapy providers who have experience with ASDs and the age group of the person seeking treatment.

Sensory Integration (SI)

This is practised by occupational therapists, who contend that many behaviours exhibited by children and adults with autism are an attempt to avoid certain types of sensations or to seek preferred stimuli, in order to balance out their nervous system. There are different strategies that are used. Occupational therapists who are well trained in sensory integration have designed individual programmes that have led to improvements in behaviour and skills by assisting individuals with ASDs to process and use sensory information. Data from patient records show these improvements. SI can be a valuable intervention, integrated into a child's programme, depending on the person's sensory issues.

Contact
Sensory Integration International
PO Box 5339
Torrance
CA 90510-5339, USA
Tel: (1) 310 787 8805
Fax: (1) 310 787 8130
Email: info@sensoryint.com
Website: http://home.earthlink.net/~sensoryint/

Books
The Out-of-Synch Child by Carol Stock Kranowitz
Facing Autism by Lynn Hamilton

Auditory integration training (AIT)

These methods were developed by Dr Guy Berard and Dr Alfred Tomatis, and are based on the theory that some people have a hypersensitivity towards certain sound frequencies, making some common sounds painful to hear. In AIT, individuals wear head-phones and listen to modulated sounds and music with certain frequencies filtered out. This is done over a period of time. It is not known exactly how it works physiologically speaking; however, individuals have reported benefits from these listening methods. Other listening programmes have been developed that can be used at home without any special equipment. The Society for Auditory Intervention Techniques is a great resource for information on various types of auditory therapies. A review of 28 reports of studies between January 1993 and May 2001 on AIT, as developed by Dr Berard, was undertaken by Dr Edelson and Dr Rimland. They concluded that 'The balance of the evidence clearly favors AIT as a useful intervention, especially in autism.' However, the Tomatis method does not appear to be supported by any published research studies.

Contacts
Society for Auditory Intervention Techniques
PO Box 4538
Salem
OR 97302, USA
Email: info@sait.org
Website: www.sait.org

To purchase EASe home audio discs, a type of listening programme you can do at home, contact:

Vision Audio Inc.
611 Anchor Drive
Joppa
MD 21085, USA
Tel: (1)888 213 7858 or (1)410 679 1605
Email: visionaud@earthlink.net
Website: www.vision-audio.com

Book

The Sound of a Miracle by Annabel Stehli (about her daughter's recovery from autism through AIT)

Irlen lenses

These were developed by Helen Irlen for individuals with a sensory perceptual problem known as Irlen syndrome. Irlen's theory is that people with reading problems and perceptual difficulties are very sensitive to white-light spectrum wavelengths, which overstimulate certain cells in the retina, resulting in incorrect signals being sent to the brain. She found that by placing different-coloured overlays on printed pages, light sensitivity and perceptual distortions were reduced. These colours were then applied as a tint on glasses. There is no strong empirical research to support the use of Irlen lenses as an autism-specific therapy; however, coloured overlays on printed matter and tinted glasses have been shown to be helpful for a number of school children. There is anecdotal evidence that some people with ASDs have light sensitivity, and have reported a major difference in their sensory processing when wearing tinted glasses. It would be interesting to study if tinted lenses available for use as sunglasses have the same effect as Irlen lenses.

Contact
The British Dyslexia Association
98 London Road
Reading RG1 5AU
Tel: 0118 966 2677
Fax: 0118 935 1927
Email: admin@bda-dyslexia.demon.co.uk
Website: http://www.bda-dyslexia.org.uk/main/information/extras/x01eyes.asp
Direct link to more information about light sensitivity and the use of coloured lenses and overlays as well as helpful resources.

Tito and Soma: Never Underestimate the Power of a Parent

Tito Rajarshi Mukhopadhyay is a teenager from India who is severely autistic and writes eloquently. His mother, Soma, raised him and educated him with little help from anyone else. When he was two and a half he was diagnosed as autistic and she was told to keep him busy. Soma did just that. She read to him from texbooks on subjects ranging from science to literature when she wasn't engaged in teaching him other skills. Any physical activity, such as riding a bicycle, she had to teach him by physically motoring his body through the motions. She taught him to write by attaching a pencil to his fingers with a rubber band as he was unable to hold it on his own. She taught him to point to numbers and letters, also by physically prompting him through the tasks. By age six he was able to write independently.

In December 1999, Soma took Tito to England, to Elliot House (the Centre for Social and Communication Disorders run by the National Autistic Society), where he was observed and assessed by Dr Lorna Wing, Dr Beate Hermelin and Judith Gould, among others. Tito at the time was 11, yet reached the level of a 19-year-old on the British Picture Vocabulary Scale administered by Dr Gould. His story, from India to the UK and back home again, is the subject of a BBC programme, *Inside Story: Tito's Story*. The National Autistic Society subsequently published a book written by Tito entitled *Beyond the Silence: My Life, the World and Autism*.

Since the autumn of 2001, Tito and Soma have been living in Los Angeles. Brought over by Cure Autism Now, Tito graciously consented to undergo extensive testing by experts such as Dr Michael Merzenich, a neuroscientist at the University of California at San Francisco Medical School. Much is being learned through Tito about people with severe autism and their brain functioning. For example, in perception testing where lights are flashed on a computer screen at the same time as the sound of beeps is issued, most people can sense the beep and the light at the same time. However, Tito cannot see the light on a computer screen unless it appears a full three seconds after the beeps. He explains that he can only use one sense at a time, and has chosen to use his ears. This is in marked contrast to Dr Temple Grandin, a professor at

Colorado State University who holds a doctorate in animal science and has autism. Dr Grandin explains that she thinks totally in pictures, that thinking in language and words is incomprehensible to her, and that she has difficulty with her ultrasensitive hearing because she cannot tune out unwanted noise the way most of us can.

Meanwhile, Soma has been working with a class of severely autistic children using the method she developed with Tito, which she calls the Rapid Prompt Method. Soma demands rapid responses from the children in order to keep their brains from disengaging from the task or lesson at hand. She physically motors them through responses, gradually fading the prompt until the child is able to respond on his own. Cure Autism Now has been videotaping the progress of the class over a year in order to ascertain if Soma's method can help others like her son. More research is needed, but neuroscientists such as Dr Merzenich are hopeful that this teaching method will help many. For more information, contact Cure Autism Now (see resources section at the end of the book).

The Irlen Institute website has information about Irlen lenses and the location of different test centres in the UK: http://www.irlen.com/

Book

Reading by the Colors by Helen Irlen

DIETARY AND BIOMEDICAL INTERVENTIONS

What follows is a basic overview of some of the dietary and biomedical interventions that are being used to treat ASDs. Some of these interventions have empirical research to back them up. Some have much anecdotal testimony. Some of these interventions are non-invasive and worth trying; others should only be done under the care of a knowledgeable health professional.

These types of interventions are effective in helping people whose metabolic systems may not be functioning properly. It may be that their systems are not processing essential nutrients properly, possibly because of a food allergy or intolerance, or a 'leaky gut' (where the wall of the intestine does not do its job of keeping its contents separate from the bloodstream), or high levels of mercury or other toxic metals. It is possible to check for food allergies by adding or removing the suspected culprit from the person's diet and taking data before and after on their behaviour. Essential nutrients can be tested in the same way. However, there are specific tests and analyses that can be done which are more indicative of what is going on in the metabolic system.

More and more health practitioners are learning about these interventions and how to treat patients with ASDs from a dietary and biomedical perspective. In the last few years an increasing amount of credence has been given to the positive effects of these interventions on many individuals with ASDs. And although more research is needed, it is important to note that the discovery of many of these interventions has been due to a strong collaboration between parents and medical professionals. At times it was parents who convinced health practitioners or researchers to think 'outside the box' in searching for answers to their child's behaviours. At other times it was medical professionals who dared to look beyond the confines of traditional medicine. Together they have formed a strong partnership, widening the prism through which autism is viewed and treated from the medical perspective. To them we owe a resounding thank-you.

Dietary and biomedical interventions can be confusing for anyone who is not medically inclined. Please keep in mind that what follows is not a complete analysis of all the possible interventions. Before attempting any of them, I would strongly suggest that the reader obtains a more complete understanding of this area of intervention by reading or consulting the following:

Facing Autism by Lynn Hamilton. As mentioned earleier, her explanations about dietary and biomedical interventions are easy to read.

'The Sunderland Protocol: A logical sequencing of biomedical interventions for the treatment of autism and related disorders' by Paul Shattock and Paul Whiteley. This is a more complete overview in

---

FOOD FOR THOUGHT
The Power of Sharing Knowledge

'Thirty years later, Dr Rimland and I had lunch down the street from my home and office in Connecticut. I expressed how inadequate I felt in understanding the digestive and immune system problems of the autistic children I was seeing in increasing numbers. I asked Dr Rimland if he could gather some smart people to brainstorm the problems. I knew one smart person, Jon Pangborn. Bernie knew dozens around the world. Within a few months he had organized and named the first DAN! (Defeat Autism Now!) meeting, an extraordinary gathering of 30 practitioners, researchers, and parents who found common ground in a new map of the landscape that emerged from the mirage that once simply cast blame on mothers.'

Sidney MacDonald Baker MD, *Defeat Autism Now! 2002*, Conference Presentations Book.

---

a 14-page document that walks the reader through the steps of eliminating or adding different substances, explaining the reasoning and research at each level. In this manner, it is possible for a parent or practitioner to try different interventions and assess the effects on a particular child.

'Biomedical Assessment Options for Children With Autism and Related Problems – A Consensus Report of the Defeat Autism Now! (DAN!) Scientific Effort Autism Research Institute'. This is the most complete and detailed of the sources. Some of it is easy to read and some is a bit mind-boggling for the non-medically inclined. Look on the Autism Research Institute website (www.autismresearchinstitute.com).

'Parents Ratings of Behavioural Effects of Drugs and Nutrients'. Since 1967 the Autism Research Institute has been collecting information on the usefulness of the interventions parents have tried on their children. See Appendix at the end of this book.

For those wishing to read studies regarding dietary and biological interventions for ASDs, Karyn Seroussi of the Autism Network for Dietary Intervention (ANDI) has compiled most of them on this website: http://www.autismndi.com/studies.htm

Gluten free/casein free (GFCF) diet

This has been developed for individuals who have allergies or a toxic response to gluten (found in wheat, oats, rye and barley among others) and casein (found in dairy products). Some indications of allergy or a toxic response to gluten and casein are diarrhoea, constipation, hyperactivity, red face or ears, breaking wind frequently, pale skin. (However, it is important to note that these symptoms can be an indication of other problems.) Basically, peptides that are derived from an incomplete breakdown of certain types of food are affecting neurotransmission within the central nervous system.

Research studies as well as hundreds of anecdotal reports have shown dietary intervention as a useful treatment for alleviating some of the symptoms of autism in children. It is less clear what the effect is on adults.

This type of treatment, though constraining in terms of diet, is not harmful and it may be worth removing your child from gluten and casein to see if it has an effect on his behaviour. However, there are urine and blood tests which can give information as to the level of peptides your child has, which would be a helpful indicator of before and after trials to see if the diet is helping.

Contact
Autism Research Unit
School of Health Sciences
University of Sunderland
Sunderland SR2 7EE
Tel: 0191 510 8922 or 0191 515 2581
Fax: 0191 567 0420
Email: hs0psh@orac.sunderland.ac.uk or aru@sunderland.ac.uk
Website: http://osiris.sunderland.ac.uk/autism/

Websites
http://www.shopping-guide.co.uk/uk_supermarkets/index.shtml
On this website you can access major supermarkets and search their
sites to see what foods are available in their stores.

Allergy Induced Autism: http://www.autismmedical.com/

GFCF diet website: http://www.gfcfdiet.com/

Coeliac disease and gluten-free diet on-line resource centre:
www.celiac.com

Autism Network for Dietary Intervention (ANDI): http://www.
autismndi.com/

Books
There are many interesting books on gluten- and casein-free diets, as
well as recipe books. The above websites give details of many of them.
In addition, the following are worth looking at:

A User Guide to the GF/CF Diet for Autism, Asperger Syndrome and AD/HD
    by Luke Jackson and Marilyn Le Breton. A book by a teenager
    with an ASD who is on this diet.
Unraveling the Mystery of Pervasive Developmental Disability by Karen
    Seroussi
Special Diets for Special Kids by Lisa Lewis
*Autism as a Metabolic Disorder: Guidelines for Gluten and Casein-Free
    Dietary Intervention* by Paul Shattock, Paul Whiteley and Dawn
    Savery, offers a more complete look at the science behind GFCF
    diets and guidelines on how to get started on the diet in the UK.

Anti-yeast (fungal) diet
This is helpful for those individuals who have an overgrowth of yeast
(*Candida albicans*) in their system. Children who have autism and have
had frequent ear infections treated by antibiotics may be likely to have
an overabundance of yeast in their gut. While the antibiotics may

reduce the bacterial flora naturally present in the gut, the candida increases, as it is not affected by the antibiotics. Physical symptoms of yeast overgrowth may include gastrointestinal distress, headaches, skin rashes; behavioural symptoms may include irritability, confusion and hyperactivity. As these may be characteristics of other difficulties, testing for yeast overgrowth is advisable.

Anecdotal reports show that this diet has been effective in over 50 per cent of cases. There are some antifungals such as luzoconazole that may be useful for more persistent yeast overgrowth.

Books
Feast Without Yeast by Dr Bruce Semon and Lori Kornblum
The Yeast Connection by Dr William Crook
Biological Treatments for Autism and PDD by Dr William Shaw

The Feingold diet
This diet was developed by Dr Ben Feingold to treat hyperactivity in children. In his book *Why Your Child is Hyperactive* he recommends removing artificial colourings and flavourings, salicylates and some preservatives from children's diets. Salicylates are a group of chemicals related to aspirin and found in certain fruits and vegetables. His hypothesis was that more and more children were being seen and treated for hyperactivity at the time the book was published, due to the increase in artificial ingredients being added to our food and the increase in the consumption of processed foods.

Website
The Feingold Association of the United States: www.feingold.org

Book
Why Can't My Child Behave? Why Can't She Cope? Why Can't He Learn?
by Jane Hersey

The ketogenic diet
This diet has been developed for people who have seizures. It is high in fat, low in protein and carbohydrates. When the body burns fat for

energy instead of carbohydrates, it creates ketone bodies, which in turn suppress seizure activity. This is not a healthy, balanced diet, it is difficult to undertake and it has to be tailored specifically for each person. It is usually considered to be a last-ditch effort when medications are no longer effective, and should not be attempted without the supervision of a neurologist and with the help of a knowledgeable dietician.

Websites
The National Society for Epilepsy http://www.epilepsynse.org.uk/pages/info/leaflets/keto.cfm#how
Pediatric Neurology Division at Stanford University School of Medicine http://www.stanford.edu/group/ketodiet/

Book
The Epilepsy Diet Treatment: an Introduction to the Ketogenic Diet by John M. Freeman, Millicent T. Kelly and Jennifer B. Freeman

Mercury detoxification treatment (chelation)
There has been growing concern over the last few years about a possible connection between mercury and ASDs. Mercury is present in dental amalgam, certain types of seafood, and in Thiomersal, a preservative found in some vaccines. It is highly toxic and some individuals are extremely sensitive to it. If the mercury exposure has been fairly recent, urine, hair and blood analysis may show some trace. However, provoked excretion of mercury and heavy metals is necessary to estimate the amount in the body. Defeat Autism Now! and the Autism Research Institute brought together the expertise of 24 experienced physicians and researchers to come up with a mercury detoxification protocol, published in June 2001. It is suggested that before starting the mercury detoxification treatment, patients must correct as much as possible any nutritional disturbances, or 'leaky gut' problems. This is because many of the drugs and supplements used for mercury detoxification can increase the growth of bacteria and fungi.

Resource
'Mercury Detoxification Consensus Group Position Paper' on the ARI website: www.autismresearchinstitute.com

Vitamin B6 and magnesium
This is one of the treatments you can try without worrying about possible negative effects. Since 1965, 20 studies on these supplements have been published. These studies have shown benefits to taking vitamin B6 (often combined with magnesium) and none have shown harm. Some of the benefits reported have been: improved eye contact, improved language, reduced self-stimulatory behaviour, reduced aggression, and reduced self-injurious behaviour.

Website
The Autism Research Institute: www.autismresearchinstitute.com

Dimethylglycine (DMG)
This is a naturally occurring substance in the body and is implicated in a number of important biochemical reactions. Much anecdotal evidence exists that DMG has been helpful for some people with autism, although there have been no scientifically valid trials to show efficacy. Reported benefits are: positive changes in behaviour, improved language and even in some cases reduction of seizures. Some parents have reported increased hyperactivity, and in those cases it is suggested that small amounts of folic acid be added to alleviate the problem. As DMG is not harmful, it is one of those therapies worth trying. For information, contact the Autism Research Institute.

Fatty acids
It has been recognised that fats have a very important role to play in the metabolism and development of the body. However, due to the way our foods are now processed and the widening use of antibiotics which alter the intestinal flora, plus the fact that we do not swallow a daily spoonful of cod liver oil the way our grandparents did, it has become apparent that most of us are not getting the fatty acids our bodies need.

Omega fats, cod liver oil and evening primrose oil may be of benefit to all individuals, not just those with autism. Cod liver oil has the added benefit of containing vitamin A.

Sulphate ions

Dr Rosemary Waring at the University of Birmingham has been studying the levels of sulphates in children with autism, and was the first researcher to produce scientific evidence of abnormal sulphate levels in such children. (It was the UK parent group Allergy Induced Autism that first brought concerns of a possible link between sulphation and autism to the attention of Dr Waring.) Some children with ASDs show a deficiency of sulphates in their plasma. Sulphate is a substance the body produces that helps break down and get rid of compounds it no longer needs, such as the residues that are left once medication has done its job. This deficiency may contribute to 'leaky gut'. Sulphates appear to be important for hormone effectiveness as well as good intestinal function. As sulphate ions are not easily obtained from food but may be absorbed through the skin, magnesium sulphate (Epsom salts) is added to bathwater as a way of facilitating absorption.

Enzymes

The stomach enzymes of some people with autism may not be working properly. It could be that in some there are insufficient levels of peptidase enzymes, or insufficient acid in the stomach for the enzymes to break down proteins. Some parents of children with hyperactivity have for many years been using enzymes taken orally to help with some of the problems associated with hyperactivity. Enzyme therapy is usually administered in conjunction with other dietary interventions.

Secretin

This is a hormone involved in gastric function. It stimulates the pancreas to produce substances that aid in the process of digestion, among other functions. It was originally made from the intestines of pigs. Secretin as a therapy for autism was discovered by accident in 1996 as a result of an endoscopy performed on Parker Beck, a non-verbal child with autism who suffered constant chronic diarrhoea.

Parker's parents noticed dramatic changes in their child after this procedure, in which secretin had been used, and they pushed for medical professionals to look into the possibility that it might be beneficial to other children. Some doctors and parents have seen dramatic changes in some children with autism after treatment. No one really knows how or why it works. At time of publication of this book, clinical trials are being conducted in the US to evaluate the safety and efficacy of synthetic secretin.

Website
Repligen: www.repligen.com

Intravenous immunoglobulin (IVIG) therapy
IVIG is a blood product that is tested and processed and given to the person over a period of months. No one is quite sure how it works, but it appears to have an effect on the immune system.

More resources for biomedical interventions
For those interested in consulting general practitioners in the UK implementing the Defeat Autism Now! consensus report on biomedical interventions, the Autism Research Institute has posted a physician referral list on its website: www.autismresearchinstitute.com

For those interested in a 'one-stop-shop' treatment plan, Dr Jeff Bradstreet of the International Child Development and Resource Center in Florida (where the UK's Dr Andrew Wakefield is Director of Research) has developed a three-step procedure for the testing and treatment of developmental disabilities, including ASDs. This treatment plan includes all the necessary analyses and an individualised treatment plan. The service is now available in the European Union, as well as an online training course for parents and health professionals called 'Open Windows Essential Training Program'. Information is provided for entitlements to costs for treatment and testing within the European Union.
Website: http://www.newlifelearning.com/3step_index.htm

General reading for those interested in biomedical interventions:

Biological Treatments for Autism and PDD by William Shaw
Children With Starving Brains: A Medical Treatment Guide For Autism Spectrum Disorder by Jaquelyn McCandless
Treating Autism: Parent Stories of Hope and Success, edited by Stephen M. Edelson, PhD and Bernard Rimland, PhD

FOOD FOR THOUGHT
Tips from Temple Grandin

Temple Grandin is a woman with autism who has a successful international career designing livestock equipment. Temple completed her PhD in Animal Science at the University of Illinois in Urbana and is now an Assistant Professor of Animal Science at Colorado State University. She credits early intervention, starting at age two and a half, for her recovery from autism.

Temple has written two books, *Thinking in Pictures* and *Emergence: Labeled Autistic* (with Margaret Scariano), as well as many informative articles, which can be found on the website of the Center for the Study of Autism (CSA) at www.autism.org

Over two phone conversations, Temple shared with me the following important information about what can help people with autism spectrum disorders to learn.

Therapies, treatments and interventions: As every person has different areas of strengths and challenges, what works for one person may not work for the next. For each person, finding the right balance of strategies is important. Donna Williams, who has many sensory challenges, uses a combination of strategies to offset the difficulties she encounters. She wears Irlen lenses, is on a gluten- and casein-free diet, and is now taking a tiny daily dose of Risperdol (a quarter of a milligram a day), an anti-psychotic. Temple takes Norpramin, an anti-depressant, and still uses the 'Squeeze Machine' she invented years ago. Temple designed and built this machine as a teenager after observing the calm effect a squeeze chute had on animals at a relative's farm. This was in response to her need for deep pressure, under her control, that she craved and that helped her cope with anxiety.

Educational strategies: Temple has accumulated much information and experience over the years about what is effective in helping others to learn (see p.184). The most important point she makes is that intensive and early intervention with the right kind of teacher is crucial, more important than the type of programme.

Medication: Temple reports that medications have helped her tremendously over the years. In her book *Thinking in Pictures*, she includes a chapter on the different kinds of medications and how they can be helpful. She has recently reviewed this chapter and found the information still to be valid, although more recent developments, such as the newer atypical antipsychotic medications, are not listed. When treating with medications it is important to look at the benefits of the medication versus the risks, especially with children, whose bodies are still not fully developed and to start with tiny doses. Temple says that a good rule of thumb in deciding whether or not to continue using the medication is to look at the 'wow' factor. If a child is put on a medication and there is an obvious dramatic, positive change in him (e.g. a non-verbal child can now speak) then the benefit may outweigh the risks.

For example, Temple told me that she recently attended a conference with Donna Williams and was amazed at how Donna was able to tolerate sitting and having dinner with her and other people in a noisy environment. If Donna lapses from her gluten- and casein-free diet now, the effects are not so severe. This way she can travel and eat in restaurants. Her improvement is attributed to the tiny amount of Risperdol she takes daily.

However, it is important to find a doctor who is knowledgeable about autism and medications, and to try medications only under the guidance of such a person. Ask your local autism chapter for names of doctors who are familiar with medications, doses, and the effects on people with ASDs, as again, this treatment needs to be individualised for each person.

Psychopharmacologic treatments (traditional medications)

Medications can be used to treat some of the behaviours associated with autism. Certain drugs are used to control seizures. For some people, drugs can be helpful for reducing anxiety, obsessive–compulsive behaviours, hyperactivity, self-injurious behaviours, attention deficits and depression. Medications used include anticonvulsant drugs, stimulant medications, tranquillisers, antidepressants and opiate antagonists. No medication should be tried without the advice of a knowledgeable physician familiar with ASDs and the person being treated. Most of these medications should be tried in very tiny doses, less than the manufacturers' recommendation. Care should be given especially when treating young children, as many of these medications have been researched for use in adults only.

Resources

For more information on particular drugs read the book *Essential Psychopharmacology* by S.M. Stahl or the sections on medication tips and medication in the book *Autistic Spectrum Disorders: Understanding the Diagnosis and Getting Help* by Mitzi Waltz. Also, the Autism Research Institute has developed a chart outlining how parents rate the effectiveness of many drugs and nutrients they have tried (see Appendix in back of book). In addition, you may wish to call MIND, as they also have knowledge on many of these drugs, on 020 8519 2122, ext. 275.

TREATMENTS BASED ON FORMING INTERPERSONAL RELATIONSHIPS

These treatments are mainly concerned with facilitating attachment and bonding as well as a sense of relatedness, which are seen as the cornerstone on which the normal development of the child is built. These approaches vary in how they can be used in conjunction with other therapies and how they are accepted and utilised by the majority of families and professionals.

The floor-time approach

This was developed by Dr Stanley I. Greenspan as part of his developmental approach to therapy. Parents and floor-time therapists help children master the emotional milestones needed to develop a foundation for learning. The approach is based on his belief that emotions give meaning to our experiences, as well as a direction to our actions. Floor-time seeks to have the child develop a sense of pleasure in interacting and relating to others, and is done through play, based on the child's interests, and creating an increasingly large circle of interaction between the child and an adult. Parents and therapists work on four goals: encouraging attention and intimacy; two-way communication; encouraging the expression and use of ideas and feelings; and logical thought. This method is often used as the play component for children who are in ABA programmes. An analysis of the charts of 200 children has provided some data to validate its effectiveness. Floor-time looks promising for helping children with autism relate to others. As this is a relatively new technique, more empirical research is needed.

Website
www.polyxo.com/floortime/buildingplaypartnerships.html

Book
The Child With Special Needs: Encouraging Intellectual and Emotional Growth by Stanley I. Greenspan and Serna Wieder

The Portage early education programme

This is not autism-specific, and is a home teaching programme for families with pre-school children who have special educational needs. The main focus is on supporting the development of young children's play, relationships and communication, as well as encouraging the child to participate in everyday life at home and in the community. Trained Portage visitors set goals with the family for the child's development through stimulating activities, and provide training on these activities. Between visits, the parents or carers may practise the activities with the child. Progress may be recorded if desired with checklists and activity charts.

Contact
The National Portage Association
PO Box 3075
Yeovil
Somerset BA21 3FB
Tel: 01935 471641
Email: npa@portageuk.freeserve.co.uk

Gentle teaching

This is one of those therapies based on the belief that adults need to show unconditional acceptance of the individual with autism, and interact in a warm and caring way to develop a bond. Inappropriate behaviours are ignored or redirected to show children that they are unconditionally loved. Some behavioural techniques such as prompting, reinforcement, and task analysis, are used. One five-year study showed that 86.3 per cent of the 73 adults who had exhibited self-injurious behaviours showed none of these behaviours on discharge after receiving gentle therapy. However, this result has not been replicated, and other researchers have suggested that the approach is ineffective and can be harmful. More information can be obtained at www.gentleteaching.nl

Options

This therapy, known as the Son-Rise Program in the US, is not autism-specific and was developed by the parents of a child diagnosed with autism. They spent every waking hour with their son with the goal of developing a bond. Since the least stimulating room in the house was the bathroom, that was where they spent most of their time, and starting out by imitating his ritualistic behaviours. After three years, he was showing no sign of autism and is now an Ivy League university graduate. The key to this treatment is to join in the child's repetitive behaviours, showing unconditional love, thereby enticing the child to emerge from his world, and eventually utilising his motivation to advance learning. Options offers training programmes in this method for parents, and they are expensive. There are some case studies and testimonials claiming that other children with autism have improved dramatically. However, research has yet to be done on the effectiveness of the method, which appears to be more about making parents feel good about themselves than actually teaching the child.

Contact
Autism Treatment Center of America (the Option Institute)
2080 S Undermountain Road
Sheffield
MA 01257, USA
Tel: (1) 413 229 2100
Fax: (1) 413 229 3202
Email: correspondence@option.org
Website: www.Son-Rise.org

Books
Son-Rise and *Son-Rise: The Miracle Continues* by Barry Neil Kaufman

Holding therapy

This is based on the belief that body contact and physical contact must be re-established with the child who is refusing to make eye contact with the parent (usually the mother). Advocates of this therapy believe that autism results from a broken symbiotic bond between mother and child, and that when the child begins to cuddle and make eye contact with the parent, his development will proceed normally. This therapy is touted as a 'cure' although few studies have been done. Again, this appears to be one of those 'let's make the parents feel better' methods. (Holding therapy is not to be confused with deep-pressure or 'squeeze' therapy which Temple Grandin advocates, and which has a physiological base.)

Psychoanalysis

Until recently this was the main treatment on offer in some countries, namely France and Switzerland. Up until the mid-1990s France still considered autism to be a mental illness rather than a developmental disability; children with autism were denied an education, and psychoanalysis was the recommended treatment. As late as 1993, some parents in the UK were led to believe by certain professionals that their child's autism was due to bad parenting. Not only did psychoanalysis cause the parents to feel guilty, it offered no practical strategies to help them with their children. Although counselling and psychoanalsyis may be used as a treatment for depression in people with ASDs, it is not to be considered as an effective treatment for autism in itself.

Combined Treatments

In this category are placed the better-known programmes that use a combination of different approaches. These programmes work on improving skills, include physiologically based approaches to help with behaviours and have a relationship component to them. Note: At times it is unclear whether the relationship component is about making the parents feel better, or actually trying to teach the child how to relate to others.

NAS Early Bird programme

This autism-specific, parent-focused early intervention programme bridges the gap between diagnosis and school placement. The three-month parent training programme includes group training sessions and individual home visits including the child, with video feedback to help parents apply what they learn. This style of training programme is taken from the Hanen programme, for parents of children with speech and language impairments. Parents have a weekly commitment to the three-month programme, which aims to offer support in the period between diagnosis and placement by helping parents understand autism, structure interactions to encourage communication to develop, and learn how to pre-empt or handle problem behaviours. It uses techniques of the SPELL approach (see opposite), the TEACCH approach (p. 117), and PECS (p. 87). A pilot study found evidence of significantly reduced stress, as well as a modified communication style and more positive perceptions by parents of their children. However, it is unclear about what gains the children themselves make.

Contact
Early Bird Centre
3 Victoria Crescent West
Barnsley
South Yorkshire S75 2AE
Tel: 01226 779218
Fax: 01226 771014
Email: earlybird@nas.org.uk

SPELL

This is the educational approach being developed by the National Autistic Society and is used in NAS schools and adult centres. SPELL stands for Structure, Positive, Empathetic, Low arousal, and Links. This approach provides continuity, order and appropriate expectations coupled with positive attitudes. A teaching programme is designed specific to each person, and is taught in calm and uncluttered environments. Links to the community and with parents are fostered, and the National Curriculum is accessed in order to maximise the children's opportunities for inclusion in mainstream schools. As the SPELL approach is still being developed, it is being monitored and assessed.

Contact
National Autistic Society
393 City Road
London EC1V 1NG
Tel: 020 7833 2299
Fax: 020 7833 9666
Email: nas@.org.uk
Website: www.nas.org.uk

TEACCH

The Treatment and Education of Autistic and related Communication handicapped Children was developed by Eric Schopler at the University of North Carolina at Chapel Hill in the early 1970s. TEACCH started out as a parent and child psychoanalysis group and quickly became a skill-based approach dependent on a strong parent–professional collaboration. It focuses on teaching functional skills while modifying the environment to facilitate the needs of the individual. Structured teaching and the use of visual materials and schedules are used to enhance the acquisition of skills, by providing a stress-free environment. Vocational preparation is a strong component of this programme.

The effectiveness of individual components of TEACCH has been validated in a number of studies. However, there appears to be a lack of research in terms of individual gains. Adapting the environment for the person does make it easier for them, but in doing so it may remove some of the natural 'stresses' that create opportunities for learning. TEACCH strategies are very useful for the visual learner, but may not be as suitable for those who are auditory learners. Sometimes classrooms based solely on TEACCH principles appear to be about making the class easier for the teacher to handle, and appear to lack social interaction and social skills development, which many individuals with autism need.

Contact
Division TEACCH Administration and Research
CB# 7180
310 Medical School Wing E
The University of North Carolina at Chapel Hill
Chapel Hill
NC 27599-7180, USA
Tel: (1)919 966 5156
Fax: (1)919 966 4003
Website: http://www.teacch.com/

Daily life therapy
This treatment originated in Tokyo with Dr Kiyo Kitahara over thirty years ago. It was introduced in the United States when the Higashi School in Boston was opened in 1987, and a number of schools in the UK have also incorporated some of the approach into their curriculum. Daily life therapy incorporates physiologically

based interventions and skill-based treatments using systematic instruction. An important focus is physical education, which is viewed as a bridge to social development. Vigorous exercise helps the children to gain control of their bodies and sleep better, and leads to a decrease in self-stimulatory behaviour as well as hyper-activity. Children learn self-help skills and the ability to follow directions, as well as language, maths, art and music, depending on the interest of the child. This therapy is lacking in objective scientific validation; however, its effectiveness is supported by numerous testimonials from parents. More information can be found at http://www.bostonhigashi.org/home.html

Other Therapies

Listed here are some adjunct therapies, usually used to target a particular skill area, or as part of a wider programme, and potentially extremely useful depending on the individual's needs. Again, it is important that the therapist be knowledgeable and experienced with ASDs.

Speech therapy
Language delay is often one of the primary concerns that parents of a young child raise that may lead to assessments and diagnosis of an ASD. Speech therapists play an important role by evaluating the child's level of functioning, using a developmental approach. Once in school, speech and language therapy should be a part of the child's educational provision.

Contact
The Royal College of Speech and Language Therapists
2 White Hart Yard
London SE1 1NX
Tel: 020 7378 1200
Fax: 020 7403 7254
Website: www.rcslt.org

More Than Words

This is the Hanen programme for parents of pre-school children with ASDs and was developed by the Hanen Center, a Canadian charity. It involves a three-month group training programme led by a speech and language therapist that teaches parents how to promote social interaction and communication in their children. Parents learn to use strategies shown to be helpful with young children with ASDs.

Contact
Anne McDade, Coordinator, Hanen UK/Ireland
Tel: 0141 946 5433
Email: uk_ireland@hanen.org

Occupational Therapy

Depending on the age, ability and need of the individual, occupational therapists provide different services. Their aim is to help the person meet goals in areas of everyday life that are important to them, such as self-care, work and leisure. Assessments are carried out initially to discover the needs of the individual and provide support to learn skills in those areas. Some therapists are specifically trained in sensory integration (see p. 96).

Contact
The College of Occupational Therapists
106–114 Borough High Street
Southwark
London SE1 1LB
Tel: 020 7357 6480

Music therapy

Most people respond favourably to music, including people with ASDs. Music is motivating and enjoyable. In music therapy, goals are tailored to the needs of each individual and may include: increasing non-verbal interaction such as turn-taking and eye contact; exploring and expressing feelings; being creative and spontaneous. Many parents have reported that their children began to learn to speak as a result of being taught nursery rhymes and other songs.

Contact
Association of Professional Music Therapists (APMT)
26 Hamlyn Road
Glastonbury
Somerset BA6 8HT
Tel: 01458 834919
Website: http://www.apmt.org.uk

American Music Therapy Association: www.namt.com

Assistive technology
Broadly this means any item, piece of equipment or product system that is used to increase, maintain or improve the functional capabilities of a person. It can be a high-technology item such as a Lightwriter to help someone type what they cannot say verbally. Or it can be low technology such as picture icons used to communicate something a person wants, or larger letters on keyboard keys. Check with knowledgeable speech therapists or your local autism group for information about items they have found useful, and with the latest research and computer specialists to see what is new.

Website
Inclusive Technology, the Special Needs People: http://www.inclusive.co.uk/infosite/autism.shtml

Computer software
There are many software programmes around that can help people master certain skills. This area is constantly changing.

Websites
Fast ForWord: http://www.scilearn.com/prod/ or http://www.abilities-center.com/html/fast_forword.html

Laureate Learning Systems: http://www.laureatelearning.com/

Inclusive Technology, the Special Needs People: http://www.inclusive.co.uk/catalog/softlist.shtml

Closing the Gap: Computer Technology in Special Education and Rehabilitation: http://www.closingthegap.net/ctg/rd/allinline.lasso

Book
Autism and ICT: A Guide for Teachers and Parents by Colin Hardy, Jan Ogden, Julie Newman, Sally Cooper. This book may help you through the maze of Information and Communications Technology (ICT).

CHAPTER SIX

Family Life

Family life can be a test of love and resilience, so taking good notes and understanding each other's needs and wants are vital to the success and survival of any marriage. After children arrive, there is a balancing act between caring for their needs and putting time and effort into the maintenance and growth of the marriage. This rite of passage in the development of family life is challenged still further by disability or chronic illness.

ROBERT A. NASEEF, *SPECIAL CHILDREN CHALLENGED PARENTS*

I was raised in a French Catholic family, one of six children. As my parents had emigrated to the United States from France, we had no extended family, but we were very close. We did everything together: ate dinner as a family every night, rode our bikes, played tennis, watched TV (the few hours a week we were allowed), went to church and socialised with other families. We had very little time on our own and were not encouraged to join clubs that would take us away from our family activities.

So I had always expected that when I had a family, though it would be much smaller, it would be the same kind of close-knit family life with shared activities. This was important to me. However, having two children who are basically living on separate planets (one is severely autistic, with poor motor skills; the other is very social and athletically gifted) makes it tough to have the kind of family life I grew up with. I had to learn to let go of my expectations, change my perception of what family life meant, and figure out what we could still do together as a family, and what we would have to do separately. We have had to create our own version of family life. But we are still a family; we just do things differently.

AUTISM SPECTRUM DISORDERS AND THE FAMILY

Having a child with an ASD has a major impact on the family. Besides the stress associated with bringing up a child who needs more attention and care, children with autism are not as social as other children, and do not reach out to parents in the same way that other children do. This lack of spontaneous signs of affection from one's own child is very difficult for a parent.

Often families tend to isolate themselves either because of concern over their child's socially inappropriate behaviours, or from fear of being embarrassed by some of the child's behaviours, or because of the extreme fatigue most parents of children with an ASD suffer from. Families stop doing what they did before the ASD was very apparent. Single-parent families find themselves alone with their hands full and no free time to keep up any kind of social life, increasing their isolation. Being a single parent, adoptive parent, step-parent, foster-parent or grandparent raising a child with an ASD adds even more difficulties to an already precarious situation.

A marriage or relationship with a significant other can deteriorate due to added stress, fatigue, and differences of opinion on how to handle certain situations. Often one or both parents are having difficulties coming to terms with having this child and are on different parts of the grief cycle. Add to that the searching for support and trying to get an appropriate education for the child and it is easy to see how many couples come to call it quits.

Siblings can suffer from being raised in a family with a child who has an ASD. Not only do they have a sibling who is hard to understand, has limited interests, and is not social; they also have to deal with some pretty wild behaviours. And they also feel the stress their parents are under, as well as the fact that inevitably more of the parents' attention is taken up by the sibling with an ASD.

It is difficult bringing up a child with an ASD. But first and foremost you are raising a child, not a disability. No matter how bad the behaviour or situation, there is always a solution. And mainly it is the parents' attitude that will make the biggest difference. In this section, practical suggestions on family life are offered.

FOOD FOR THOUGHT
Beam Me Up!

It's a Wednesday morning and I am volunteering at the jog-a-thon at my daughter's school. As we await the start of this event, other mothers are standing around talking. I approach a few I know and hear a bit of their conversation. 'Oh, I hear Pasqual got voted off.' 'Oh no, he was my favourite!' 'Mine, too.' I move in and ask, 'What are you talking about?' They look at me as if I have just landed from another galaxy, and say, '*Survivor!*' I say, 'Oh, you have time to watch that?' and as they look at me, one replies, 'We *make* time, the whole family!'

They continue to talk about *Survivor* and I drift away. I am left with the usual feeling of being an alien on another planet. Is it because I have a son who is severely handicapped by his autism, leaving me with a lack of time for trivial time-fillers, that I don't fit in?

It's hard to feel as if you fit in when you don't have the same points of reference. The parents huddle around waiting to pick their children up after school, talking about their daughter's latest piano recital, her high scores on her SATs, or how their son is representing the school at the county science fair. Somehow, the highlights of my 14-year-old son's week (he sat in his mainstream class and participated appropriately for a one-hour stretch, and hasn't wet the bed once) don't seem like the kind of information that I can just slip into the conversation and share as an accomplishment.

What are my time-fillers? Filling out paperwork to explain why I still need respite and other services; preparing for my son's annual review at school and documenting why he needs OT and ABA; explaining to the medical insurance company why my son needs a certain treatment; attempting to keep him from 'redecorating' the family room; making picture icons; trying to reach the neurologist about seizure medication; reading up on the latest research; making my son clean up the mess he made when he did redecorate; sending letters to politicians; attending voluntary board meetings; taking my son for a swim or a run because he is too hyper; cleaning spots off the rug, the couch and the walls you really don't want to know about; and oh yeah – trying to earn a living.

I don't share the same cultural points of reference as most of the other inhabitants of this suburb. My reference points are those of autism: talk to me about ABA, OT, MMR, IEP, NAS, GFCF, DTT, ASD; I'm sorry, I don't know how to talk reality TV.

Family Life With Children With ASDs

The sooner you realise that your family life will not resemble *The Waltons*, the better off you will be. Take heart from knowing that your family life would probably never have resembled that perfect ideal, and if it had, you would have been bored out of your skull. Think of the Addams Family and how much more fun they seemed to be having regardless of the daily household disasters.

Life for your family will never be boring from this point on. It may get monotonous, but it will not be boring. Start buying rubber gloves, cleaning liquids, disinfectants and carpet stain removers in wholesale quantity, as you will be using them often. I wonder if the sales figures for cleaning materials rise at the same rate as ASDs diagnoses. But I digress.

It is not easy striking a balance between family life and all that is inherent to having a child with an ASD. It is true that you probably will not have the family life you envisioned. But many people who do not have a child with an ASD do not either. People get divorced, lose a partner or a child. They grieve, but then they move on and rebuild another kind of family life. And families with a child with an ASD need to do that as well. Grieve about the loss of your expectation for the family life you envisioned, and then start building the one you will have. You owe it to the rest of the family. It will be hard work, but you can do it. To start with, here are some basic guidelines to keep in mind.

Do not isolate yourself and your child: Primarily, parents must take care that the family does not become isolated. This is vitally important for all members of your family. Now, more than ever, you need to be surrounded by relatives and friends, and so does everyone in your family. Isolation occurs because you are too tired to go out, you cannot handle your child in public and you are embarrassed by your child's behaviours. People soon stop inviting you over, either because you have previously turned down invitations from them, or because of your child's behaviour, or because you are obsessed about ASDs and that is all you can talk about. You stop inviting people over because you are too exhausted to play hostess and you are embarrassed by your child's behaviours. Do not be one of those people who says, 'I remember when I used to have a social life. Look, I even have pictures to prove it.'

Get over caring what other people think: Do not be intimidated by looks and remarks when you go out in public, and do not feel you have to justify your actions to family members and friends. If you are too embarrassed to take your child out in public, then you need to analyse why you feel that way. If it is because of your child's behaviours, and they are very disruptive or unsafe, then you need to work on those behaviours. If it is because you feel uncomfortable that your child appears 'odd', then I suggest you get over it. Your child is here to stay, and he needs your support. And the general public need to be reminded that none of us is perfect.

Get your child's worst behaviours under control: This is never easy and can sometimes be extremely difficult. However, this child is your responsibility now. You need to help him. First you need to try and understand what is causing the behaviour. If you can eliminate the cause, that's great. If not, you need to try and get disruptive behaviours under control. It is not fair to the rest of the family, nor will it make you friends out in the community. There are positive behaviour techniques that can be used to decrease and eventually eliminate the worst behaviours, and with practice a parent can learn how to use them. Your local authority or GP should be able to provide you with a professional who can help you. If not, there are various books you can consult that will explain in simple terms what to do. They are listed in the resources section at the end of this book.

Keep your sense of humour and take time to laugh: Surround yourself with uplifting media. No matter how bad things are, you can and will make it through today. Play good upbeat music, not the tunes that make you feel even more depressed. If you have ten minutes to read or watch TV, make sure it is something amusing. Don't waste it on reading or watching the news. Usually the news is depressing, and you can't do anything about it. Keep entertaining videos around the house, as well as light reading. Humour helps, even if it is gallows humour. You may not be able to control the situation you are in or solve your problems, but keeping your mood uplifted will help you have a more positive frame of mind.

Do what you can to stay healthy: Take care of your physical health. Try to eat properly, catch up on sleep when you can and exercise regularly. Even just a 20-minute walk three times a week will keep your body healthier and will make you feel better. Your physical health affects your mental health, which in turns affects the whole family.

Remember that you are only human: You may try to act like a superhuman and do the impossible. That is OK, if you are feeling up to it. However, watch out for burn-out. Revert to acting human and do not feel guilty for only doing what you can. Think of all you have accomplished, not what you wish you had done.

How To Continue Doing The Family Activities You Enjoy

Most parents think that family activities should be done as a unit. Parents of a child with an ASD may try to include the child in all family outings, hesitating to leave him at home while everyone else is out enjoying themselves. Others may rarely take their child out in public. What is needed is a balance. Pick activities to share as a family unit that will be enjoyable to all, and schedule other activities or family outings that can be done separately with individual members of the family.

Parents need to look at the activities they enjoyed doing before, and what they would like to continue doing now. See how you can adapt them for the home life you have now. Analyse whether it is easier to change the activity, or to change your child's behaviours, or to drop the activity. You will probably have to do a bit of all.

The following basic suggestions will be helpful to some of you, especially parents of younger children, and parents of children severely impaired by an ASD. These strategies are included here for those who have no supervised behaviour programme, and need to teach their child some basic skills. If your child has a behaviour programme, he is probably already learning these skills.

Teaching your child basic communication

The first skill your child should learn is how to communicate. Some children with ASDs are verbal and are able to communicate effectively, others may have enough speech to at least get their basic needs met. Many have no speech whatsoever, or had speech and then lost it.

Not being able to communicate is very frustrating and can lead to major tantrums and disruptive behaviours. Teaching some basic communication skills can alleviate a lot of this frustration. PECS is a wonderful system for helping children to communicate (see p. 87). At the basic level it teaches the child that by giving you a picture of an item that he wants, he will get that item. Without professional help, you can teach your child to give you or point to pictures that represent what he wants or needs. This will not inhibit him from learning to speak and is a good practical starting point to help you at home.

For example, start by cutting out the labels of food or drink items your child enjoys. When you first introduce this concept, have another person help you. The first step is to pick a moment when you know he wants a particular item. Make sure you have a picture of that item. Hold up the item, and have the other person physically help the child to hand you the picture. In exchange you can immediately give him the desired item. This will only work if he really wants that item, and if he can't reach it without your help. You can add more pictures, perhaps laminate them, and put them somewhere easy for the child to find, stuck to the refrigerator, or on the kitchen table. You can keep adding pictures so that he can request to go outside, in the car, watch TV, listen to music.

If you wish to learn more, look on the PECS website (www.pecs-uk.com) to find out when a workshop is planned for your area.

Teaching your child to wait

Another skill your child will need to master to make home life easier is waiting. At home, he needs to wait for someone to help him, he needs to wait for dinner, he needs to wait to go out. In the community he needs to learn to wait at the doctor's, wait at the supermarket check-out, queue to get on a bus or a plane. Learning the concept of waiting (you will get what you want eventually) will help to lessen the number of tantrums.

Make or find a picture that will represent 'waiting' to your child. We have used a simple line drawing of a person sitting in a chair, with the face of a clock next to it. Write 'waiting' clearly on the card. Laminate the picture and place a piece of Velcro somewhere on it. Next, make sure you have pictures of whatever items your child usually requests or wants immediately (favourite food, toy, ride in the car), backed with Velcro, and a seconds timer. The next time he requests an item put the relevant picture on the Velcro on the waiting card, then turn the timer on for a few seconds. Say, 'We are waiting' or 'Waiting' and point to the card. When the timer goes off, immediately give him the desired item.

Some children need to start with a wait of only three seconds, and work on up from there. Some can start at ten seconds or more. Once your child has learned to wait for those few seconds, add more. You know your child, so you will have to gauge where to start. Eventually, he will understand that he *will* get what he wants, it is only a matter of time.

Schedules

Another helpful tried and trusted method is schedules. Posting pictures or words about the day's activities in the kitchen or by the front door can be helpful for a child having difficulty making sense of the world around him. Knowing what will happen and in what order is comforting. It also helps those who have sensory problems in some areas to get ready for a not so pleasant onslaught of sensory input. For example, I have noticed that if my son is forewarned that he will be visiting the dentist or the hairdresser, he appears to have an easier time of it, as if he has prepared himself mentally. If I have forgotten to put it on the schedule earlier in the day, and then show him the picture just before leaving the house, he appears to be anxious and unhappy often refusing to get in the car, which he usually loves.

If your child is very young and home all day, you may find it helpful to establish a routine of activities that will fill part of his day and use a schedule to show what that routine is (eating, getting dressed, free play inside, napping, TV).

Food for Thought
Learning to Share

'Having to SHARE my parents with two older brothers was the main thing. I see too many families where the needs of the autistic person run the day. There has to be a balance, between that very needy person and needs of parents and siblings. I don't care how needy he is, he has to learn that he is not the sun with the rest of the world as planets revolving around his every tantrum. I was very lucky to have two older brothers and two parents whose egos weren't totally tied up in what I thought of them or how I succeeded.'

Jerry and Mary Newport, *Autism – Asperger's and Sexuality*

Consistency

For any behaviour changes that you are trying to make with your child, it is important that you follow through and be consistent, and that the other family members do so as well. If you introduce a way to communicate and then do not respond to his attempts to approach you, you will be doing your child a disservice. If you teach him to wait, but do not give him the item he is waiting for, he will not learn the concept, and will be even more confused.

Travelling and going on holiday as a family

Travelling can be trying even at the best of times when you have small children. Travelling with a child with an ASD can be even more of a challenge. Airports and train stations are areas that involve lots of waiting. Leaving the security of home for a new place can be off-putting for a child with autism. How you prepare your child depends on his age and how the ASD affects him. Some suggestions are given here that you can adapt for your own child's needs and level of ability. Remember that the first time you use this he may not understand, but over time, he will.

- Teach your child the 'waiting' skill if he does not have it.

- Put up a monthly calendar and check off each day until it is time to go. Bring the calendar with you and mark off the number of days in the new place, always having the departure indicated.

- Put together a 'travel book' of pictures (and/or words) of the means of transport you are going to be using to travel (aeroplane, boat, train), who you are going to see (relatives, friends), where you will sleep (hotel, Grandma's house) and what you will do or see at your destination (swimming, playing outside, visiting monuments). Go over this with him as often as you like in preparation for the trip. A three-ring binder is best, because you can add extra pages or insert the calendar mentioned above for use on the trip.

- Put together a picture or word schedule of the actual journey to take with you on your trip. Add extra pages to the travel book. Use Velcro to attach pictures or words in sequence. Add an empty envelope to put the 'done' pictures in when you have finished that step of the journey. For example, if you are flying to Paris, start with a picture of the taxi or car that will take you to the airport. When you are at the airport, have him remove the taxi picture and put it in the envelope. Then have a picture of the airport, followed by the waiting picture, and then the aeroplane, and so on.

- Think of your child's daily routine and the items he likes or needs for it, and bring them along to make him feel more at home. Bring whatever foods and drinks will keep him happy on the trip.

- Buy some small inexpensive toys that he can play with. If he only plays with one favourite item, try to find a duplicate and see if you can 'break it in' before the trip. Do not wash any toys before you go, as your child may find comfort in the 'home' smell of his cherished item.

- When staying in a hotel, it is a good idea to call ahead and ask for a quiet room. You may wish to explain about your child's behaviour if there is a good likelihood of him exhibiting it in the public part of the hotel. The same with a friend or relative's home. It can be a bit disconcerting for everyone concerned if your older child takes his clothes off and races through a friend's house stark naked.

- Make sure your child has an ID tag attached to him somewhere, with current phone number and 'autism' written on it. You can order medical bracelets, necklaces and tags to attach to shoelaces. If you can persuade your child to keep it in his pocket, also make an ID card with current photo and date, plus home and mobile phone numbers and the number of where you are staying. Indicate that your child has autism. Be sure to add any other important details: allergies, medications, and any specific information, for instance, whether the child is non-verbal.

Tips for travelling by plane

- Call the airline as far in advance as you can, and tell them you will be travelling with someone who has special needs. Explain about the ASD and some of the behaviours that can inconvenience other travellers, for example rocking in the seat. Request bulkhead seats and explain how it will be more convenient for the other passengers if your child has no passenger in front of him.

- If you will need help, perhaps because you have other children and your child with an ASD is a handful, request in advance that assistance be provided after you check in, to get you to the plane, and upon arrival. Remember, the person you speak to may not understand about ASDs. They may tell you that assistance is only for the physically handicapped. Explain that your child cannot move from one place to another without physical assistance. Always be polite but insistent.

- Talk to someone at the airline about avoiding the long queues at security and check-in. Some airlines will send you a medical form for you or your GP to fill out. They may ask questions such as 'Can the person walk?' The correct response would be, 'He needs help to move from one place to another' or 'He is unable to move from one spot to another without assistance.' It may be helpful to attach an explanation of behaviours or challenges with travelling, always stressing the inconvenience that the other passengers will experience, e.g. 'When waiting more than 5 minutes he will scream at top of lungs and will not stop for 20 minutes which can be annoying to other passengers.' Attaching a brochure or information sheet about ASDs from the National Autistic Society could be helpful as well.

- Let the airline know ahead of time if your child has food allergies or sensitivities. They may be able to accommodate his special diet.

- Make sure the child is wearing clothes that are loose, comfortable and easy to pull off and on if need be. Bring any medications, pull-ups or nappies, baby wipes, assistive communication tools, food and drink and books and toys the child likes.

- If you are travelling with an adolescent, or are helping an adult plan a trip, you may wish to read an article entitled 'Autism and Airport Travel Safety Tips' by Dennis Debbault, on the NAS website at www.nas.org.uk/family/parents/airtravel.html

This may all seem a bit daunting, but it pays to plan ahead. The experience will be so much more enjoyable for all involved, including fellow travellers.

Other areas to be addressed

There is not enough room in this book to address all the important areas that parents may need to work on to make life easier at home. Those listed here are important, but many books are available to help you with others. Here are some suggestions.

Toilet training: Can be difficult for some, easy for others. Some children who have sensory processing issues and poor muscle control may not 'feel' when they have the need to urinate, or have the necessary motor control. It can take a long time to toilet-train some people. There are books specifically about toilet training that are good, and *Steps to Independence* (B. Baker and A. Brightman) and *One on One* (Marilyn Chassman) have sections on toilet training as well as many other areas you may wish to address. *Steps to Independence* explains how to teach functional living skills to children at home, and *One on One* is the best book I have seen for teaching skills to the less able child with autism.

Chores: Teaching a child to do chores not only gives him independence, but also makes the statement to siblings that everyone contributes to the household. Both books mentioned above have ideas for you to try.

Desensitising: Some children with sensory processing issues have a terrible time getting their hair cut, their teeth checked by the dentist, wearing a hat, etc. Teaching a child to get used to an item or sound little by little is helpful. Anyone who has a practical knowledge of ABA can devise a system. *One on One* has a good section about how to teach your child to tolerate stimuli that are difficult for him.

Behaviour plans: Are an important part of making life easier at home and teaching a child responsibility for his actions. Again, these are ABA techniques and *Steps to Independence* has a section on them.

Teaching your child safety: Many children with ASDs do not have any notion of safety. It needs to be taught. *Dangerous Encounters: Avoiding Perilous Situations with Autism* by Bill Davis and Wendy Goldband Schunick has some good suggestions for all types of safety issues at home and in the community.

FOOD FOR THOUGHT

'As time went on, the world of professionals, friends, acquaintances, and strangers became divided into two camps: those who rendered things more difficult, and those who helped. The first camp was far more heavily populated than the second. But notwithstanding the sometimes painful lack of sympathy Marc and I and Anne-Marie encountered, we were fortunate – indeed, blessed – in the people we did find who helped, each in his or her own way.'

Catherine Maurice, *Let Me Hear Your Voice*

ADOLESCENT ISSUES IN ASDs

Some adolescent issues will be discussed in Chapter Seven on education, and the reader may wish to consult that chapter as well. Jerry and Mary Newport, Luke Jackson, Claire Sainsbury and Liane Willey, all authors with ASDs, have written about their teenage years and how their ASD affected them in contrast to their neurotypical peers. Parents should read some of these accounts. They will give you information you can share with your child's teacher.

Puberty and hygiene

Puberty is usually an awkward time even for neurotypical people. Bodies are changing, hormones are raging, moods are swinging. All children nearing adolescence need to have an understanding of what is going on in their bodies. Children with ASDs need even more information and input from parents at this time. Things to keep in mind:

- Boys usually start puberty around age 11 and it may last until age 17. They start producing testosterone, which leads to changes in the body such as hair growth on the face and legs and under the arms, developing muscles, growth spurts, deepening of the voice, growth of penis and testicles, and development of the Adam's apple. Boys need to be told about how their bodies are changing, about erections and 'wet dreams' that can happen while they are sleeping, and that ejaculation can happen when their penis is rubbed, or they may be perplexed and wonder what is wrong with them.

- Girls generally start puberty before boys, beginning sometimes as young as nine years old. In girls, overall body shape starts to change as breasts and hips begin to develop, the menstrual cycle commences at some point, and hair begins to grow on legs and pubic area and under arms. It is important that girls are told about the menstrual cycle before their first period, so they are not confused and upset and think there is something physically wrong. They will also need to be told who are the appropriate people to discuss this with (parents, a teacher, a girlfriend) and that it is not necessarily a lunchtime conversation topic in a mixed group.

- Seizures may appear during puberty for one in four individuals with ASDs, possibly due to the increase of hormonal changes in the body. Sometimes the seizures are associated with convulsions and are noticeable, but for some they are very minor and may not be detected by simple observation. You may wish to keep an eye out for the signs that indicate seizure activity. These signs are: little or no academic gain in contrast to doing well during the childhood years; losing some gains academically or behaviourally; and showing behaviour problems such as severe tantrums, self-injury, or aggression. You may wish to discuss any such changes with a knowledgeable professional.

- Hygiene is an area that needs to be addressed at this time. Puberty brings the onset of sweat, and some teenagers will develop acne as a result of intensified amounts of oil in their glands. Good habits need to be developed. Daily face-washing and the application of deodorant are good places to start. Boys need to be told about shaving facial hair. Girls will need to learn how to use feminine hygiene products.

- Teaching about puberty depends on the level of understanding your child demonstrates. Some will need things explained and pictures shown a few times; others will need to be motored many times through the various aspects mentioned above. If your child learns very slowly, an early start will be helpful in the long run.

Sexuality

Sexuality is a topic that many of us would rather skip talking about, even with our neurotypical children. However, sexual feelings are natural and everyone has them, regardless of their level of ability. Children become adolescents and then young adults. Some individuals with ASDs want intimacy and to get married; some do not. Many want friends and to date; some may not. But as adults, it is up to them to choose, and it is up to us as parents to help them develop the social skills they will need and teach them about self-esteem and self-respect and about relationships and sex.

Even if your young adult is not interested in relationships or intimacy or sex, this subject needs to be addressed. Sadly, people who have intellectual disabilities are at a high risk of sexual abuse and of catching AIDS. Even if your child does not have intellectual disabilities, the very nature of ASDs makes it difficult for someone with the condition to read the social cues and understand appropriate versus inappropriate behaviour. These cues need to be taught. There are different ways to teach them, depending on the person's level of ability. It may take a lot of time and effort on your part, but it will be well worth it. You will not always be around for your child; he needs to learn these things from you.

This is the time, while he is still living at home, to be teaching your child about appropriate behaviour. Even if as an adult he chooses not to have a sexual relationship, he needs to know what is appropriate and inappropriate behaviour towards him, about giving or withholding consent, how to say no to others, and how to let others know if he needs help or support. He needs to learn to be able to tell a responsible person about any inappropriate behaviour that someone might be doing to him. It is imperative for your child's safety that he be able to identify appropriate places on his body where people can touch him. Not only does your adolescent need to understand about behaviours, he needs to understand what is behind it.

Here are some concepts that every adolescent needs to learn.

Modesty – private versus public: If your child has not mastered the concept of modesty, now is the time to teach him. He needs to learn the appropriate place for private acts (such as dressing or being naked). If he does not understand through an explanation of the concept, then perhaps visual icons will help. Pick an icon or colour to represent public and one to represent private (do not confuse him by using smiley and sad faces). Put the private icon on his underwear drawer and his bedroom and bathroom doors, and the public icon on the doors to the rest of the rooms and going outside. If he gets dressed in a place other than the bathroom or his bedroom, or if he runs around the house with no clothes on or in his underwear, now is a good time to teach him what is appropriate to wear in public and in private. Perhaps you don't really mind at home, but think of when he will be living with others and how inappropriate it will be then. He needs to learn now, or he won't understand what the fuss is about years down the line. If he comes out with no clothes on, you can remind him by showing him to his room or bathroom with the appropriate icon, and pairing it with the icon on his clothes drawer. Also, your child needs to learn about using the toilet on his own with the door closed.

For some children, social stories will be effective in teaching about what behaviours are to be done in private, and which ones are okay in public. This concept of private versus public is crucial to the child's learning about the body parts that are okay for others to touch, and the parts that are private and should only be touched with his permission.

Masturbation: This is one of those activities that needs to be explained as okay to do, but in private. Your adolescent needs to understand that it is a normal behaviour, but only in private. Many individuals with ASDs practise self-stimulatory behaviour, and masturbation is the ultimate such behaviour, so a parent needs to accept the inevitable and make sure it is done in private. If your son starts touching himself in public, he needs to be told that that is a private place, not to be touched in public.

Teaching to say or communicate NO: Some children with ASDs are compliant and have learned through years of special education to follow instructions and rules of behaviour. However, for safety reasons, now that your child is becoming a young adult, he needs to learn to say 'no' even to you and people of authority. One way to do this is to give him choices (e.g. does he want a bar of chocolate or carrots). When he states his choice, give him the other choice and teach him to say 'No, I want the . . .' This needs to be generalised to all kinds of subjects. Then you can make a list of situations to say 'no' in, some serious and some funny to make it fun (e.g. a stranger asks you to get in the car; your dad wants you to eat worms). You can also teach him to say 'go away' by invading your child's space when you know he doesn't want you there (e.g. when he has closed the door to his room and is watching TV). Stand very close to where he is sitting, and when he does avoidance behaviour (pushing you away, moving to another spot), prompt him to push you and say 'Go away'. When you are teaching the concept of 'no' and 'go away' you must respect his right to choose, but do not confuse him by asking instead of telling in a situation where he really has no choice (e.g. 'Do you want to get ready to go out now?' instead of 'Time to get ready to go out.'). You can, however, create choices (e.g. 'Time to get ready to go out. Do you want to wear your blue jacket or your red sweater?') that he really has.

Relationship boundaries: Can be a difficult concept to teach. First your child needs to learn about the various relationships (husband, wife, sibling, aunt, colleague, close friend, neighbour, shopkeeper, etc.). Next comes the concept of appropriate types of conversations and behaviours. One way to teach this is through the idea of Circles (p. 264 in Resources). Draw a dot in the middle of a big piece of paper, with ever-increasing circles surrounding it. Each circle defines the acceptable behaviour of people in that circle. The circle closest to the dot represents behaviours of people you are extremely close to, and when first introducing the concept write in 'close hug' in this circle, then in the next circle 'big hug', and so on with 'handshake', 'wave', etc. 'Stranger' will be the largest circle farthest out. Hang this up in your child's room and add the people (by name or picture) he knows to the different circles, discussing the concepts at his level. Then, when he meets new people, you can add them to the circle.

Grooming and dressing

In the teenage years, how you are dressed and how you present yourself are extremely important. Luke Jackson and Jerry and Mary Newport in their respective books talk about the importance of looking right. Jerry and Mary say that right from the first day at school it is important to not look like a misfit. ASD teenagers need help in this area. Reading parts of *Freaks, Geeks and Asperger Syndrome, Autism – Asperger's and Sexuality* and *Your Life is Not a Label* can be very helpful to the teenager. The different aspects that need to be taught to your child are: what matches and what doesn't; what's 'in' and what's 'out'; and the importance of basic hygiene and cleanliness. Parents, your teenager needs your support here. First impressions are crucial. Jerry Newport talks about the importance of looking right to avoid bullying, in addition to making friends. If you have no other teenager in the house, get a friend's teenager to tell you and your child what is hot and what is not. Often the brand name is important. If you have a very small clothing budget, it is better to buy the right thing from a charity shop than the wrong thing brand new. Find out what the current hairstyles are and teach your teenager how to have that look. See if your teenage fashion adviser can go shopping with you and your child to help with getting the right look.

Teenage emotions

With raging hormones come feelings that your child may not be familiar with. Jerry and Mary Newport, Luke Jackson, Claire Sainsbury and Liane Willey all describe how their ASD affected their teenage years in contrast to their neurotypical peers. Reading about their experiences will help you understand about the thinking processes of many people with ASDs, and give you ideas on how to help your child get through this crossroad in his life.

Teenagers with ASDs may physically be maturing at the same rate as their teenage peers, but emotionally they tend to mature much later. Early adolescence is when most young people seek more independence from their parents, seek even more approval from their peers, and try to fit in with the crowd. Teenagers start showing an interest in romance, start dating and perhaps getting physical with members of the opposite sex. Thus, while their peers are interested in romance and start testing the system, the teenager with an ASD may continue to stick to the rules and value high grades.

The young person with an ASD who as a child had difficulty with meltdowns and aggression may calm down at puberty. However, adolescence is often a time when tantrums appear or reappear. Usually these are due to frustration, which is a normal feeling to have when you have an ASD and don't understand the social cues and changes in your non-ASD peers. Another change is that usually in primary schools the children are in the same classroom with the same teacher for most of the day. In secondary school the teenager has to deal not only with different teachers, but also with moving around to different classes. These issues are discussed in Chapter 7.

There is a risk of depression during these years as it becomes apparent to the teenager with an ASD how different he is from his peers. As he becomes more interested in socialising, he may be teased and scorned by others due to his lack of required skills. Your child may be experiencing feelings of anxiety, depression or the 'blues' that will go unrecognised if he is not encouraged to talk about his thoughts with you. Your child needs to know that these feelings are normal and how to recognise and identify the different feelings he is having. For those less able, picture icons or simple drawings of happy and sad faces can initially help the non-verbal person to communicate how they feel.

Research has shown that there is a higher incidence of depression or manic depression in families with a child with an ASD, perhaps due to a biological predisposition. It is important that a person with an ASD who is depressed is treated by a professional knowledgeable about the condition.

Tony Attwood has outlined some strategies for communicating about emotions and learning about friendship in *Asperger's Syndrome: A Guide for Parents and Professionals*, and Patricia Romanowski Bashe and Barbara L. Kirby in the *Oasis Guide* also offer advice on adolescent issues. See also the Resources section at the end of this book.

Bullying

Bullying is a significant problem in secondary school, and for this reason I have written about it in Chapter Seven, on education, which the reader may wish to consult. However, a few suggestions are in order here for parents.

There are a number of things that can be done about bullying. Luke Jackson suggests in his book that if bullying occurs from the teacher, the student should go up the hierarchical ladder, to the head of the year, or the headteacher, or another teacher he trusts.

If it is fellow students who are doing the bullying, the parents may need to step in and sort it out, but Luke suggests seeing the teacher or an authority figure in private. For a parent to speak to the bullies themselves will only aggravate the situation as soon as the parent is gone. This situation has to be dealt with seriously, but discreetly.

Bullying is very upsetting for the victim and should not be treated as a fact of life that everyone deals with, because in reality it is only people who are different who are bullied. Teenagers need to learn what is responsible behaviour and how to be tolerant of others. If they don't learn this in school, where will they learn it?

As a parent, you can request that the school teach social skills to your child as part of his educational provision. You can also try to teach the social skills to your child that will make him understand more about neurotypical teenagers and the behaviours and conversation that they expect from your child. There are resources in the back of this book for you to consult.

Luke Jackson also mentions that learning Taekwondo helped him in many ways, including impressing his would-be tormentors. It not only helped him with his motor skills, it boosted his confidence and made him feel better about himself.

Social skills and dating skills

Even if your teenager prefers to spend a lot of time alone, he will need some social skills. In Chapter Eight, ideas for actual situations or places for socialising are discussed. Again, social skills should also be taught at school, but dating may be a subject you want to discuss at home.

For the able teens and young adults who are interested in dating, Jerry and Mary Newport offer many words of wisdom in their book *Autism – Asperger's and Sexuality*. Have your teenager read certain sections (this can be done by photocopying the section in question, which is authorised by the book's publisher for this specific purpose, then you can discuss them with him and provide any support he needs. Luke Jackson's book is a good resource for the early teen years.

FOOD FOR THOUGHT

'One way to help our young men is to help them learn a few stock social scenarios. Support groups should have practice sessions in introductions. Family members can go on "dates" with their daughter or son with autism. The practice of any social activity is a good training ground.'

Jerry and Mary Newport *Autism – Asperger's and Sexuality*

Siblings

It's not always easy to be a sibling, but having a brother or sister with an ASD has added challenges. These challenges can have both positive and negative effects on a sibling. Parents need to be aware of the sibling's feelings in order to develop strategies of support to help him adjust.

On the positive side, many siblings develop a maturity and sense of responsibility greater than that of their peers, take pride in the accomplishments of their brother or sister and develop a strong sense of loyalty. Siblings of ASD children are usually more tolerant of the differences in people, and show compassion for others with special needs.

On the down side, many siblings feel resentment at the extra attention the child with autism receives, and some feel guilt over their own good health. They may also feel saddled with what they perceive as parental expectations for them to be high achievers. Many siblings feel anxiety about how to interact with their brother or sister. Often there is a feeling of resentment at having to take on extra household chores, coupled with restrictions in social activities.

Living with a brother or sister with an ASD

Because of the behavioural characteristics inherent to autism, living with a brother or sister with an ASD is not easy. It is hard to foster a relationship with a sibling who does not show any interest in being your playmate. After a while the sibling stops making attempts to interact with the brother or sister. It is hard to harbour tender feelings towards someone who invades your personal space and tears your favourite art project off the wall, or twirls the tail right off one of your favourite stuffed animals. And how can a sibling feel comfortable inviting friends over, knowing her older brother with an ASD may come running down the stairs with no clothes on at any moment? Some of the behaviours exhibited by children with ASDs would be typical of a younger child's behaviour, but it is hard for a sibling as time goes on and the behaviours continue (or are replaced with other more interesting ones) to feel anything but resentment.

My Brother Jeremy

by Rebecca Sicile-Kira, 11 years old

Jeremy is my older brother. He is 14 years old and has autism. He likes to watch TV, spin tops, twirl toys, and play computer games. He also likes to go for car rides and go swimming at the pool and the beach. He enjoys watching the TV show *Sponge Bob Square Pants*. He used to not like that show but he has gotten used to it because *Sponge Bob* is my favourite TV show. Now sometimes he watches it with me. His favourite foods are french fries, cheese, pasta, rice, salad, strawberries, cookies and chocolate. He is in 8th grade. He has some friends that he hangs out with at school. He also goes to school dances. When he goes, he goes with one of his aides.

I like playing games with my brother a lot. I'm usually busy, but when I am free I try to play with him. We play games on the computer as well as board games. Some of the games we play are babyish, so they can get really boring after a while. One of my good friends Rozlin plays with my brother, too. She plays with him when she comes over, and at the Boys and Girls Club.

Sometimes I get mad at my brother. If I don't lock the door to my room while I'm not in, he will mess up my whole room! He is constantly playing with my toys. If he sees one of my toys lying around, he will pick it up and twirl it, until he finds something else to twirl. After a while that gets very annoying. I also can't leave my toys out because he might break them. It's not often that he breaks my toys, but when he does I get really mad.

Now that Jeremy is learning how to type, he is able to communicate more with us. I like this because now we can ask him a question and get an answer. Unlike when he couldn't type and we couldn't ask him anything. Sometimes he types something about me or to me. I like this because when he says something about me, it is usually something nice. I do not mind that he is autistic too much. He has gotten better at many different things. He does not hit as much as he used to. He is also a lot more patient. Even though he is autistic, I like having him as my brother.

Concerns of the siblings

Some of the concerns siblings feel are about the ASD itself. They wonder what autism is, if they can catch it, and if their brother or sister will get better or not. Many feel that the parents spend more time with their brother or sister, and thus feel that the child with an ASD is loved more. They can be resentful of the special treatment the other child receives and of the extra burden and responsibility they feel they have. As they get older, siblings are more and more concerned about the reactions of their friends.

Factors contributing to how a sibling adjusts

There are different factors that affect how a sibling adjusts, including the family size, the severity of the brother or sister's impairment, the age of the sibling at the time of the diagnosis, as well as the gender and age of the sibling, and their place in the birth order.

An older sister may well feel responsible for a younger sibling with an ASD and try to 'mother' or take care of him. On the other hand, a younger sibling may find herself caring at times for an older brother, in contrast to the traditional roles that she may be observing in other families. This can lead to feelings of resentment. All in all, the parents' attitudes and expectations have a strong bearing on how a sibling adjusts.

How parents can help

There is much a parent can do to help a sibling adjust and experience more positive than negative effects. Here are some tips:

● Keep the lines of communication open. Knowing that they can ask questions and talk about their feelings is the most important thing for siblings. Let them know their feelings are normal.

● Remind siblings that just because you give more of your time and attention to the child with an ASD, it does not mean that you also give him more of your love. Let them know you love them just as much and that they are just as important. They need to hear it.

● Make sure that siblings have a private, autism-free zone to call their own. Install locks to make sure they have a secure place to keep their precious objects. Siblings need to feel they are safe and have privacy.

● Set out consequences for the child with an ASD if he wrecks or ruins siblings' belongings.

● Teach siblings how to play or interact with their brother. When they learn the skills of getting his attention and getting a response from him, they will be able to interact with him on his level and that will make them feel good about him.

● Make time on a regular basis to spend with siblings alone. It doesn't have to be a long period of time, even a 15-minute breakfast alone. Schedule a special outing every once in a while.

● Do what you can to try and get the behaviours of the child with an ASD under control.

● Make sure siblings have some time when they can have friends over and spend time with them without having to always include their brother or sister with an ASD.

● It may be helpful for siblings to meet or talk to children in the same situation. Check with your local organisations to see if a support group for siblings exists in your area. If not, see if there is any interest, check out the Sibshop website and book (see Resources) and start your own.

HOW TO KEEP YOUR MARRIAGE OR SIGNIFICANT RELATIONSHIP INTACT

Many couples look forward to having children, and all parents know the effects those little bundles of joy can have on your relationship with each other. It is put on the back burner as the new addition to the family takes centre stage. When children enter the picture, the

---

FOOD FOR THOUGHT

'Anything you read about autism almost always says that the
parents' marriage suffers more than anything. A lot of people
separate. Men especially seem to have trouble. I think men suddenly
feel they are not the head of the family anymore . . . If I was going to
believe in what I was doing, and allow my wife to take hold of her
growth and help my son, then I was going to have to step out of
traditional roles and complement her.'

Bill Davis, *Breaking Autism's Barriers*

---

couple may realise that they don't see eye to eye on everything, and
there are squabbles about child-rearing: how the children will be
disciplined, what the appropriate bedtime is, how much TV the
children can watch, what constitutes an acceptable diet, and the
importance of table manners. Add to the mix the household division
of labour (who does what), plus the monotonous day-to-day routine
of running a household, and often the relationship starts to resemble
two partners of a company gone bad rather than the romantic liaison
it once was.

The same is true of a couple who have a child with an ASD.
However, there are more ingredients added to the pot: the emotional
turmoil of the grief cycle when a diagnosis is pronounced; the lack of
positive support from the community; the waiting for information
from professionals; the incredible demands brought on by the
behaviours characteristic of ASDs; and the struggle to find and
obtain an appropriate education as well as other essential services.
For many, as the child gets older, the demands of caring for him do
not lessen as they do with neurotypical children, and the difficulty of
finding someone to care for those older children with challenging
behaviours so you can have some time alone sometimes becomes a
challenge in itself.

This is a lot for any couple to survive, no matter how strong.
However, this is the life you have now, so it is up to you, the couple, to
do what you can to keep your relationship or marriage afloat. Here are
a few basic suggestions:

Arrange for scheduled time alone on a regular basis: The first step in being a parent, whether an ASD is a factor or not, is to find someone to watch your children on a regular basis even if only for an hour or so, to have a beer at the pub. Even when the children are not all-consuming, it is easy enough to fall into the trap of never having free time alone. Use this time to do something that you always enjoyed doing together before you had children. Granted, it is not always easy to find someone to care for your child. Your concern should be for your child and the carer's safety. You will need to tell any person helping you about the behaviours your child has and what they should do about them. Here are some tips:

- You know your extended family. Can you ask them to watch your child?

- Do you belong to a church or community group? You may find some volunteers who may wish to help you.

- How well do you know your neighbours? Are they likely to know someone?

- You may be eligible for respite services from your local authority (see Chapter Four).

- Call the local university and ask them to put a notice up that you would like to hire a college student.

- If you need to pay for the respite and do not have deep pockets, apply for and use the Disability Living Allowance or other benefits (see p. 71). If all else fails, barter a service in return. Perhaps you can exchange hours with another couple needing a few hours off at the pub.

For more tips on finding and hiring carers, see Chapter Eight.

Discuss and decide what the division of responsibility and work will be: There is a lot more to be done when you have a child with an ASD. It is rare to find a partnership that naturally absorbs the extra work and stress without one of the partners feeling as if the burden has been placed on them. Usually, one person jumps right in and takes over (usually the mother). This will lead to burnout, and even more disengagement on the part of the other partner. Sometimes, when one parent is working to support the family and the other is the homemaker, the extra burden falls on the homemaker, while the breadwinner tends to be around less and less, as the workplace starts to seem more fun than the home environment at the moment.

Find someone to talk to: Sometimes, talking to other couples in the same situation can be helpful. Just being with another couple who know what the two of you are living every day can make you feel better. Perhaps you can help each other out by sharing information or tips, or just meet up to relax amongst understanding grown-ups. You can meet other couples through your local support groups.

Go to couples' counselling: If you are having a difficult time and feel that your relationship is severely suffering and heading the wrong way, couples' counselling can be helpful. Don't wait till things are so bad you are talking divorce. And if your partner refuses to go, then go alone. Contact your GP for a referral. Try and find a counsellor who has experience with ASDs. Ask your local support group for the names of any professionals they may know.

PARENTS: HOW TO PROVIDE FOR YOUR CHILD FOR WHEN YOU ARE GONE

Thinking about what will happen to our children when we are gone is not always pleasant and something we'd rather not have to think about. But the reality is, no one lives for ever and provision needs to be made. No matter the ability or needs of the child, there are always challenges you know they will face. Whether your child is still a toddler or approaching middle age, a plan needs to be created. Here are some suggestions.

Write a 'letter of intent': This is a document that describes what kind of living situation you envision for your child. You will need to consider the age and ability level of your child, lifestyle issues such as your ideas for where he will live, the education he will receive, what kind of employment he will have, and the social life you wish him to have. Your ideas on religion, medical care, behaviour management, advocacy and/or guardianship, trustee and final arrangements should be noted.

For individuals needing a high level of care or supervision, detailed instructions should be provided for assisting the person with functional living skills such as bathing, dressing, feeding and toileting. Making a videotape showing how the person needs to be assisted would be most helpful, and take less time than writing it all out.

For those who have minimal communications skills, note down their likes and dislikes, what they like to do and see, how to contact any friends or relatives they may have. Imagine how much easier the transition will be if you have everything written down in one place.

Do some legal planning: Seek the advice of someone competent and experienced in the area of providing for disabled children. Look into wills, discretionary trusts and guardianship. Having a discretionary trust set up is a way to put money or assets aside in a trust that belongs to neither the parents nor the child. Money in this type of trust is not considered when assessing entitlement to state benefits. Guardianship may be necessary for some individuals who are unable to take responsibility for themselves.

Look into government benefits: You want to make sure that your child will be taken care of, and so a basic understanding of all government benefits is necessary. Make sure that it is clear what your child is qualified to receive and that he will not lose funding because of any assets received as gifts from other family members or friends.

Do some financial need planning: Simply put, to have an understanding of how much your child will need to supplement his benefits or income, a monthly budget is drawn up and calculations made. The result is an idea of how much needs to be put aside in the discretionary trust fund, and the family can identify what resources to use to fund the trust.

CHAPTER SEVEN

Educational Needs and Provision

It would be nice to think that things had changed since my school days, but, in discussions, teenagers still at school today described the same problems and issues as people in their thirties and forties (many of these school problems, incidentally, were described in Hans Asperger's original paper in 1944). In the 80s and 90s awareness and research into Asperger's syndrome increased dramatically, but it is still taking considerable time for this new knowledge to reach teachers and others 'on the ground'.

CLARE SAINSBURY, *MARTIAN IN THE PLAYGROUND*

I really hated to do it, but I had to file for due process, the US equivalent of an appeal to the Special Educational Needs Tribunal. I did not want to go through the cost in time, energy, stress and money we didn't have. But there comes a time when you have to take a stand. My son was regressing, and there was abuse and neglect occurring in the classroom, which had been documented.

The special needs class he was in was being taught by an untrained substitute teacher, and there were different untrained special needs assistants in there every other week. They were barely providing babysitting services, let alone a safe environment or an appropriate education. Meetings with the school district administrator just supplied us and other parents with unkept promises. The advocate we had hired said she had done all she could.

I removed my son from school, started a home programme and filed for due process. At home, Jeremy gained back his lost skills, and learned new ones. We wanted to avoid going to a tribunal, so we attempted mediation. The school district came to the bargaining table with no alternative or compromise for us to consider, and was chastised by the mediator for wasting everyone's time. We were obliged to proceed to fair hearing. On the first day, the new administrator (the old one had gone) agreed that the school district would refund us the money we had spent educating our son at home, and agreed to provide an appropriate provision for him, including training for staff, stating that none of this should ever have happened.

THE STATE OF EDUCATION:
THE SOBERING FACTS

If you are an older parent or a professional who has been in the trenches for a while, this chapter will ring a few bells. If you are a parent of a newly diagnosed child, or a general reader, you may be surprised by what you are about to read. And if you are a responsible person at a local educational authority or in a position of power in the Government, I would hope that you will read carefully and reflect long and hard about the state of education for children with ASDs in the UK today.

This chapter is different from the other chapters in this book. Being an optimist, it is against my nature to write about a problem and offer no practical solutions. But when it comes to a challenge as all-encompassing as the education of our children, there are no easy solutions to suggest. Parents and educators alike know and live this crisis every day.

But parents and educators should not be the only ones concerned. These children with ASDs will become adults who will be contributing members of society. If they do not receive a proper and intensive early intervention, if the educational system does not provide adequate resources for the educators teaching them, and proper resources for preparing the adolescents to transition into real adult life, society too will suffer. Not only will the costs to support these individuals all their lives be greater than those of a proper education, but society will lose out on the valuable contributions they could have made.

Someone once wrote: 'The history of man's progress is a chronicle of authority refuted.' In this, I am a true believer, and in terms of education, it is time to make some progress.

The challenges, expectations and demands

Worldwide, the number of children being diagnosed with ASDs is rising at an unbelievable rate. Every country has different laws and acts governing education. The settings may be different, but the challenge is the same: parents and professionals everywhere are grappling with the issue of how to educate an increasing number of children in the best possible manner. And more and more, as the struggle intensifies the expectations of the parents and the budgetary policies of administrative officials, it is the frontline teaching staff who get caught in the crossfire, and the children who are the casualties.

In the UK over the last few years the expectations of the parents have increased drastically. This is due to both the Education Act 2002 and the Special Educational Needs and Disability Act 2001 taking effect in 2002, an increase in the number of teaching methods and strategies known to be effective for children with ASDs, and the access to knowledge that parents now have thanks to the worldwide web. Regardless of ability, parents expect their child to be treated with dignity and respect, and to be given the opportunity to learn, using the methods known to be effective. Parents believe that every child has the right to reach his or her potential, no matter their ability. And rightly so.

As the parents' expectations for their children have changed, so have the demands on the teaching staff.

What surveys and reports show us about these challenges – some numbers

Facts and figures can be boring to read. However, it is necessary to take a look at a few in order to understand how the educational system is performing, keeping in mind the White Paper 'Excellence in Schools' (1997), which described the 'Government's vision of excellence for all children' (Quinquennial Review of the Special Needs Tribunal, DfEE, August 2000). Schools are supposed to be preparing the children of today with special educational needs for their roles as contributing adults in the future. A great majority of them are expected to contribute not only to society but to the economy as well. Here are some facts from two NAS surveys and one review of the Special Needs Tribunal:

Survey: Inclusion and Autism: Is it Working? (National Autistic Society, 2000)

- This survey found that 21 per cent of children with Asperger's syndrome and autism were excluded from school compared with an estimated 1.2 per cent of the total population. However, 29 per cent of the more able children with autism were excluded from school at some point. Parents attributed this to a lack of training and understanding on the part of staff. Parents of more able children noted that sudden changes in curriculum or classroom organisation were common causes of problem behaviours and could be avoided.

- This same survey showed that teachers are often having to send home children with autism of all abilities, either for the whole day or for certain classes, because of a lack of the necessary expertise, time and specialist support.

Quinquennial Review of the Special Needs Tribunal (DfEE, August 2000)

- Increasing expectations and knowledge on the part of parents has led to more dissatisfaction with the educational provision given to their children. When parents are not in agreement with the provision that their child is receiving, and the local education authority (LEA) is not budging, their only option is to file an appeal with the Special Educational Needs (SEN) Tribunal . In 1994/95, there were 1,161 appeals registered at the Special Educational Needs Tribunal. In 1998/99 there were 2,412. In four years, the number of cases has more than doubled. (SEN Tribunal Report 1989/99).

● An interesting fact is that when asked, 68 per cent of the parents who had appealed to the SEN Tribunal reported that their child's provision had improved as a result of lodging an appeal. However, for those who were dissatisfied, implementation issues figured prominently.

● The cost of the SEN Tribunal has risen from £499,000 (not including central service overheads which includes another £1.25 million per annum) in 1994–1995 to £3,045,000 in 1999–2000. While administrative costs have gone down, judicial costs have gone from an average £201 per SENT appeal registered in 1994–1995, to £713 in 1999–2000.

● It has been recognised that it is the interests of the child that is the determining factor for outcomes of SEN Tribunals. However, LEAs are concerned that the tribunal does not take into consideration the very real constraints that they are placed under in terms of budget and difficulties in getting specialist help from other statutory bodies. Some LEA officials stated that if they provided the appropriate provision for one child, it could be at the expense of another.

Survey: Autism in Schools, Crisis or Challenge? (National Autistic Society, 2002)

● This survey reported the views of teachers in seven LEAs in England. Two-thirds of the teachers felt that there were more children with an ASD now than five years ago, and this was consistent regardless of age or educational provision (special and mainstream). The rate of autism reported by teachers was three times higher in primary schools than in secondary schools.

● Of the schools, 72 per cent were not satisfied by the extent of their teachers' training in autism. In terms of specialist support, 44 per cent of schools which identified children with ASDs said that significant numbers of these children were not getting the specialist support they needed. 47 per cent of those responding would like to see training and advice provided through the LEA. Speech and language therapy was unavailable to 31 per cent of schools with children diagnosed with an ASD.

- 55 per cent of schools responding felt that support was not forthcoming because of delays in statementing or diagnosis.

- It is interesting to note that 32 per cent of the schools with inadequate training in autism were negative about inclusion, in contrast to only 19 per cent of schools where autism training was felt to be sufficient.

Food for Thought
Taking Responsibility

Everyone needs to take responsibility in an emotionally intelligent way. Parents need to take responsibility for not accepting less than an appropriate education for their child, while supporting the educational staff whenever possible and having good communication with all concerned.

Teaching staff need to accept responsibility by stating their needs to their superiors and refusing to provide services without the proper training and specialist support as well as asking parents for information that can help them understand the child's learning style.

And finally the headteacher and LEA officials need to take responsibility for leading the way by listening to what the front-line teaching staff are telling them, understanding the educational needs of the child, and making some effective changes. With the increasing numbers of children being diagnosed with ASDs today, this challenge is not going away.

As parents, educators and administrators, we are responsible for the future of all individuals with ASDs. It is our responsibility to work together to ensure the best preparation for the future of these children. They are counting on us and we must not let them down. As neurotypicals, we should be able to handle the pressure, communicate effectively, empathise and understand each other enough to work together. Aren't we the flexible, socially cognisant ones?

What these numbers mean

What the parents are saying: Parents expect their child to learn, regardless of the child's ability or whether he attends a mainstream or a special school. They expect teaching staff to demonstrate a working knowledge of different teaching methods and strategies proven to be effective in teaching children with ASDs. Parents expect adequate supports for the child included in a mainstream school, and for the staff there to be provided with necessary specialist support or training. They expect their child to stay in school for the whole day, just like any other child.

More and more parents, who have no other option, are lodging an appeal with the SEN Tribunal, not an easy decision considering the cost in stress, time and money. However, there is a good chance that even if there is a decision in their child's favour, it may not be implemented, and their child will still not be getting adequate provision.

What the teaching staff and schools are saying: Teachers in special schools may be expected to teach children with autism using the latest methods and strategies, yet do not have the expertise or adequately trained special needs assistants to do so.

Mainstream schools are at times having to send children home due to a lack of adequate support. Teachers in mainstream schools are expected to have children with ASDs included in their class, often with no special training, extra time for preparation or specialist support. Most schools wish the teachers had more training in autism.

Most schools who have teachers that are adequately trained feel that inclusion is working. However, teachers are seeing more and more children with autism in their classrooms, with no adequate support. Schools would like to see the statementing process take less time (some children have been waiting for years), because with no statement there is no money, and with no money the school cannot provide the support the child needs.

What the local educational authority officials are saying: LEA officials expect staff at both mainstream and special schools to learn more teaching methods known to be effective with autism, yet are not able to provide the necessary training or specialist support. Though local schools are seeing more and more children with an ASD in the primary grades, LEAs are not providing enough specialist support or training. LEA officials are not able to keep up with the statementing requests because of constraints in budget, policy and dependence on other statutory bodies (such as the health system). Even when a decision has been rendered by the SEN Tribunal in regard to a child's provision, often LEAs do not take, or are unable to take, the steps necessary to implement the decision.

Conclusions about the state of education for children with an ASD

- The parents and school staff would like to have the training and specialist support in order to provide an adequate education in the best interests of the child. The local educational authority officials feel that they are constrained by policy and budgets and therefore may not always be able to make adequate provision for these children.

- At a time when the Government and the LEAs are concerned about budgets, it is interesting to note the amount that is spent on the SEN Tribunal: £4,075,000 (including costs of central service overheads) 1999/2000. Imagine how much training that would provide, how much expertise and specialist support could be bought for such a nice sum of money, and how many children's educational provision would be enhanced.

- The Government is unable to change the educational system overnight, and may not be willing to spend more money on providing appropriate provision. However, the state of education is changing, slowly but surely. More and more parents have appealed to the SEN Tribunal. Although there has been some lack of implementation, the process has worked for a good many children in getting them the education they need. In some cases, these appeals have set legal precedent and allowed other families to ask for and receive appropriate provision for their child. The message is clear: if you want an appropriate education for your child, and you live in certain local authorities, you must be willing to fight for it. Remember, parents, every step you take for your child also paves the way for the others behind you.

Hope for the future

The Special Educational Needs and Disability Act 2001 (SENDA) could bring about major improvements in the educational opportunities offered to children, adolescents and young adults with ASDs. The Special Educational Needs (SEN) parts have been in force since September 2001, and the Disability Discrimination Provisions have been in effect since September 2002.

FOOD FOR THOUGHT
The Ongoing Struggle to Provide for Pupils with ASDs in Mainstream Schools
by Leslie Macdonald

Two years ago I was headhunted by my son's mainstream secondary school special educational needs coordinator (SENCO) to become a senior teaching assistant leading on ASDs. How on earth did I, a 55-year-old ex-accountant, arrive at this point? The answer goes back some 13 years, to the day when my growing fears about my two-year-old son were confirmed by a local paediatrician. He had a rare condition, about one in a thousand, they said, a social communication disorder. I had apparently described this perfectly in detailing my worries about him. I didn't even know what a learning difficulty was, let alone a social communication disorder.

My consequent distress was alleviated by a mother of twins, both with Kanner autism, who persuaded me to join a group of mums who were trying to set up a support group, and I never looked back from there. I spent the next nine years helping to set up and run the charity, becoming the first 'named person' in my county under the 1981

Education Act, where I worked with scores of families of children with ASDs, who gave me my education in ASDs, together with the many professionals who came to talk to our growing society.

I came to my present mainstream school from a resource for pupils with Asperger's syndrome in another mainstream school, which I had helped to save by raising funds for a new building. I 'cut my teeth' in the hands-on education trade here, and I learned the basics under a truly humanitarian headteacher and a dedicated resource lead-teacher. I joined my son's school and started the new internet-based Birmingham University autism course practically at the same time. My boss, the school SENCO, and I had high hopes for our ASD pupils. Almost two years later we have built a sound reputation with parents and the local education authority for good mainstream provision for ASDs. Sadly, we even have to turn some pupils away, but we are still a long way from providing what pupils with Asperger's syndrome really need, and an equally long way from convincing our own school of the true value of our work.

The SENCO is a strong lady who never flinches from arguing her corner for 'special kids', so a school that was unaware of ASDs has now become aware through talks I have given at in-school training days and through the high profile of some of the pupils who we are now admitting. Attitudes towards 'special children' are, however, variable, with some teachers showing acceptance for inclusion and willing to be flexible when it come to bending school rules and changing systems, while others are clearly sceptical and make it clear that they don't like to make 'exceptions'.

Special educational needs still gets given the fuzzy end of the lollipop when it comes to the need for flexibility and providing the equipment and resources required to meet real needs. After all, good SEN provision never put any school high in the national league tables.

Training and supervising teaching assistants in working with pupils with ASDs, observing and assessing existing and incoming pupils, and drawing up suitable programmes to allow them to integrate into school life and access the curriculum do not challenge school dogma too much. However, pupils with ASDs need other things, like social skills training, anger management, thinking skills and self-esteem work, and this requires time, staff, space and some initial capital outlay. Additionally, if pupils are being taught social skills they are missing some part of the academic curriculum, and this is where schools really start to feel the challenge. If timetables are inflexible it is impossible to put together a group of suitable children where at least one of them isn't missing out on a core subject that day. This doesn't meet with the approval of teachers and often not of parents either. Yet sending a 16- or 18-year-old out into the world with severely deficient social understanding doesn't seem to worry anyone very much.

I sometimes feel that our now considerable skills of supporting and protecting these children, predicting and heading off problems, and working within an inherently structured system are doing them no favours when it comes to arguing their need for additional and different provision. Although there are many pitfalls for the pupil with an ASD in a mainstream school, there is also a lot of structure there, and if staff have an understanding of ASDs and good internal communications, and if they modify the curriculum and the environment in even a fairly modest way, then life becomes a lot easier for most children. Even parents can then start to feel more confident and think about passes in GCSEs. However, in my experience this is lulling both parents and teachers into a false sense of security, because the outside world and all mainstream tertiary education is very far from making similar adaptations and accommodations to the person with an ASD.

This is why the way ahead for meeting the needs of pupils with ASDs can only be through the provision of specially resourced units where ongoing, long-term teaching of social skills, life and thinking skills is an integral part of the programme. Our small and economically challenged LEA will not commit funding for a resourced unit in our local authority area despite heavy bills to send their more challenged pupils to private residential schools for ASDs. Only parents can change this by getting together to challenge their local authorities and councillors to provide for their children, as the law requires. But this rarely happens because parents still do not properly understand their own or their children's rights, and slowly improving provision is dissipating most parents' worst nightmares – until, that is, their child leaves school.

SENDA has established legal rights for disabled students and should have a major impact on pre- and post-16 education. The Act makes it unlawful for education and training providers to discriminate against disabled students.

SENDA also gives the renamed SEN and Disability Tribunal the power to order training for staff and changes to policies, practices and procedures. The government is making monies available through the Schools Access Initiative over three years to provide incentives to schools to come up with comprehensive accessibility strategies and plans.

Although there are some concerns on the part of the NAS and other Special Education Consortium members on the practical guidance issues to LEAs and schools on implementing the SEN Code of Practice, it is hoped that the consequence of this Act will be to promote genuine supported inclusion in mainstream schools for students of all ages.

PARENTS: HOW TO GET THE EDUCATIONAL PROVISION YOUR CHILD NEEDS

Although this section is intended primarily for parents, teachers and front-line staff may find it interesting reading.

In Chapter Five, various types of therapies and teaching methods were discussed. To determine a child's educational needs, information-gathering must take place. Different professionals will do assessments, but as parents spend the most time with their child, they can learn a lot about his abilities and learning styles just by observing him. Regardless of whether your child is a baby or school age, you will need to form your own opinion, based on your observations of your child in his daily life.

How to know what your child's educational needs are

Negotiating the Special Education Maze: A Guide for Parents and Teachers by Winifred Anderson, Stephen Chitwood and Deidre Hayden is an excellent user-friendly book that has good advice on becoming an educational advocate for your child. Although the book is written with the American educational system in mind, much of the information and advice on how to make observations and collect information, and what questions to ask when visiting prospective schools and classrooms, is applicable to the UK. The various charts and questionnaires to use as guidelines to gather information are useful. Teachers may find the book helpful as well.

FOOD FOR THOUGHT

'As you prepare to explore the special education maze, you will need to know how the process of special education works. Your knowledge of the school system's procedures and your skills in communicating information about your child are essential to becoming an effective educational advocate . . . As parents going into school meetings, you are moving into a situation where the people you meet use a language and a body of knowledge you may not understand completely.'

Winifred Anderson, Stephen Chitwood and Deidre Hayden
Negotiating the Special Education Maze: A Guide for Parents and Teachers

---

Observing and recording

This kind of information is invaluable when thinking about your child's needs, and what kind of educational provision would serve him best. Yet planning an appropriate provision for a child requires documented and specific facts about the child, not just impressions and concerns. Parents need to learn to observe their child, to organise the information they glean and to make sense of it.

Anderson, Chitwood and Hayden give suggestions on recording observations on how the child acts in different environments, and how he relates to objects and people. These observations need only take five to ten minutes at a time. A good way to do this is to step back from your role in the family and watch your child, and how he does without your help. For example, can your one year old sit himself up without your help? Does he know and respond to his own name? If your child is five, does he understand the rules of games and does he follow them?

Different developmental areas: Once you have written down your observations (e.g. 'Sam can eat with a fork', 'Debra can do long division unaided and correctly'), you can organise them into the different developmental areas they pertain to. These areas are: senses and perception, movement, self-concept and independence, communication, thinking skills and social relationships. Your child will have different abilities in the different developmental areas. Knowing about these different areas will be helpful for you in identifying problems in your child. In regard to young children from birth to five, a good resource is the NHS Direct Online at http://www.nhsdirect.nhs. uk/SelfHelp/info/advice/normalchilddevelopment.asp or telephone NHS Direct 0845 4647 to ask for printed materials. Another good source is the GP Notebook at http://www.gpnotebook.co.uk/cache/-623902671.htm For school age children, your child's teacher as well as general practitioner should be good sources of information as to what is considered normal development.

Your child's learning style: Children are different from each other, and so is their learning style. Think about yourself. Do you learn better by hearing information or by seeing it? Do you work best in a neat environment or a messy one? Do you work long and hard, or do you take frequent breaks?

Now think about your child, and what you have learned about observing him. Observe him some more if you are not sure, thinking about how he learned to do the things he does. Does he like watching videos and has he learned some phrases from the programmes he watches? Does he copy an action he sees someone else do? Does your child do homework better alone or in the company of friends? Does he do his homework in a quiet environment or a noisy one? Sharing this kind of information with those who will be or are teaching your child will enable them to create the best possible setting for him.

What this means about your child's educational needs

The observations you have noted down about your child's abilities, challenges and learning styles will help you in your quest for the right educational provision. Now that you know about your child, you can look at what is on offer (and what is not!) and decide if it is an appropriate provision for him. This will also help you in your quest for educational strategies and therapies that could be useful for your child.

The Meek Shall Inherit the Earth, But Only the Bold Will Get a Decent Education for Their Child With Autism

This chapter may be difficult reading for those who are used to abiding by authority and professional opinion. I mean no disrespect, but after living in three different countries with my son, I can tell you that one must be polite, but not be meek, when it comes to getting the education your child needs. If you do not fight for your child, who will?

The status quo will not change unless parents become proactive, learn about their rights and responsibilities and convince the local educational authority that they know what the effective teaching strategies are for their child with an ASD, and that they won't go away until they get them, regardless of the school or ability level of the child.

Be careful of the words of assurance from people in positions of power. Get promises in writing. If people don't call when they are supposed to, keep calling until you get them on the phone. Document everything. Be polite, but be insistent. And most of all, be brave.

Special educational needs (SEN)

Perhaps you are the parents of a pre-school child, or you have an older child who is experiencing difficulties. It may be that you are a teacher who has concerns about a child in your class. A child may have been identified as having special educational needs before attending school, when he starts school, or when he starts encountering even more difficulties as he gets older. Sometimes the teacher has concerns; sometimes the parents; or perhaps a young person is having anxieties about their own ability to progress or difficulties in certain areas.

Basically, in England, the local education authority (LEA) has responsibility for identifying the children who need special educational provision in their area. For children under five, a health authority, primary care trust or National Health Service trust has a duty to tell the parents and the LEA if they suspect that the child has special educational needs. For children under two, parents may request an assessment, but a statement of special educational needs may not necessarily be made.

The law on special educational needs is different in Scotland and Northern Ireland. In Wales, while the law is the same as in England, the regulations and guidance may be different.

It is not my intention to give legal advice, or an in-depth explanation of how the system works, as each person's situation is different. Parents need to inform themselves about educational provision in their LEA. Teachers as well should be aware of their rights and responsibilities. There are wonderful resources available, for both parents and schools, and they are listed at the end of this book.

Whatever the situation, there is a possibility of assessment resulting in a statement of special educational needs. It is also possible for help to be given to those with special educational needs who do not have a statement. The Special Educational Needs Code of Practice provides a model for this help to be given. An individual education plan is developed that sets out ways of helping the child with his difficulties, and some individual short-term targets that he needs to meet in certain areas. Statements are reviewed annually and the individual education plan should be reviewed at least twice a year.

If a parent has concerns about a child's progress, they should ask for a meeting with the teacher to begin with. If you have already discussed them with the teacher, and still have concerns, you should approach the headteacher or the school's special educational needs co-ordinator (SENCO).

General advice for parents going through the special education needs process

It may be that you are one of those lucky individuals living in an LEA that is truly knowledgeable about autism spectrum disorders and what works best for these students, and you have a wonderful early, intensive programme with good trained staff and appropriate supervision. Or perhaps your older child with an ASD is included at the local school with specialist support, teachers who are knowledgeable and have the support they need to help your child, and not a bully in sight.

However, you are probably one of the many who is obliged to persuade your LEA about what is best for your child. If you have other children, you may already have experience with the educational system. However, when you have a child with special educational needs, you are entering unfamiliar territory and you need to learn a new set of navigating skills.

FOOD FOR THOUGHT

Bear in mind that:

- The statement is not the 'end all'; rather, it is the beginning of ensuring a suitable education for your child. Maintaining the statement is a continual process, just like education is. As a parent, you may need to monitor the statement or individual education plan that is being implemented.

- Risk-taking is an integral part of life. Many people are timid by nature and do not like to risk the ire of those in power by questioning authority or professionals. However, you are the expert on your child. What is it that you want for your child, what do you think he needs to learn and how does he learn best? If you are not in agreement with what others think is best for your child, you need to think about what the risk is of not speaking up. Think about what you would do if you were not afraid, then do it. Do you want to spend the rest of your life thinking, 'What if I had taken the risk of speaking up?'

- Parents who have a child with a disability have more stress than other parents. Dealing with the systems that are in place to 'help' your child often creates even more stress than the child himself does. These feelings will overpower you (remember the grief cycle?) from time to time. You will find that you take your frustration out on the wrong targets, usually the systems and people who are actually there to help you. Learn to recognise when you are not in control of your emotions or your stress level is high.

Over the last few years I have written and given workshops with Merryn Affleck, president of the North County chapter of the Autism Society of America. Our workshops are about developing the skills to become an advocate for your child, and creating a good working relationship with your child's school. Whatever your situation might be, as a parent you will need to follow these suggestions derived from our workshops to ensure that your child is getting the provision he needs.

Get to know how your child learns: For a pre-school-age child, observe how he interacts with people and objects. Does your child imitate others? Does he try to do new things with different toys; does he appear curious about his environment? For older children, look at what your child's track record says about his learning style. For example, does he learn new concepts only with one-to-one instruction? Is he able to focus with 29 other students in the classroom? Does he need a communication device? Does he learn by imitating others? For how long can he successfully be integrated into a mainstream school with support? What has worked in the past for your child and what hasn't? What has worked for other children like yours?

Learn about the educational strategies that work for ASDs: Join local autism groups, look at resources on the internet, read books, talk to other parents and professionals. Read Chapter Five for a general overview on treatments and therapies, and the section for teachers later on in this chapter (p. 176), as well as Chapter Six on family life. You will find plenty of information about educational strategies and what research has to say about the various techniques, plus resources to find out more. ASDs are a spectrum; all children are different. Find out about which particular teaching methods and strategies have been proven to be most effective with children like your child.

Learn about the law and what it says about LEAs' duties and parents' duties with regard to the education of children: Live by the motto 'Always be prepared'. You and your child are consumers of the education system, and have certain rights as well as responsibilities. As a consumer you need to be informed as to what those are. You need to be as astute on the law as your LEA is. As mentioned earlier, there are resources to help you. Every parent of an autistic child in England needs to get a copy of the *Special Education Handbook: The law on children with special education needs*, published by the Advisory Centre for Education (ACE). There are similar resources available for other geographical areas (see Resources). This handbook should become your bible. It is user-friendly, available in different languages and explains the law in layman's terms. There are plenty of other books, organisations and websites out there that can also advise you, and they are listed in the ACE handbook.

Learn about your local education authority: Education authorities vary on what kind of provision or specialist support they have given in the past and are geared towards providing. There are regional differences, and some are better about hearing the need of the child versus the budgetary constraints. Again, it is up to you to think outside the box. Don't depend on the authority giving your child what he needs; more often than not you will have to ask for it. Remember, your child's statement should be about meeting his educational needs, not what the education authority is used to providing. Find out from other parents what your LEA's track record is with children with autism spectrum disorders.

Familiarise yourself with the different types of school: Community schools, specially resourced units, voluntary schools, foundation schools, special schools, nursery schools, portage schemes, city colleges, specialist schools or colleges, independent schools and residential schools are all explained in the ACE *Special Education Handbook*. Basically the community school is your local mainstream school, and special schools are schools specifically for children with special education needs. Some mainstream schools have specially resourced units.

Visit mainstream schools, special schools and specially resourced units: Before making a decision regarding educational provision, visit special schools and mainstream schools. There is a tendency now towards educating autistic children in mainstream schools, and if that is the case you must be sure that proper support for your child and the teacher is provided. There are many factors to consider when making a decision about your preference. At any school, the appropriate questions to ask would include:

- How many children are in a class?

- Do the staff have appropriate skills and access to training to help your child?

- Are there any specialist resources?

- What kind of experience do they have with children with ASDs?

- What teaching methods and strategies specific to ASDs are the staff trained in?

- Is the school prepared to fit their systems around the child rather than being concerned about how a child will fit into the school system? For example, in a mainstream school, does a child have to go to assembly if they cannot tolerate confined spaces and noise? Can a child be taken out of a lesson to go to a 'safe' place if they are feeling overwhelmed and stressed? Can school rules about eating in the dining hall be bent so that vulnerable children and their friends can eat together and have a lunch-club in an empty classroom?

It is critical to ask specific questions about the teacher's experience with and knowledge of ASDs. Flexibility is also important. A teacher may not have much knowledge about ASDs, but be flexible about the needs of your child, and willing to learn what is necessary to make this a positive experience for your child.

Do not be comforted by a good ratio of staff to children in a special school, unless you know that the special needs assistants or support staff can demonstrate a functional knowledge of teaching methods proven to be effective with children with autism. Even the best teacher cannot be effective if she has untrained staff, unless she is given the resources to train them.

As autism is a spectrum, the staff may have had experience with a different ability level from that of your child, or a different severity of autism. You want to make sure the staff have a working knowledge of your child's type of difficulties, or ensure that specialist support will be provided by someone with that level of knowledge.

Develop good relationships: Develop and maintain good relationships with everyone you meet. If your child is already in school, make sure you have open lines of communication with the school staff. There should be a good flow of information going in each direction to make sure that you are all on the same page when it comes to behaviour plans, toilet training and homework. Often the front-line staff have their hands tied. By working together you may be able to get resources for your child or the classroom.

Learn about intensive behavioural treatment: This has been shown to be the most effective treatment for young children. If you wish your local education authority to provide this type of treatment, contact Parents for the Education of Autistic Children (PEACH) for information, or other ABA providers (see p. 84). Contacting other parents who have managed to obtain this type of provision can be very useful in terms of information.

Make sure you have copies of any assessments, reports, individual education plans and statements: Keep good records. Keep all assessments and reports in chronological order; they will be easier to find. Make sure you get copies of any assessments the LEA has requested on your child's behalf.

Keep good notes of any phone calls, meetings and conversations about your child: Keeping a notebook for this purpose is a good idea. Sometimes it is easy to forget suggestions professionals may make that are helpful, or when someone at school has told you something they are doing for your child, so writing notes including with whom and when you spoke is very helpful. This is also a good way to jog people's memories about timelines and follow-through on actions that need to be taken. It is also an ideal place to note attempts that were made to contact individuals who are having a hard time getting back to you.

Do not be afraid to ask questions: If you don't understand certain expressions or jargon, or what someone said, ask for an explanation. If you are unclear about who is saying they are doing what when, ask specific questions. This is especially true in something as important as a statement. Make sure the wording is specific. For example, what does 'help on a regular basis' mean? Does that mean once a year, once a month or once a week? How small is a 'small group'? If you are told that a particular professional will monitor a programme, the question begs to be asked, who is devising the programme, carrying it out, and how often? Sometimes the wording is vague in order to allow flexibility. However, it should be specific enough so you know who is responsible for what, and how often it should happen.

Always have someone accompany you to important meetings: Most people find it intimidating to meet professionals. Discussing your child's education can make you feel emotional and stressed. If you are meeting with more than one person, you may feel overwhelmed by the sheer numbers, and a warm body that you know next to you can be very reassuring. Bringing someone you know and trust with you (a friend or relative) will make you feel more at ease and confident. More importantly, this person can take notes to make sure you don't miss any information you may not remember in detail afterwards. A person who is not so emotionally tied into the situation may be able to give you better feedback about the meeting or to support you when you speak up.

Remember, you are the expert on your child. Never feel intimidated or that your input is less valuable than that of the teaching staff, other professionals or the LEA. If you feel intimidated, learn more about your child, his disability and abilities. Knowledge is power.

Keep focused on your goal: an adequate provision for your child: Although you do want to develop good relationships, remember that this is not about whether people are 'nice' or trying to do what they can. Either your child is getting an appropriate provision (meaning staff are knowledgeable and trained or given the specialist support they need if necessary) and is showing progress, or he is not, and that is the crux of the matter.

Monitor your child's progress and educational provision: Education is a continual process, including review and assessment: you review what is supposed to be happening, and you assess its effectiveness. Parents of mainstream children monitor their children's progress all the time. Parents of children with SEN may need to be more vigilant. There are a variety of ways to achieve this. Base your monitoring method on your relationship with your child's teachers, therapists and school administrators.

Develop good relationships in the community: Being on the board of governors of the school your child attends is an excellent way to meet other parents and to network with the professionals. I encourage those of you out there with extra energy and time on your hands to get elected. This is where decisions are made regarding local school issues. Our children need to be represented. You *can* have a positive impact on your community.

What to do if you are in disagreement with the LEA: If you are truly unhappy with your child's educational provision, and discussions with the powers that be are going nowhere, you have the option of making an appeal to the SEN and Disability Tribunal. This can be extremely stressful, and I would recommend it only as a last resort. However, remember that you have to live with whatever risk you take: the risk of not making an appeal and giving up if it is your last resort, or the risk of making an appeal and having a chance of obtaining the provision you feel is appropriate for your child. It's your call.

Some LEAs have independent conciliation facilities that can be used to try and avoid having to go to the SEN and Disability Tribunal but in no way take away your right to proceed with making an appeal to the Tribunal. I would advise attempting conciliation. Again there are resources and organisations who can help you with legal advice. ACE and other parents can give you the names of reputable and experienced barristers.

FOOD FOR THOUGHT
Autism-Specific Training is the Key

What makes a difference in the education of a child with an ASD is not whether the child is integrated into the local school or special needs school, but whether the school he is attending has autism expertise and specialist support. Mike Collins, the National Autistic Society (NAS) Education Advisor, reported that 'Parents of children in autism-specific units and schools – where exclusions rarely arise – are twice as likely to be satisfied with provision as those whose children attend mainstream or special education schools. Autism is a complex condition, with children having difficulties in relating to people and communicating their needs. Parents are telling us that *everyone* involved in the day-to-day running of schools needs specific training to recognize and support their children.'

(News release from NAS, 15 May 2000.)

FOR THE SCHOOLS: TEACHING THE CHILD AND ADOLESCENT WITH ASDs

Whether you teach in a special school or at a mainstream school, you will have students with autism spectrum disorders in your class. This section is written particularly for those who work in education; however, parents will find this section informative as well.

As indicated earlier in this book, the incidence of ASDs is rising and is not going away. Perhaps you already have a lot of practical experience or knowledge of the best teaching strategies for children with autism, and you work in a local education authority that is supportive of your need for specialist support or access to knowledge in order for you to use strategies proven to be effective with children with ASDs. If so, hurrah!

FOOD FOR THOUGHT
Be Precise

'For any classroom assistants or teachers reading this, then please, please try to realize that instinctively knowing where to go or who to talk to, and what to do next just isn't possible for a kid on the autism spectrum. If a teacher says "now get out your books and turn to page 10" and doesn't say "and now start answering those questions," then the AS kid is not likely to know, so to tell them off for doing no work that lesson is unfair.'

Luke Jackson, *Freaks, Geeks and Asperger Syndrome*

However, not all LEAs or schools give the same level of access to autism expertise or specialist support. Young teachers fresh out of college may not be aware of the politics of education, and some administrators will convince them they know enough to run a class and teach the children with little or no specialist support or autism-specific training. There are also the teachers who do not see the need to acknowledge that students with ASDs are differently wired, or the need to learn strategies effective with students with ASDs, or who have a difficult time with being flexible enough to accommodate the needs of these students. However, all educators, by the nature of their chosen field, ought to recognise that you can never stop learning nor have too much knowledge.

FOOD FOR THOUGHT
The Educational Environment

'There are many things that people with "autism" often seek to avoid: external control, disorder, chaos, noise, bright light, touch, involvement, being affected emotionally, being looked at or made to look. Unfortunately, most educational environments are all about the very things that are the strongest sources of aversion.'

Donna Williams, *Autism: An Inside Out Approach*

The basics everyone working at any school needs to know
Make no assumptions: Remember, every child is different, and every child deserves the same respect, whether they are non-verbal and severely handicapped by their autism, or very able with idiosyncratic behaviours. Just because someone is unable to talk doesn't mean they don't understand what is going on around them. And just because someone is verbal doesn't mean he understands more than the literal sense of what you are saying. Assumptions about a child's intelligence cannot be made because of his lack of communication or social skills.

ASDs are unlike any other disability: Some children with ASDs do not have imitation skills. Imitation is how most people learn. Many children with mental retardation or learning disabilities have imitation skills and are social. They may pick up social behaviours and language 'naturally' by being put in a class of their peers. This is not true for the most part for children with ASDs. Many have a good academic understanding of social skills but are not able to apply them. They need to be taught how to apply, in everyday situations, the social skills that most of us take for granted. The challenges that people with ASDs have are due in part to different wiring in the brain. They are not just being 'difficult'. Obviously, there are different ability levels in children with ASDs, but regardless, all have problems with social skills, communication and understanding more than the literal meaning of words.

ASDs-specific training is necessary: It does not matter how many years you have been teaching developmentally delayed children, or how many children with ASDs you have seen in your class, you need to learn more. It is only in the last decade that the results of effective teaching methodologies and strategies are being seen and recognised. Currently these strategies are still being developed or refined or built upon. Your headteacher or special educational needs co-ordinator or local authority needs to be convinced of the need for specialist training and support.

This is true no matter what type of school you are working in, no matter the level of disability or ability.

Special needs assistants and all staff working with the child need to be trained: A person who does not have the skills to do the job properly will not be an effective person to have around. Giving people the right skills to do their jobs will make them effective, confident and provide more job satisfaction, which makes for a low employee turnover rate. And that is always a good thing.

Peers need to be informed about disabilities and taught tolerance towards those who are different: Peers need to be given information so that they understand why people are different and why they act the way they do. This is true for all disabilities, not just ASDs. However, an ASD is an 'invisible' disability as you can't see it and the person may act neurotypical in most ways. Peers need to be told that they will benefit from having students with differences as their classmates. If there is concern about 'labelling' on the part of the parent or the student, it is possible to talk about the issues without naming the disability. For example, peers could learn about how 'social communication' is a challenge for some. Just as the student with an ASD is learning new appropriate ways of behaving, the peers need to learn to be more accepting of the differences in others. If they don't learn this at school while they are young, how will they learn to be tolerant and responsible members of society? A good resource is the book *My Friend with Autism* by Beverly Bishop.

The headteacher sets the tone: Tolerance and flexibility are key words that should be practised in every school towards any student who is 'different'. Headteachers should show by their own actions and attitude that bullying will not be accepted, and that staff are expected to be flexible to meet the needs of these children.

Communicate with parents: Keeping lines of communication open with the parents can help alleviate a lot of stress at both ends. Many parents are willing to follow any suggestions you may have to help their child. Any behaviour plan should be explained to parents so they can enforce them at home as well. Parents, out of necessity, have become more and more knowledgeable about their children's disabilities and can give you information on ASDs and their children that can be useful to you.

A must-read for teaching staff, the headmaster, the SENCO, the LEA...

An essential text for anyone working at a mainstream school or a specially resourced unit is *Freaks, Geeks and Asperger Syndrome: A User Guide to Adolescence* by Luke Jackson. It describes what it is like to be a child or teenager with an ASD, from one person's perspective, attending a school where the staff and other students have no understanding of this 'invisible disability'. There are specific examples of how someone who is academically very capable can only understand the literal meaning of words unless taught otherwise, and needs to be taught social skills to be able to act normally in a neurotypical world. This book also shows us, sadly, how youngsters with ASDs are routinely bullied by their peers as well as ignorant teaching staff. This alone should put the book at the top of all school educators' and headteachers' reading lists.

Another good book is *Access and Inclusion for Children with Autistic Spectrum Disorders: Let Me In* by Matthew Hesmondhalgh and Christine Breakey. The authors describe the challenges they faced in setting up a resource unit at a mainstream secondary school. Besides teaching the regular school curriculum, they also taught additional life skills in the community, and some students participated in a work placement scheme.

Bullying

Bullying is a major problem for students with ASDs attending a mainstream school or a specially sourced unit at a mainstream school. It is apparent in primary school, but becomes a significant problem in secondary school. Bullying, which can range from verbal taunts to actual physical encounters, is very upsetting to the victims and should not be treated as a fact of life.

Kenneth Hall, Jerry and Mary Newport, Luke Jackson, Claire Sainsbury and Liane Willey, all authors with ASDs, discuss bullying in their respective books at some length. Luke Jackson writes about how he was chased and pinched, shoved and hit many times. He also describes having personal school items such as rulers and pencils taken from him, having his lunch grabbed and stepped on, and doors being slammed in his face. More distressing are his stories about teachers making fun of his difficulties and calling him names such as 'thicko' or 'dopey' in front of the class.

Bullying occurs for a number of reasons. It can happen simply because the teenager with an ASD appears different to the neurotypical teens because of his dress and grooming. Often it is because as the other teenagers start to question authority, the ASD teen is still in the mentality of following the rules and thus seems to be 'nerdy'. Sometimes bullying is due to the misinterpreted behaviour of the ASD teen. Many children with ASDs have monotone voices, and sound rude, or mimic the person they are speaking to, which makes it appear as if they are poking fun. Many children with autism have mindblindness; they do not understand that others have different thoughts from theirs, and so are unable to anticipate what others may say or do, which creates problems in social behaviour and

---

FOOD FOR THOUGHT

'Another reason I think I have been bullied in the past and am prone to being picked on is that I just don't want to "run with the pack". I never have and never will. I don't see any point in pretending that I like things when I don't. I think this is one of the reasons why other people don't want to make friends with me or hang around with me.'

Luke Jackson *Freaks, Geeks and Asperger Syndrome*

---

communication. As mentioned before, some of the bullying comes from teachers who are uninformed about ASDs. It is hard for teachers and other students to comprehend that someone who is verbally astute and gets good grades for his work is unable to pick up all the non-verbal cues most people take for granted.

A teenager with an ASD may appear sneaky or manipulative because of some of his body language when stressed (avoiding eye contact, shifting from foot to foot, speaking in a flat voice). The teen with an ASD, usually a stickler for rules, may correct another student or tell off a child who is breaking a rule, thus enraging the teacher, who does not realise that he has no sense of hierarchy, only a sense of what is right. If a person with an ASD has good language skills, others tend to forget that his comprehension of the language is different, that he only has a literal understanding of language which can lead to trouble. Claire Sainsbury, in her book *Martian in the Playground*, talks about a teenager who was told by a teacher to 'pull their socks up' and who literally bent over and did just that, much to the astonishment and displeasure of the teacher, who thought she was being ridiculed.

Mainstream peers need to be told about ASDs, and how they manifest themselves. It needs to be made clear that bullying will not be tolerated. Having an ASD is like having an invisible disability. If a student is having difficulties with bullying, his teachers and classmates need to be educated about ASDs and how they affect people.

Besides giving information about ASDs, forming a 'circle of friends' has been found to be effective. In 1997, the Leicestershire Autism Outreach Team established seven such circles. The results were very promising. Not only did the child with an ASD show benefits, but so did the six to eight children who volunteered to form each circle. The benefits also extended beyond the immediate circle. For more information contact the NAS website (see Resources).

Sensory processing issues

Most people with an ASD suffer from sensory processing issues, which is part of the reason why they have difficulty with transitions and need schedules so they can anticipate what is going to happen next. They may easily experience sensory overload, which can lead to meltdowns. Sensory processing can affect learning, as some students have challenges in their auditory processing, some in visual, and some in both. This is also important in understanding how the learning material should be presented to the student. For more information, see page 213.

Social skills

If a child or teenager with an ASD prefers to spend time alone, parents and teachers need to respect that. However, some social skills are called for, because we all live in society and have to deal with people at one time or another. All children, no matter the age and ability level, need to learn some social skills. School resembles a mini-society and it is one of the first places where people first learn how to interact with other people.

For a more able autistic child in a mainstream school, this is an area where a lot of support will be needed. Teaching the student some social skills can help him avoid some of the bullying he may be prone to as a result of not knowing what neurotypicals expect in terms of behaviour.

Transitions

Transitions are another challenging area for students with ASDs. Whether transitioning from one school to another, one teacher to another or one classroom to another, it needs to be prepared for. Another change is that usually in primary schools the children are in the same classroom with the same teacher for most of the day. In secondary school the teenager has to deal not only with different teachers, but also with moving around to different classes. For some individuals with spatial difficulties, this is an added stress. Picture or word schedules can help in this area.

The section on finding your way around on page 236 gives suggestions for how to enable students to move around from class to class. Transition from one school to another needs to be carefully prepared. One way of doing this is through social stories; another way is through creating a scrapbook with pictures and descriptions of what will happen so the student can go over it. Teachers who are going to have the student in their class need to be prepared. Information can be given to them about the student, and the student could have a picture and a description of the teacher for his scrapbook.

Adolescent issues

Adolescence is a difficult time of life for most people. Hormone levels start flaring, the body changes in weird yet wonderful ways, and teenagers are in a state of flux. Puberty, hygiene, sexuality, dating and social skills are areas that create special challenges for the adolescent with an ASD. Adolescent issues are discussed at length in the previous chapter (see page 136) which should be consulted by teaching staff as these areas affect school life.

In primary school, the student usually had one principal teacher, and that teacher had to be able to recognise the warning signs of a possible meltdown, and how to defuse it. However, in secondary school there are many different teachers. If the teachers do not all recognise when a student is nearing meltdown, then more tantrums and unfortunate incidents may occur.

Arranging for a quiet place where the student can go to calm down if he feels overloaded, stressed or confused is very helpful. School staff should seek advice from experts knowledgeable about ASDs and put effective strategies in place as a preventative measure, rather than waiting for a major incident or crisis to occur.

Teaching Tips from Temple Grandin

As mentioned earlier in the book, Temple Grandin is a woman with autism who has a successful international career designing livestock equipment and is a world-renowned speaker on the condition. The following is her advice on what can help people with ASDs to learn, based on what was effective for her and information she has accumulated over the years about what has worked for others:

● Intensive and early intervention is very important.

● Having the right kind of teacher is more important than what kind of programme you are doing. The teacher needs to be structured and clear in what is being requested and what the correct response is.

● Talents and special interests can be used to motivate a child to work and learn, and as he reaches adulthood it can be transitioned into a line of work. For example, if a child likes trains and is studying maths, ask him to calculate how long it takes to go from Bristol to London by train.

● Some people cannot process visual and auditory input at the same time. Their sensory processing system cannot process visual and auditory input simultaneously. These individuals should only be given either an auditory or a visual task.

● Having rooms that are quiet and have low distracters is important. Carpeting on the floor is good for noise absorption. Fluorescent lighting is terrible for many people with autism. Temple suggests using a lamp at each desk with an incandescent light bulb.

● Children who are echolalic and repeat commercials or jingles do so because they are hearing it in the same tone each time and that makes it easier for them to learn. Be thrilled the child is echolalic. You can teach this person by using flashcards with both the picture and the word on the card, and saying the word in the same tone to begin with. When the child has learned the word in one tone, then teach it using a different tone. Teach nouns first. For verbs and other words, illustrate the action by modelling (i.e. jump while saying jump, or making a plane take off from the desk to teach 'up' and also visually showing the word going up) or by having the word look like the action (i.e. write falling as if it were falling).

- Some people with auditory processing issues cannot 'hear' consonants, and therefore cannot reproduce them verbally. Overemphasising consonants when teaching words is necessary for them to hear and reproduce them.

- Some individuals respond better if words or sentences are sung to them. People with sensitive hearing will respond better to being spoken to in a low whisper.

- Laptops and the new flat-monitor computers are better for people who have visual processing problems, as some individuals are distracted by the flicker of the screen.

- For people who like to rock, sitting on a therapy ball or a T-stool (made from two pieces of wood nailed together like a T) that the person balances can be helpful.

Learning about educational strategies

How does a teacher go about learning more? If you are not getting adequate information about ASD-specific training and conferences from your local authority or school, there is still hope; there are resources out there. Look on the National Autistic Society website. Become a member of the NAS and local chapters and get on their mailing list. Read their newsletters and find out about workshops and conferences and when they are being held. Contact the organisations or companies that offer information and training on certain techniques you want to know about (PECS, ABA, social relationships). There are more and more universities offering courses on autism, some of them online. For example, the University of Birmingham has developed an online programme of training in ASDs. You can consult the website at www.webautism.bham.ac.uk For other possible training courses, check with the NAS or do a web search.

Food for Thought
More on the Politics of Education

For six years I served in a voluntary capacity on a state-mandated community advisory committee made up of parents, educators and administrators. For two of those years I sat on the executive board. Our mandate was to give input and advice to the special education directors and school superintendents of the 14 member school districts, who were obliged by law to listen to, but not necessarily to follow, our recommendations.

One of our most important tasks was to draft a list of priorities for special education in the districts for the coming year. The administrators would look at the priorities and address these areas of concern, then report back to the community advisory committee about what they had done to address those concerns.

One year, a major concern drafted into a priority was about the exodus of qualified special education staff. Our suggestion was that each school district develop and implement strategies to attract and retain competent staff. At the end of the year, we sent a questionnaire to the directors of special education to ask them what strategies they had come up with. One special education director actually wrote back to say that he had done nothing, because staff left because of the parents. This reply begged the question 'What are the parents doing that makes staff leave?' Here are some prossible answers:

● *The parents were expecting their child to learn.* For some reason, there appears to be an assumption by some school administrators about severely handicapped children: as long as the child is happy and loved, and goes home with his nose clean and his pants dry, the school has done its job. Often, good teachers who want to teach this population recognise when there is a lack of support from above and leave to go and work in a more supportive environment (possibly a neighbouring school district).

● *The parents were expecting that staff demonstrate a knowledge of teaching methods and behavioural strategies that were proven to be effective with that child.* Often special needs assistants are thrown into classrooms with no prior training or knowledge. This is detrimental to the child and the teacher who is running the class, and also to the teaching assistant herself. If people do not have the skills to effectively do their job, they will eventually be unhappy and leave.

● *The parents were expecting that the teacher be given some information about their child and his learning methods.* Inclusion will not work if specialist support is not given to help the teacher. Teachers need to be given the tools and training to do their job; they cannot be expected to be knowledgeable in all strategies simply through osmosis.

Many school administrators like to play the game of convincing the staff that the parents are too demanding. People in a position of power will convince staff that yes, they can do the job, they don't need specialist support or to learn new educational strategies. Then the parent is put in the uncomfortable position of explaining why the teacher (or other school professional) is not able to provide for the child's educational needs. The administrators pit the parents and the teachers against one another, when in reality they should be partners. If you are the only proactive parent in that class, then you also get the reputation of wanting 'special treatment' for your child. However, the way the process works, you can only ask for provision for your child, not the whole class. In essence, by requesting that a staff member be properly trained, you *are* helping the whole class, and smart teachers will recognise this.

A Reader's Digest condensed version of effective educational strategies
This is by no means an exhaustive list, but rather suggestions based on what is known to be most effective and practical. For more information on certain techniques, look at Chapter Five as well as the resources section at the back.

Applied Behaviour Analysis (ABA): Regardless of what kind of school you work at or ASD ability level you teach, all teaching staff should have a working knowledge of ABA. It is the cornerstone of all effective teaching techniques for people with ASDs and, for that matter, all students.

Most people think of Lovaas when they think of ABA, but while Lovaas developed a particular intensive teaching programme for young children, ABA has been around for many years and is useful in all contexts. In fact 25 years ago, before Lovaas was known to the world at large, I was trained to use some aspects of ABA, such as task analysis, prompting, shaping and rewarding, in order to teach the developmentally disabled adolescents I was working with.

ABA can be used with all types of students, not just those with ASDs. For example, plans can be drawn up for unruly students to teach them appropriate behaviours, and students with cognitive disabilities can have academic skills broken down into smaller teachable steps. So ABA is a good general method that all teaching staff could learn that would be useful in all aspects of their work, regardless of the student population they are teaching.

Specifically, ABA techniques such as task analysis and discrete trial teaching can be adapted to teach academic skills, life skills, communication, anger management and so on. Many of the effective techniques for students with ASDs (such as PECS, social skills training and TEACCH) are based on or use some behaviour principles. If you know basic ABA, you will be more effective in applying these other strategies and with practice will be able to adapt techniques and curriculum for all types of children.

Some good books to teach general practical ABA techniques are *Steps to Independence* by B. Baker and A. Brightman, and *One on One* by Marilyn Chassman. To learn basic discrete trial teaching read *Teaching Developmentally Disabled Children: The ME Book* by O. Ivar Lovaas. See Resources section for more.

Behaviour plans: Behaviour plans that are clear, precise, fair and written down are necessary to address inappropriate behaviours and replace them with appropriate ones. Bad behaviour will not just go away, and a student with autism cannot understand what all the fuss is about. He needs a systematic way of understanding how to behave appropriately. Consistency is necessary for behaviour plans to be effective. They can be drawn up to encourage or eliminate specific behaviours, once the behaviours have been analysed and the

.dents identified. It is important that anyone working with a student knows what the behaviour plans are in order for them to be effective.

One last word about ABA and behaviour plans. Many people are under the impression that ABA turns people into little robots or that it does not take into account people's feelings and emotions. That is just not true. For example, if you have a student who is kicking the back of someone's chair in the classroom every day, you will analyse why he is kicking the chair, and then you will teach him an alternative appropriate behaviour. Perhaps he is kicking the chair because he can't stand the sound of the squeak every time the student moves. He needs to learn to appropriately tell someone, and then the squeak will be fixed. However, if it is discovered that chair-kicking is one of many behaviours he is exhibiting because he has anger management issues, you will use ABA techniques and teach him to express his anger in an appropriate manner. The student will have counselling sessions about why he is angry, and what can be done about it. But he still needs to learn in a clear, concise, on-the-spot way which behaviour has to stop and what can replace it.

Picture exchange communication system (PECS): For non-verbal children, PECS is very useful. It immediately teaches the child a basic system of communication, and can convey many academic concepts too. This method is wonderful for small children, but even non-verbal adults who have never developed a communication system can learn to use it. See page 87 for contact and resources.

Schedules: Schedules and structure are necessary for students with ASDs. Clarity and precision are the key words. Schedules can be pictures or words, simple or complex, depending on the student's need. A good book about schedules is *Activity Schedules for Children with Autism: Teaching Independent Behavior* by Lynn E. McClannahan and Patricia J. Krantz.

TEACCH: Certain elements of TEACCH, such as schedules, are very effective and can be adapted for use at many different ability levels in all environments. However, classrooms that use only TEACCH techniques appear to be about making it easier for the teacher to teach a certain number of children, and appear to be lacking in offering social situations or opportunities for teaching communication. See p.118.

Social behaviour and social skills training: Because of the impairment of social skills that people with ASDs have, it is very important to teach these. Social skills are used in every aspect of life, and are necessary to be able to function even basically in society. People with ASDs don't just pick up these skills by rubbing elbows with their peers. They need to be taught systematically. Again these can be geared towards various ability levels. Social stories can be developed with the student. Social skills groups teach social skills by breaking them down and providing practice in a safe environment. The Social Use of Language Programme (SULP) is useful in developing interpersonal and social abilities from a thinking skills and communication perspective in the student with high-functioning autism or Asperger's. See p. 94.

Self-esteem training: Working on self-esteem is a necessary component of education with children and adolescents with ASDs. They need to learn about ASDs, the challenges as well as the strengths. An interesting book with good worksheets is *I am Special* by Peter Vermeulen.

Preparing for Life After Secondary School: Transitions to College or Work

Just like any student, plans have to be made for the future. A transition plan should form part of the first annual review after the child's 14th birthday, and any subsequent annual review. The purpose of the plan is to gather information from a variety of individuals at the school and different agencies in order to plan for the teenager's transition to adult life. Some students may wish to go on to specialist colleges, training courses or university, or move directly into employment. Those who are in special school provision may stay until they are 19. However, the issue of transition still needs to have been addressed at an earlier date.

Food for Thought

'There is so much more to the life of an autistic than just being on SSI and safely tucked away at home, sheltered from the world. That is minimal existence, and I know from my conversations with people with autism and Asperger's that many of you want more than that out of life. You would like to make some money, hopefully doing something you enjoy. I'm here to tell you that it's possible to be gainfully employed, but to accomplish this, you need 1) an idea of what you would like to do, 2) some sense of the availability of jobs in that area, and 3) an appropriate education that will prepare you for working in that field.'

Mary Newport, 'Education and Jobworthiness'
(article in *Autism Asperger's Digest Magazine*)

Person-centred approach

In the White Paper *Valuing People: A New Strategy for Learning Disability for the 21ˢᵗ Century*, 2001, the Government set out proposals for a person-centred approach to planning services for adults with learning disabilities. A person-centred approach means that the individual's aspirations and wishes are pivotal to the process. He has more choice and control; it's more about making the services fit his wishes and goals than about making him fit into an already existing option.

By 2003, local agencies will be expected to introduce person-centred planning for all young people moving from children's to adults' services. This means that individuals with learning disabilities will be given more choice and control over their options.

Sadly, in England and Wales, the definition used by the Government specifically excludes people with ASDs where there is no accompanying learning disability. (In Scotland, ASDs have been included in the Scottish Parliament's Learning Disability Review *The Same As You?*, published in May 2000.)

Connexions Services

Connexions Services partners different Government agencies and the private sector to assist young people in making a successful transition to adult life. Comprehensive services including information, advice and guidance, opportunities for personal development and learning are provided to young people aged 13 to 19 who are at risk of not making a successful transition to adulthood.

Connexions Services have personal advisers to help with transition planning. For those students with statements of SEN who have a learning disability, an adviser must be invited to attend annual reviews of Year 9 students. Then, when a learning-disabled person is 19, Connexions is responsible for arranging a review and continuing support through a transition into adult services at 25.

For parents of students with Asperger's who do not have a statement of SEN, contact the National Autistic Society or your local chapter to find out if the local Connexions Services has been helpful for teenagers such as yours. Find out what resources have been helpful in your area.

Although services for those with Asperger's are sorely lacking, there is hope for the not too distant future. In 2002 the NAS published *Taking Responsibility: Good Practice Guidelines for services – Adults with Asperger Syndrome* written by Andrew Powell. These guidelines are a result of the Avon Asperger Syndrome Project 1999–2002 and was funded by the Department of Health. The NAS, along with other groups such as the All Party Parliamentary Group on Autism (APPGA), are working hard to have these recommendations implemented.

As well as the above-mentioned document, two good books for transition planning are: *Life Beyond the Classroom: Transition Strategies for Young People with Disabilities* by Paul Wehman; and *Community-Based Curriculum: Instructional Strategies for Students with Severe Handicaps* by Mary A. Falvey.

CHAPTER 8

Community Life

I . . . had trouble learning the rules to the games that other children played and I often played the wrong way, causing the other kids to avoid me as well or tease me . . . My reactions to various situations were not quite what people expected . . . I knew that I did not act right but I was often at a loss to know what I was doing wrong . . .

CLARE SAINSBURY, *MARTIAN IN THE PLAYGROUND*

My son often goes to the shops with college students who help him with his afternoon activities. We started off by teaching him appropriate behaviour in shops, such as how to walk up and down the aisles without pulling the price tags off items. He then took an interest in finding his favourite food items and taking them off the shelves, so we taught him shopping skills. This included looking at a modified shopping list, finding the items he wanted to buy, queuing up and paying for them. One day my son and I were shopping and when we reached the checkout counter the relatively new cashier said, 'Hi, Jeremy, how are you? Oh, are you his helper for today? Wait, he can empty the shopping cart himself.' I laughed, feeling good that the cashier knew him, knew what he could do and was looking out for him. It's a small thing, but it's connections like that that make the place you live in a community.

CREATING TIES IN THE COMMUNITY

Most people go through life easily developing all sorts of relationships, from the casual relationship with the shopkeeper to relationships with colleagues, classmates and a partner for life. Like a garden, all relationships take a certain amount of tending to grow and maintain.

And like gardens, the more intense the relationship, the more tending is involved. No matter the age or ability of a person, having relationships and ties in the community is vital. Though we all like to think of ourselves as independent, none of us is self-sufficient; we all rely on other people in one way or another.

The same holds true for people with autism. However, because of the very nature of ASDs, developing community ties can be mind-boggling. For those of an age and ability where they are on their own, it can be frustrating and seem unnecessary and illogical. For parents of children and the less able, it is another reminder of how their child does not fit in, and how society on the whole is geared towards the competitive neurotypical person. Creating relationships in the community can be hard work, but it is worth it and necessary.

Community ties are the threads in the fabric that binds society together. Whether your child is shopping at the grocery store or an active participant in the Boy Scouts, he is engaging in some form of social relationship. Adults with ASDs also have different levels of contacts in the community. By creating these ties, no matter how small, you are laying the foundations for being a part of the community you live in. This is important for many reasons, not the least of them being safety.

For an adult, community ties can provide a support network you can fall back on if you ever need assistance. For a parent, they can help create the foundation of the relationships your child will have as he gets older, and perhaps be there when he is an adult and you are no longer around.

How to create community ties

Community ties can be developed at different times on different levels. Remember that a person has different relationship needs at different times of his life, but all people need friendships and feelings of security and safety. As people with ASDs are in the minority, it is still up to individuals with ASDs and/or their parents to educate others and create those connections. Here are some tips.

Identify what the needs and desires are: If you are an adult with an ASD, you need to think about what your comfort level is, and what you would like to do in the community. If you are a parent, you will need to identify your child's abilities, challenges and interests, as well as what community skills he needs to learn to prepare him for adult life.

Identify what information or skill the person needs to develop that community relationship: If a person likes to go shopping but doesn't have the patience to queue, then he needs to learn the skill of waiting. A person who likes to go to the library to look at books will not be fostering good community relationships by taking all the books off the shelves and dumping them on the floor.

Identify what information people in the community need in order to facilitate building relationships: Perhaps the adult with an ASD does not need any special consideration; it all depends on the individual. For a child learning to shop, perhaps the shopkeeper will need to call him by name and ask him for the money. An activity leader will need to know about any behaviour challenges, and how to handle them.

FOOD FOR THOUGHT

It's Getting Easier

Twenty-five years ago I worked with adults with severe autism and other developmental disabilities living in a state hospital. Some of these individuals were going to be de-institutionalised and live in group homes. My task was to help them learn self-help and community living skills, including how to act in public. Along with other staff, I would take them out to restaurants, and teach them safety skills such as how to cross the street. Currently, with my own son, I am faced again with trying to figure out how to find programmes and activities that my son will enjoy, as well as finding ways to teach him community living skills. It is not an easy task, but definitely not the challenge that it was decades ago.

EVERYDAY LIFE IN THE COMMUNITY

Regardless of a person's age or ability, we all need to learn how to go about everyday life and be safe in today's society. Creating community ties is necessary for that to happen. Think of all the skills you use just to function every day and the skills you use to keep safe: shopping for food, stopping at the kerb, ordering in a restaurant, asking for directions, going to the movies, having a friend over, locking your door. These are the skills everyone should learn. Children and adolescents with ASDs, and adults as well, all need to learn basic community skills. Some of them can be taught or addressed at school.

Safety is an area that everyone needs to learn about. Children with ASDs do not have some of the natural survival skills that neurotypicals do; these need to be taught. A good resource for this is *Dangerous Encounters: Avoiding Perilous Situations with Autism* by Bill Davis and Wendy Goldband Schunick.

Leisure activities for children and adolescents

When a friend in Berkshire read the original heading for this section 'How to find community programmes that are a good fit', she remarked caustically, 'Oh, that will be a very short chapter!' Her point was well taken, as the title was misleading. In reality, integration in community programmes is not about finding the right fit, but about searching for possibilities and creating opportunities for involvement in existing programmes or out in the community. It's really about *making* a good fit.

A person who is severely autistic, even if he has no aggressive behaviours, will not be able to participate in any community programmes without a helper. This means finding an activity that will accept an individual who has a helper present. In the end, this person may have an easier time, in that he will always have someone watching out for him and guiding him through the experience. A more able person may benefit more from the actual experience, but if he is not accompanied by an aide, he may be vulnerable to, at the very least, misunderstanding by the group leader; and at the very worst, bullying by his peers. This is why it is so important to choose activities carefully.

Where to create community ties

Every community offers opportunities for integration. Some places to look are leisure centres, Scout and Guide associations, swimming pools, churches, libraries and sports clubs.

Activities have many benefits to them besides integration. Luke Jackson, in his book *Freaks, Geeks and Asperger's*, writes about the benefits he derived from tae kwon do. Not only did he learn a new skill; it helped him improve his motor skills, increased his self-confidence and self-esteem, and made him feel safer when threatened by others.

There are also activities designed with individuals with disabilities in mind, or certain times designated at centres. To find out what is on offer in your area, contact your local council, your local support group, other parents and school.

How to find the right activity or programme

Depending on where you live, you may have few options or many. The most important thing is to make this a positive experience for your child, as well as the activity leader and the other children. The first thing to do is to look at your child and where his interests lie. Here are some questions to ask yourself.

What are your child's likes and dislikes? What makes him tick or motivates him? Does he like music? Computer games? Obviously, if the individual is verbal or able to communicate in some form, you will be able to ask him his opinion as to what he likes or doesn't like, what he would like to learn to do or participate in. Never assume that because you know this person, you know what he wants to do. Sometimes we make assumptions and we need to ask the right questions to know more.

What are your goals for your child with this activity? Are you looking for an opportunity for your child to socialise with others his own age? Are you looking for him to develop a hobby or learn how to play an instrument? Do you want to offer him the opportunity to strengthen an existing skill?

Does your child have gross and fine motor challenges? Some activities may not be a good choice for the individual with these challenges; however, some activities that appear challenging may be just the thing for him to enhance or improve those areas he may be clumsy in. A martial art such as tae kwon do may be a good choice.

Does your child easily imitate and learn by watching others? Does he need to be 'motored through' an activity (physically prompted) many times, or can he learn with minimal prompting and by watching others? Choose activities where his learning can be adapted to the situation.

Does your child have behaviour problems that may prevent him from participating in certain activities? To make a community experience a positive one for all involved, the child should not be a danger to others. Behaviours such as hitting and tantruming do not necessarily mean that he should be excluded; however, a behaviour plan should be in effect and working, which can then be transferred to the community programme. Identify any problems, and look at how they affect him working in a particular activity. Then work on those behaviours. In addition, skills such as turn-taking and waiting are usually a prerequisite for taking part in activities, and can be successfully taught at home.

Does your child have sensory integration or processing issues? Some activities may seem appropriate, but may be taking place in a physical environment that is bothersome to the individual with autism. For example, if your child has a hard time with noise or bright lights, then a location with an 'echo' to it or fluorescent lighting may make the activity difficult to participate in. Perhaps he will be able to get acclimatised to it; perhaps not. It all depends on the individual.

How to analyse the different options available

Once you have short-listed some options depending on your child's desires, needs and capabilities, going without your child to observe an activity or programme in progress is the next step. Questions you should be asking yourself when observing are:

What is the activity leader's style? Does the leader seem authoritative? Does he appear to make allowances for the different types of children? Is he patient? How would the leader's style mesh with your child's personality?

How many other participants are there? Is it a small group or a large group? Is that conducive to your child? Make sure you find out if that is the usual number.

What is the physical environment like? Are the lights very bright? Is it noisy? Is the space large or small? Are there lots of distracting posters and artwork up on the walls? Do you think your child would be comfortable and able to participate here? Would your child need some desensitisation to the environment?

How to approach the activity leader and what to tell him

After observing, if you consider this activity to be a possible match with your child, talk to the leader and see how receptive he is to having your child in his programme. You will need to gauge how much or how little to tell the activity leader at this point. The more able the child, the less you may want to say at this time. If your child needs to have a shadow aide or helper with him, you will need to tell the leader. You should ask if you can bring your child to the activity on a trial basis, and arrange the most practical time for all of you.

At some point, you may need to give the activity leader more information. It all depends on your child, the activity and the leader. You may have your own personal philosophy and comfort level about what to divulge. Obviously, if your child is severely affected by his autism, the leader and others in the group will need to have at least some basic information about him. When placing a more able child, the activity leader (and peers) need to be aware of how your child is different. Luke Jackson (author of *Freaks, Geeks and Asperger Syndrome*) and Clare Sainsbury (author of *Martian in the Playground*) talk at length in their books about the bullying and misunderstanding they were subject to, all because the teacher and their schoolmates had no knowledge of their condition.

Here are ideas for what you may want to talk about with the activity leader:

Talk about the positive attributes of your child: Any special gifts or interests your child may have that could pertain to the activity would be a good thing for the leader to know. Even if they do not pertain to the activity, they will be a point of contact.

Talk about the challenges of your child: If your child is a 'runner' or bolts out of the door when he hears the fire drill bell, the leader needs to know that. Does your child have any behaviour challenges? The leader needs to know what to do in situations that might arise.

Explain about the ASD and how it affects your child: It is a personal decision whether a parent wants to identify their child in a group as having an ASD. My personal opinion is that as parents of children with ASDs, we should also be advocates and educate the public in a positive manner so that our children will be accepted everywhere. However, not all parents feel the same. Some parents who have very able children do not want to use any label. To each his own opinion. However, the important thing is that even if you do not use the word 'autism' or 'Asperger's', you need to explain the communication difficulties that may arise so that your child does not become the victim of misunderstanding on the part of the teacher or his peers. He gets enough of that at school, and this is supposed to be fun!

Make it clear what your goals are for your child: Are you expecting your child to participate 100 per cent in every aspect of the activity? Is your child doing the activity to learn a skill or to learn how to be part of a small group?

Explain the shadow aide or helper's role: If your child will be accompanied by another person there to assist his integration and participation, you need to explain.

Offer to come in and talk to the other participants: Again, think of your child. It is important that he does not suffer bullying because of lack of knowledge on the part of others. It is always a good idea to talk about ASDs so people will become more accepting and knowledgeable. If you explain to the others about your child's challenges and interests, they will know why he may seem a bit different and will be more accepting. They may even find any special interests he has cool. A good resource for the parent is *My Friend With Autism* by Beverly Bishop. Beverly is a parent who wrote this book to help explain to peers and teachers at the school where her child is mainstreamed about autism. You may find it helpful.

FOOD FOR THOUGHT
How We Prepared My Son for the Library and Bookshop

My son loves looking at books. Going to the library and bookshop were activities he really wanted to participate in. However, although he had quickly mastered the concept of pulling books off the shelves at home to find the one that he wanted, he had not mastered the concept of putting them back. He seemed to enjoy having 20 or more books all spread out on the floor. This may be appropriate behaviour in one's bedroom, but certainly not in public. He also had, on occasion, ripped off the flaps of pop-up books. We decided that he needed to learn that it was not appropriate to rip books and that books should be returned to shelves. These behaviours were addressed and practised at home before we allowed him to go into the community to look at books in public. Once he was able to put away books at home with minimal help, and had learned that ripping books would not be tolerated, we started taking him to the local library, and finally the bookshop. Any ripping of books or refusal to put away books and my son was immediately taken out of the library or shop. As he enjoys these environments, he has learned to treat books in a respectful manner in public.

How to prepare the child

Depending on his ability, there are different ways of doing this. Again, as discussed in earlier chapters, schedules of what is going to happen and social stories about the expected behaviour are a good way of getting your child geared for the activity. Think of what works in helping him adjust in other areas, and use those strategies here.

TUTORS, NANNIES AND AU PAIRS

Before the start of every school year, I begin my search for any tutors, nannies or babysitters I may need. At first, I dreaded doing this. After all, hiring and supervising personnel were my least favourite responsibilities when I was a TV producer. And now, I am hiring people who will be responsible for most of what my son will learn, people who will be in our house and part of our home life.

I have been doing this for ten years, yet it is still hard when people have to quit as they move on to another city to go to graduate school, or they become teachers and aren't available. But these people never really leave us; they come back at weekends and during the holidays, tell me their news, take Jeremy and his sister Rebecca out for some fun. They have become part of our extended family, and most of them will always be a part of our family's life. Inadvertently, we have created a support system in every city we have lived in, meaning that even now we have people familiar with Jeremy and his needs in the different places we return to for visits. Most of the time, I have hired individuals with no prior training in autism or applied behaviour analysis, and after their experience with Jeremy many of them have changed focus and gone on to become professionals in special education or ABA. It makes me proud of Jeremy, for he is contributing to society in a most valuable way.

People in your home

Some families with two working parents are used to having a nanny or au pair in their home on a regular basis during the children's growing years. However, few families are used to having a constant rotation of people in their home over a period of many years. If you have a child severely disabled by an ASD, two or more children with autism who are living at home, or you are running a home programme, you will need more than the usual help and understanding provided by the occasional sitter, and perhaps for many more years. Hiring, supervising and enjoying having other people in your home is not always as easy as it seems.

For those readers contemplating working as a behavioural tutor or a nanny in a family with a child who has an ASD, this chapter will give you clues as to what kind of questions you should ask the parents, how to know more about what you are taking on, and what possible challenges you should be aware of. Working for a family, especially with a child with an ASD is not like taking a job at your local Waitrose or Boots. It is hard to get used to having people work in your private home, and it takes a long time for a child with an ASD to get used to you, and for you to understand them. If you are unsure after an initial interview, and the parents are interested in hiring you, ask them if you can come back one more time and spend time with them and the child before deciding. If you explain that you do not take your commitments lightly and want to make sure this is a good match for both of you, they will be happy to have you come back.

For both the families and the tutors and nannies, the most important thing to remember is that the person being hired is there to help the child, not be a counsellor to the parents. Sometimes, parents may start talking to their tutor or nanny about problems at school, how depressed they are, or how anxious they feel, which is not appropriate. If a parent needs to talk to someone about their feelings, they should visit a friend, another parent or a counsellor. Make your home a positive work environment for the people who are there to help your child.

It is hard for families to have non-family members in their home all the time. You may feel as if your privacy is being invaded. However, if you choose the right people, and keep a positive attitude and a happy demeanour, you will grow to enjoy it.

How to hire a tutor or nanny

If you are looking for a tutor, you will want someone who has experience in or is a good candidate for training in applied behaviour analysis. However, in terms of your expectations and the issue of having another person in your home, many of the considerations will be the same as when you are looking for a nanny or au pair. These guidelines are here to give you a starting point and get you thinking about the many aspects inherent to hiring and keeping good people.

Where to place an advertisement: Many people hire nannies and au pairs through agencies. A nanny is usually specifically hired to take care of the children, not to be a housekeeper. For those families where one of the parents is home and they do not have the income to pay for a nanny, an au pair can be a good solution. Bear in mind that there are legal guidelines governing au pairs such as the number of hours they can be asked to work and the duties they are given. You must take care to make sure the person is a good match, as they will be living with you as part of the family and may not be fluent in English.

For tutors, if there is a university or teacher training college in your area, those are good places to start. Find out from other parents what places work best to put up advertisements. Put ads in behaviour therapy magazines such as PEACH, and in the newsletter of the local chapter of your autism support group, if there is one. If you are planning to have a supervisor oversee your home programme, ask if they have any advice or guidelines for hiring tutors, and if they know of tutors who might be willing to work with your child.

What to put in the ad: Take the time to write an ad that gives adequate information as to what type of person you are looking for. Some examples: 'Looking for tutors to work with my son: Parent looking for three people who love children and are dependable and flexible, to teach my son, who has autism, using applied behaviour analysis techniques. No experience necessary, training provided. Must be available 15 hours per week in three-hour increments. Hourly rate to be discussed. Please email cv or call this number.' Or, 'Looking for trained behavioural tutors to work with my daughter with autism.

Some weekend hours. Behavioural supervision provided. Pay depends on experience.' Or, 'Looking for nanny: Parent looking for dependable person who loves children and is flexible to provide after-school care for son with autism. Must be available from 3–6:30pm. Training provided. Pay depends on experience.'

Looking over a cv: If you receive a cv, you can learn a lot about the applicant just by looking it over.

- Does he have work experience?

- Has he had job responsibilities before?

- Does he know what it means to have a regular work schedule and to be on time?

- Has he worked with children of the same age group as your child before?

- What has he been studying at college and what kind of work has he done?

Questions to ask on the phone: On the telephone you may need to ask specific questions to draw the applicant out:

- Has she worked with children before? What age group?

- Has she ever babysat before or spent a lot of time around children?

- How many siblings does she have, and what is her position in her family?

- Why is she interested in working with your child?

- How long can she commit to working with your child?

- Can she provide any work references ? If she has no work references, how about personal references?

- Is she willing to submit to a police check (an administrative procedure)?

Questions to ask a person named as a work reference:

- How long did the applicant work for them?

- Is he dependable, reliable and trustworthy?

- Was he on time or often late?

- Did he often call in sick?

- Was he good at working independently and as part of a team?

- Was he flexible and able to learn and do the job they way the employer wanted?

- Did he take constructive criticism well?

- Did he show a creative streak?

- What were his most positive attributes, and his least positive?

- Would they recommend him for the position you have in mind?

Face-to-face interview: After you have screened by phone the applicants you are interested in, it is time for the interview. Schedule it at a convenient time for you and your child. If possible, do it when someone else is home working with your son. First, interview the person face to face, asking him questions to find out more about what kind of person he is. For example:

- What did she like about the job she's had in the past?

- What does she hope to pursue as a career?

- What hobbies or other interests does she have?

- Why does she want this position with your child?

- How long can she commit for?

- What schedule constraints does she have?

- Does she have any questions?

Then bring your child into the room (without the other tutor) and see how he reacts to this other person, and how this person acts towards your child.

- Does the applicant try to make contact with your child?

- Does she appear respectful of your child?

- What kind of approach does she have?

- You know your child. Does it appear that he likes this person?

If you think this could be a match, go to the child's room with the applicant. Have her watch you or the other nanny or tutor play a game or do a puzzle with your child, and then ask if she would like to try. Watch how she gets on, then give her a few directives and see how she responds to that; if she is able to change what she is doing by listening to your suggestion. Again see if your child feels comfortable with this person. After she leaves, if your child is able to tell you, find out if he liked her.

If you are comfortable with this person, then call her to come back when a tutor or nanny is around to overlap. Spend some time again with your child and the applicant, then have the applicant spend some time alone with the other person and your child. This will provide the opportunity for the applicant to ask questions of a non-family member who knows the child. It's not always easy to work for someone in their home, and you want to make sure she knows you can be trusted as an employer. Also, you will be able to get your tutor or nanny's point of view on the applicant, which is a good thing to have. They may have noticed some things you didn't. At the end of this time, talk with the person, and if you are interested in hiring her, find out if she is still interested in working with your child.

The applicant will have had two opportunities to meet your child, and a chance to talk to someone in the position she will be filling. By now she should have got a concrete idea of whether or not she really wants to work with your child.

It is recommended that the parent ask the person who is being hired to apply for a police check, which entails getting a form from the police station, filling it out and paying a small fee. The resulting documentation will then be given to you.

How to supervise and keep tutors and nannies

Somehow, our house has acquired the reputation of being a good training ground for tutors and nannies or babysitters. I often get calls from special education administrators, parents, companies that supervise home programmes based on ABA, and social workers. They call asking if anyone currently working in our home or who has worked in our home is available for working elsewhere as well. This is mostly due to Jeremy and his pleasant personality, which is so endearing.

However, in asking people why they enjoy working for our family so much, the number one response after their love of Jeremy (and his sister, Rebecca) is: we are organised. This does not mean our house is particularly clean or neat, as we do not have the time it would take to earn the Good Housekeeping Award in our neighbourhood. We do the minimum amount of cleaning so we will not be cited by the Health Department. Jeremy is particularly talented at 'redecorating' the house, and although we have attempted to teach him that he can only redecorate his own room, what he has learned is to redecorate when no one is watching.

Organised means that the wonderful people working in our home know what they are supposed to do, when they are supposed to do it, where everything is and where to put it back. Here are some guidelines to make life easier for all of you:

● Make sure responsibilities are clear. Draft a contract that outlines your responsibilities towards the person you are hiring and their responsibilities toward your child and you. The contract should cover how much they are getting paid, how often they are getting paid, whether or not you are paying sick leave and holiday pay, when pay rises will be given, and, if they will be driving your child anywhere, what they will be compensated for using their car, or any insurance details if you are providing one.

- Make sure that the hours and times they are to be present are clear. Make sure they know they are responsible for those hours, and make it clear that if they need to make a change, they are responsible for communicating that to you as soon as possible. If there are several tutors, you may wish to make it their responsibility to find someone else to work their hours.

- Make a calendar and hang it in an easily accessible area so people can see special appointments or make changes in scheduling.

- Make sure appropriate notice is given if you have a change in schedule because of a doctor's appointments, or if your child is ill.

- If you expect some degree of flexibility on their part in terms of changes in work hours, be prepared to be flexible when necessary in regard to their schedule.

- Make sure you have everything they need to do their work, and that everything has a specific place so things are easily found.

- Have a communication book located near the phone or in the kitchen where notes to each other can be quickly jotted down if need be.

- In the home environment, it is important to remember the boundaries of the work relationship and keep them clear.

- Remember that they are there to help your child and not to be your counsellor. Give them information that they need to know for working with your child, but do not overburden them with the emotional issues, school issues or legal issues that are on your mind. Those are for you to handle and get help with from someone else. The people working with your child need to concentrate on your child and helping him learn, not be thinking about your problems.

● If your tutor is working with your child at a school, clarify what their responsibility at the school is.

● Keep your rapport with the tutors respectful and professional. Never discuss any issues that are not their concern, such as any disagreements you may be having with the local school authority or another professional. Never speak negatively about other tutors or nannies who are currently working or have worked in your home.

● Make your expectations of the tutors or sitters clear.

● Do not expect them to do things you would not do yourself.

● Have high expectations of their job performance, but give them what they need to do their job well.

● Make sure any new nanny or tutor feels comfortable enough with your child to be able to handle any behavioural situations that may come up, before sending them out in public with him.

● If you have any behaviour plans for your child, or if you are working on any particular behaviours, make sure everyone who helps or works with your child knows what to do and ensure that everyone is handling behaviours in the same manner. This will make life easier for everyone and be of great benefit to your child.

● Give people working with your child information about his likes and dislikes, as well as any other pertinent information. Having this written down somewhere is helpful. This makes tutors and nannies feel comfortable with your child, and they will know more about what they can use to motivate him. Your child will feel more comfortable with someone who knows about what is important to him.

● If you are running a home programme, keep up to date and know what is being worked on. Give support when needed.

When tutors are new and having problems with a behaviour or non-compliance, or when new behaviours come up, they need to know you are knowledgeable enough to help them figure things out until they feel they can analyse it and handle the situation themselves.

- If you have any concerns or comments to make about what they are doing, talk to them privately. Explain to them your concern and ask if there is anything you can do to help. For example, think about why you have that concern and bring it up in a positive, constructive manner and not as a criticism. If you notice that one person continually asks you for materials and then leaves them out and not put away, do not assume they think it is part of their responsibility to get out and put away. Or perhaps the needed items are not in a clearly designated area. Do not wait until you are frustrated and confront the person. After this has happened a few times, say something like, 'Do you know where the items are located? It would be helpful to me if you could get the materials out and then put them away when you are done. Let me show you where they are.' Perhaps they are not thinking, but perhaps you have not made it clear that you are expecting them to do that. If that is the case, make sure you make the responsibilities clear to them.

- Feedback is always appreciated. Show appreciation of the effort they put in their work by commenting favourably on progress your child has made related to work they are doing with him, or thank them for something you noticed they did that has been helpful to you.

- Showing appreciation on birthdays and holidays is always a good way to keep them feeling that they are important to the family.

- Holding a dinner party and inviting all the past and present tutors and sitters is a fun thing to do. Over the years, the nannies and tutors get to know each other, and have this time to catch up with each other as well as get tips about college and jobs.

PUBLIC ENVIRONMENTS AND SENSORY PROCESSING ISSUES

In recent decades, we have seen more and more cases of asthma, hyperactivity, autism spectrum disorders, behaviour problems and allergies than ever before. Children are routinely given medication for hyperactivity and behaviour problems.

In Chapter Two, some of the behaviours of people with ASDs and what they could mean were discussed. Many of those behaviours can be indicative of allergies and problems with sensory integration. Every book by a person who has an ASD contains references to sensory processing difficulties, the sensitivity they have and the pain they experience from overstimulation.

Fluorescent lighting

Temple Grandin, Donna Williams, Stephen Shore and Liane Holliday Willey all write about how terrible they find fluorescent lighting. But it is not only people with autism who are affected.

In her book *Is This Your Child's World? How you can fix the schools and homes that are making your children sick*, Doris J. Rapp MD discusses the subject. As would be expected, natural lighting is best. Fluorescent lighting appears to be a major source of trouble for many people. A study of one classroom showed a decrease of hyperactivity by 33 per cent when the fluorescent lighting was replaced by full-spectrum lighting. Germany banned fluorescent lighting in its schools and hospitals years ago, whereas in other countries such as the US, people prefer to encourage the use of the drug Ritalin to counteract hyperactivity rather than looking at possible environmental factors.

In his book *Health and Light*, Dr John Ott discusses the possible health effects of different wavelengths of light. Dr Ott videotaped students using time-lapse technology, and these videos demonstrated the increase in hyperactivity in some of them.

Sensory integration dysfunction

Sensory integration dysfunction is not experienced only by people with ASDs. A. Jean Ayres, an occupational therapist, first described sensory integration dysfunction as the inability to process information received through the senses. Her two books, *Sensory Integration and the Child,* and *Sensory Integration and Learning Disorders* were not written with ASDs in mind. Neither was *The Out-of-Synch Child* by Carol Stock Kranowitz. Kranowitz talks about how some children may be labelled as inattentive, clumsy and oversensitive.

Sensory integration problems stem from the brain's inability to process correctly information received through our senses of taste, touch, smell, sight and sound. People can be hyposensitive in some areas (meaning they fail to pick up cues) and hypersensitive in others (meaning that they are overly sensitive to stimulation of a sense).

When a person's senses are over- or understimulated, it affects their behaviour as they try to compensate for a lack of stimulation or for overstimulation. Some individuals with sensory integration problems are aware of these challenges; others are not. Once a person is aware, it is possible in some cases to learn to compensate in a positive way or to undergo desensitisation over time. However, for many people, especially children, and people who are severely disabled by autism, it is difficult, as they are unknowingly put in situations where they have no choice over their environment, which may lead to displays of inappropriate behaviours.

Creating people-friendly environments

Granted, there are some environments that people with sensitivities need to and should learn to tolerate for short periods of time. However, when designing an environment where people are expected to learn or to work for long periods of time, or where people are going for medical treatment and are already not well, doesn't it make sense to look at environmental issues?

Dr Rapp's book *Is This Your Child's World?* should be a must-read for all school and hospital administrators responsible for having their buildings renovated or constructed. There are many toxins in ordinary classrooms that could be easily eliminated.

For an idea of what it is like to have sensory processing issues and live in today's man-made environment, read what some people with ASD, have to say:

I also found many noises and bright lights nearly impossible to bear. High frequencies and brassy, tin sounds clawed my nerves. Whistles, party noisemakers, flutes and trumpets and any close relative of those sounds disarmed my calm and made my world very uninviting. Bright lights, mid-day sun, reflected lights, fluorescent lights; each seemed to sear my eyes. Together the sharp sounds and bright lights were more than enough to overload my senses. My head would feel tight, my stomach would churn, and my pulse would run my heart ragged until I found a safety zone.

Liane Willey, *Pretending to be Normal*

It came as a kind of revelation, as well as a blessed relief, when I learned that my sensory problems weren't the result of my weakness or lack of character. When I was a teenager, I was aware that I did not fit in socially, but I was not aware that my method of visual thinking and my overly sensitive senses were the cause of my difficulties in relating to and interacting with other people.

Temple Grandin, *Thinking in Pictures*

And here is some advice for designing environments:

My ideal educational environment would be one where the room had very little echo or reflective light, where the lighting was soft and glowing with upward projecting lighting. It would be one where the physical arrangements of things in the room was cognitively orderly and didn't alter and where everything in the room remained within routine-defined areas. It would be an environment where only what was necessary for learning was on display and there was no unnecessary decorations or potential distractions.

Donna Williams, *Autism: An Inside Out Approach*

Imagining that one's senses are 1,000 times more sensitive than reality can help a person to design environmental accommodations for those on the autism spectrum. Considering each sense individually can assist with organization of both the issues caused by the sensitivity and the remedies for relief. In considering the sense of sight, a person with a vision hyperacuity might be bothered by the presence of fluorescent lights, because the lights cycle on and off 60 times per second in timing with the Hertz of alternating current. In such cases, a different form of illumination should be used. It is also possible that the humming from the ballast of a fluorescent lamp is irritating to individuals who are sensitive to sound.

Stephen Shore, *Beyond the Wall*

Sensory processing issues: tips from Temple Grandin

Over two phone conversations, Temple shared the following important information about sensory processing and environments for people with ASDs.

All people with an autism spectrum disorder have sensory processing problems. Some of them may be auditory, some of them may be visual. Recently scientists have been able to map out the circuits in the brain for the separate visual and auditory areas, and they see that those corresponding areas are differently wired in people who have visual or auditory processing difficulties. Temple emphasises that there are individual variations in the severity of the processing problems, and variations also depend on how tired the person is: the more tired the person is, the greater the risk of sensory overload. People with ASDs usually cannot multi-task, as they usually can only fix on one sensory process at a time.

For each individual and for each sensory processing issue there is a balance to be found between adapting the environment to fit the need of the person, and adapting the person to the environment that already exists.

If you are a parent or caregiver of someone whom you suspect has sensory processing difficulties, but who is unable to communicate that to you, Temple suggests doing the 'supermarket test'. Take the person to the supermarket and see how he behaves, using the behaviours listed below as a guideline.

The number one worst enemy for people with visual processing problems is fluorescent lighting. Some people with autism can see the flicker of 60-cycle electricity. It has the same effect that being in a disco with strobe lighting has for neurotypical people. Unfortunately because of its low cost, fluorescent lighting is present everywhere.

For people with auditory processing issues, fire bells can be particularly painful. They are very loud and you do not know when they are going to go off.

Department stores and supermarkets are particularly challenging to people with sensory processing issues, not only because of fluorescent lighting but also because of the overstimulation provided by the colours, stripes and mosaic patterns on the displays, the smells from perfumes, detergents and cleaning products and the noise level due to hard flooring.

So there are many questions that come to mind. For those individuals unable to communicate, how do you know what is creating the overload, and what can you do about it? Temple suggests observing the person's behaviour. Those with visual processing problems:

- use peripheral vision, with which they can see better (i.e. look from the side of their eyes and avoid looking directly at people or objects);

- flicker their fingers or other objects in front of their eyes;

- avoid escalators in stores and appear afraid of them;

- have difficulty negotiating stairs in places unfamiliar to them.

What you can do:

- Go shopping earlier in the day when you are not tired.

- For a temporary fix in areas that you cannot control, such as supermarkets, try wearing a hat with a brim, or a visor.

- Wear coloured lenses such as sunglasses or Irlen lenses. Some people with visual processing issues report that the lenses help not only with seeing, but with training the visual processing so that in some cases they need lighter and lighter lenses as time goes by. From what Temple has heard from people who use coloured lenses, the brownish, purplish and pinky lenses seem to work the best against fluorescent lighting.

- In areas you can control, such as your home, do not use fluorescent light bulbs; use the incandescent old-fashioned kind.

- At work stations or school desks, use individual lamps with incandescent light bulbs to offset the fluorescent lighting.

- Use laptops or the newer flat-panel computer screens. The larger, older computer monitors have a flicker much like fluorescent lighting does.

Those with auditory processing problems:

- cover their ears or leave the room when loud noises go off;

- cannot tolerate loud noises such as fire bells or school bells;

- cannot talk on the phone in large places such as airports due to the echo and resonance of the noisy crowds;

- move as far away as they can when there are too many people near them in the room talking;

- cannot pronounce the consonants of words, because they are unable to hear them properly. Hearing tests do not measure auditory detail that they may not be hearing. The hearing threshold may appear normal, but in fact they may only be hearing vowels, so they cannot produce the sound of consonants.

What you can do:

- Go to noisy places when you are not tired, earlier in the day.

- Have auditory training which helps people tolerate the frequencies that may be causing discomfort.

- For a temporary fix for supermarket shopping, wear earplugs, or white-noise busters, or listen to music on a Walkman. Temple warns that although using ear plugs and noise cancellers are OK for getting through an experience such as a trip to the supermarket, they should not be used on a regular basis, as the auditory system needs to learn to get used to and tolerate some amount of the noise which is around in the everyday environment.

- To get desensitised to the sound of fire bells, Temple suggests taping the sound of a fire bell and listening to it, controlling the volume and length of play. Every time you listen to it, the volume can be adjusted as well as the playing time, yet always under the control of the person who is getting desensitised.

- To ease the noise of scraping chairs on hard floors, pad the bottom of the chair legs.

- Put carpeting on floors and also on the walls of rooms for sound-proofing.

- To teach the consonants, emphasise them very strongly, putting the accent on them, so the person can hear them.

Some people with autism have body boundary issues. Most people can tell where they are in a space. Normally, a person can close his eyes standing in front of a wall, and put his hand on the wall, knowing where his hand ends and the wall begins. For those who have body boundary issues, they are unable to 'feel' this. Temple says that lots of brushing, massage and deep pressure can help people feel their body boundaries.

Tips from Temple Grandin on inexpensive ways of dealing with sensory processing issues

Unfortunately, many of the ways of dealing with sensory processing issues can be expensive, either for the individual with the challenge or for the person designing and outfitting a sensory-processing-sensitive environment. Temple has some tips for cheap fixes:

- For those suffering from visual processing difficulties, Irlen glasses can help but they are expensive. As an alternative, try sunglasses. Usually when a person in the family has sensory processing issues, a parent may have them too to a lesser degree, so for people unable to communicate, the parent could see what works for them and start with that. It is possible to find different shades of sunglasses to try. Another way to see what is helpful is to try different-coloured light bulbs or transparencies to overlay on written work, and see how the person works, learns or acts under those circumstances. Temple warns, however, that many sunglasses may be too dark to help with reading. She also reports that Blue Blockers sunglasses work well.

- Since laptops and flat screens are better for those with visual processing difficulties but are expensive, try finding big companies who frequently upgrade their equipment. Normally these computers are donated or sent out to be broken up and recycled, and so you may find a sympathetic company happy to give you one of their throwaways.

- Unfortunately, fluorescent lighting will not be replaced everywhere because of its low cost and efficiency. Schools who have students with ASDs should definitely remove these types of lights. However, for a quick fix for an individual work station or desk, use a desk lamp with an old-fashioned incandescent light bulb and turn off the fluorescents.

- Carpet is a good solution for minimising the loud echoey noise in some environments. If you can't add insulation, carpet on the walls also soaks up noise. A good cheap way to get carpets is to ask for remnants as donations at carpet stores, or contact major hotels who redecorate often and see if you can get the carpet they are removing and throwing away. You will have to clean it.

- To avoid those irritating scraping noises that chairs cause on hard floors, get some old tennis balls, make a slit and fit them over the bottom of the chair legs.

- To help a person who needs to rock, and avoid the cost of a therapy ball (or to avoid a child playing on it and not concentrating), make a T stool with two pieces of plywood. The person will have to rock slightly on it to keep their balance.

Food for Thought

The Curse of the Flourescent Light

Fluorescent lighting has got to be one of mankind's worst inventions. I always hated going shopping and after ten minutes I would become irritable, feel restless and get a major headache. Once home, I would be so exhausted I would have to lie down. While shopping, my husband would ask me, 'Are you hungry? Are you tired? Why are you so cranky all of a sudden?' I could never figure out why my mood would change so suddenly and how I could feel physically bad so quickly. It was not until years later when I lived in France that I realised it was the fluorescent lighting that did it to me.

Most of the time in Paris I shopped at the wonderful food markets or local shops, but every once in a while it was necessary to go to a supermarket for sundry items. The small supermarket closest to our apartment had these horrendous fluorescent lights that you could actually see flicker and hear buzz. It was horrible. The checkout girl who worked there looked poorly and so depressed all the time. One day I asked her if she was OK, she looked so ill. She told me she had constant headaches and felt nauseous at work and she thought it had to do with the lights.

Then all of a sudden it clicked. Looking at my past behaviour patterns, I could see a connection between the kinds of stores that made me feel ill, and the ones that didn't. I then started asking people around me and was surprised to find that many people suffer from the curse of the fluorescent light.

Once I realised what was causing my discomfort, I limited my outings to those kinds of stores and never planned a shopping day where I would hit more than one big shop (such as ASDA or Boots) in a day. My husband is now the designated supermarket and department store shopper in the family (he has a natural talent for this; at one time he worked in procurement). But mostly, we have taken our business elsewhere, avoiding major shops and spending money where people are more cognisant of making a comfortable working and shopping environment.

Here in California we actually have a law that prohibits smoking in public places, restaurants and even in bars, and this was done to protect the workers behind the counters as well as the customers. And of course, new buildings have to be designed with easy access for people in wheelchairs. So how about a law banning the use of fluorescent lighting?

Think of all the checkout men and women and shelf stackers working in supermarkets. And what about the teachers and physicians who are obliged to spend long hours a day under those lights? Perhaps Sensory Integration Dysfunction should be labelled a handicapping condition and no new buildings should be designed with fluorescent lighting. Then, perhaps, students will finally have a proper environment to learn in.

CHAPTER NINE

Adults Living and Working With Autism Spectrum Disorders

Once you become an adult, usually at twenty-one at the most, nobody is obligated to take care of you anymore. After that, where you live and how you live, more than anything else, depends on you and what you make of your abilities.

It will be easier for you if you prepare to accept an eventual change in where you live before failing health or death of your parents forces this reality on you. I am grateful to my parents for what they did but I have to say that I live more independently and fully now that they are gone. I had no choice.

JERRY NEWPORT, *YOUR LIFE IS NOT A LABEL*

The problem of long-term care plagues all parents of people with cognitive difficulties. People with cognitive disabilities are so vulnerable ... What parents want for their children and what they get are two completely different things. The government offices and private agencies responsible for serving them make for a huge, complicated system ... parents have mixed feelings. They know what they want in a general way, but don't know how to go about achieving it.

LINDA J. STENGLE, *LAYING COMMUNITY FOUNDATIONS FOR YOUR CHILD WITH A DISABILITY*

For a short while I worked as a case manager for one of California's regional centres, providing resources to individuals with developmental disabilities. Some of my older adult clients who required a lot of support were still living at home with elderly parents. When I visited them, I could feel the anxiety, and hear the tremor in the parents' voices, sense their exhaustion, knowing they were concerned not only about today, but later, when they would no longer be around to look out for their child.

Then I had Jeremy. Now, he is 14, and I know that although he continues to learn, he will always need some level of support. He only has one sibling, and all our relatives are spread out over the globe. The reality is that my husband and I are going to be like those ageing parents, with few options for our adult child. We can't imagine him living alone or in a residential facility or group home, where he knows no one and where he will be at the mercy of others unknown to us, or find his 'home' sold like a business and run by others. We want him to be surrounded by friends and people who love him, who can give him the support and strategies he needs to continue to learn and find his niche. So with other parents we know in this area, we are exploring options that exist, and making plans for the future.

The Reality of Life as an Adult with an ASD in the UK

In Chapter Seven, we touched upon the need for preparation in secondary school and college for transitioning to the world of work. This section is written primarily for adults with ASDs and their families or caregivers, but educators, prospective employers and those working with adults with ASDs may find it useful.

Some adults are able to live and get what they need with little or no assistance. Others, even though very able, will need support throughout the process. Even more will need support for most of their lives.

More is known about adults with ASDs than ever before. Many of the more able people with ASDs have written personal accounts of what their lives are like, and how they overcame challenges to make living in a neurotypical world easier. Their suggestions may be helpful to some readers. For the less able, the advances made in the past decade in the treatment and therapies for ASDs may be more useful.

The Government has a responsibility to all its citizens. Unfortunately, at the time of writing, not enough is available, but there is hope as people are becoming more aware of their rights and organisations are working together to improve the situation.

Particular challenges that adults with ASDs face

Over the last few years, more and more adults with autism have written books about living with the condition. It is very inspiring to read the accounts of their lives and how they overcame some of their challenges. Their suggestions on how they developed skills in order to survive in a neurotypical world can give ideas to others like them, or to parents. However, the stark reality is that most people with ASDs, even those who are very able, do not enjoy the work and living environment that these authors do.

Why is that? First of all, these individuals are exceptional people, not only in their intelligence but in their determination and motivation to live a full life. Secondly, most of these individuals had strong, supportive mothers or fathers who were able to fight for what they thought their child needed while they were growing up, and who stood by them regardless of what label they had at the time for their difficulties. Thirdly, their parents raised them in such a way as to build a strong sense of self-esteem, and if they subsequently married, their spouse continued that support. These factors helped them to overcome the challenges they had and create a fulfilling life.

Unfortunately, all these factors do not always exist. Not even all neurotypical individuals have that drive and self-motivation to succeed against all odds. For individuals with ASDs who lack the social skills and understanding to go through networking, job search and interviewing, it is a real struggle. Not all parents have the knowledge, stamina or conviction to go out and fight the powers that be for what their child needs as they grow up, and even less when they are young adults.

How to get the services you need

The Government is not very supportive either. In March 2001, they published the Learning Disability White Paper *Valuing People*, a much-heralded new strategy for the twenty-first century on how to address the needs of people with learning disabilities. Incredibly, in England and Wales the definition used by the Government has specifically excluded people with ASDs where there is no accompanying learning disability. (In Scotland, ASDs have been included in the Scottish Parliament's Learning Disability Review *The Same as You?*, published in May 2000).

Historically, the less able population of people with an ASD were institutionalised and segregated from society along with other learning-disabled individuals, and not involved in mainstream life. However, thanks to civil rights and a shifting in the views of society, it is now recognised that people with learning disabilities have the same rights and the same wants as others: their own home, friends and opportunities for personal growth. The same Government Learning Disability Paper that excluded the more able individuals with ASDs provided suggestions on how to prepare people with learning disabilities for change and transitions, and recognised the concept of a person-centred approach to planning for individuals. Self-determination and person-centred planning are important concepts that every human being should benefit from, and this is a great step forward.

However, the exclusion of the more able adult with an ASD reinforces the confusion about which agency should be providing what to adults with ASDs, as the more able adults do not fit into the supposed remit of mental health or learning disability services. The National Autistic Society published a report in 2001 entitled *Ignored or Ineligible? The Reality for Adults with Autism Spectrum Disorders*, the results of a research conducted with parents of adults with ASDs. The findings were not very positive. Parents reported being confused over which statutory agency was responsible for providing care and funding for their child. Fifty-nine per cent felt that responsibility fell between the different agencies for financial reasons.

Even more distressing was the fact that reportedly 49 per cent of the adults were still living at home with their parents, and only 2 per cent of adults on the lower end of the spectrum and 12 per cent of adults at the higher end had full-time paid employment.

Adults with a disability usually access social services by first having a community care assessment (NHS and Community Care Act 1990). However, only 38 per cent of people with an ASD have had one of these. Nearly half of lower-functioning adults have not had this assessment at all despite their visibly noticeable needs.

The report also showed the consequences of such poor support and planning on the part of the Government. A third of parents responded that their child had experienced mental ill health: and 56% of those had suffered depression, 11 per cent had had a nervous breakdown and 8 per cent had suicidal feelings. Add to this the devastating effects and emotional stress that this lack of support visits on the families, and it is a wonder that they have not invaded Parliament and wrought havoc. Many families reported having no social life, no holidays, marriages destroyed and siblings being ignored. In short, they are excluded from the everyday life that most other citizens enjoy.

In 2002, the National Autistic Society published *Taking Responsibility: Good practice guidelines for services – adults with Asperger Syndrome* by Andrew Powell. This document was the result of the Avon Asperger Syndrome Project 1999–2002, funded by the Department of Health. In this document, Powell outlines suggested guidelines for use by agencies such as social care, health, housing, secondary education and employment. The National Autistic Society among others continues to lobby for these recommendations to be adopted by the Government.

Meanwhile, it is apparent that regardless of the ability level of the person with an ASD, there are challenges and barriers to overcome in order to get the services that are needed. Although the type of need may be different, any person with an ASD who requires assistance, or their caregiver, should have access to information and advice. Here are some suggestions:

● First, if you have not already had one, request a community care assessment. The National Autistic Society has excellent information in a document entitled 'Community care: A guide for adults with autistic spectrum disorders and their carers'. It can be found on their website: www.nas.org.uk/pubs/faqs/qcare.html This document explains how to request a community care assessment, what should occur and what you should do to ensure that you receive services. If you are unhappy with the process or the services there is recourse.

● Do not allow the different agencies to bounce you around from one department to another. Make sure that there is follow-through, and that an agency takes responsibility for the support you need. You may need to gently monitor the process with a friendly phone call or two.

● If you live in Scotland, the law about community care is different there, and the NAS recommends that you read a book entitled *The Care Maze: the law and your rights to community care in Scotland* by Patrick McKay.

● Check out local colleges to see what programmes they have on offer that could be appropriate.

● Provide information on ASDs and how this affects you or your adult child to whoever is assessing needs or providing service.

● Support organisations such as the NAS and the All-Party Parliamentary Group on Autism are working hard to make changes. The laws and ensuing service will not change unless the Government hears from those affected.

● Look at what local voluntary organisations are doing to fill the gap of provision.

● Join with other parents and local support groups and create your own support system for people with ASDs who are falling between the cracks.

Never Underestimate the Power of a Group of Parents

Although it should not be up to the voluntary sector or the parents to provide for gaps in provision for adults with ASDs, the Berkshire Autistic Society (BAS) has taken an active role in doing so. Discouraged by the lack of available resources in Berkshire, the BAS has become proactive. Over the past few years, they have made the necessary contacts and set up a supported employment pilot project, organised police awareness sessions in collaboration with East Berkshire College and provided information and emotional support through their helpline.

The Support into Employment Project, modelled on the successful NAS Prospects employment consultancy, is now in its final year with plans to become a fully functioning supported employment scheme for people with Asperger Syndrome as of January 2004. An integral part of the BAS scheme is to involve a number of work preparation courses with such partners as the East Berkshire College, as well as continuing to work with job centres and careers services to provide employment advice and guidance. There are a few people currently supported in the workplace and some people on the 'Employability' course which BAS helped design at East Berkshire College.

In addition, BAS members were each sent an 'awareness pack' to give to their employers' human resource department along with an offer to arrange a free employer awareness session for those hiring a person with an ASD. Links were also created with other service providers such as Mencap, Windsor & Maidenhead Social Services, the careers service and local education providers.

Obviously, the local authority should be doing more. Imagine the amount of energy and time that parents have put into creating provision while waiting for the local authority to put into place what is needed. But think of the alternative: doing nothing and having no provision.

See the BAS website: www.autismberkshire.org.uk for more information.

What do you want to do and what do you need to do it?

Some people with ASDs have found the college or university environment a comfortable place for them to learn and even work. Others have found that particular fields of work are more conducive than others. Dealing mainly with objects and data and less with people can be helpful for those who have strong social impairments.

Many more will need help to find a job and coaching to keep it. Not only does the adult with an ASD need to develop strategies to be a good employee, employers need to know how to make the job a good match with the employee.

A book that might be useful to you is *Asperger Syndrome Employment Workbook* by Roger N. Meyer. Written by someone with the condition, this practical workbook encourages readers to engage in an exploration of their employment history, and to identify the work they are best suited for by analysing their needs, talents and strengths.

How to be successful and enjoy college

Many of the more able people with ASDs are successful at college. Some feel so comfortable that they develop their interests into a career on campus. Some of the interests or obsessions they have can be pursued in a course of study. The challenge may well be translating that knowledge or degree into a stable employment, but that is a challenge all students face.

The Special Educational Needs and Disability Act 2001 (SENDA), which has been in effect since September 2002, should have a major impact on further and higher education after secondary school. Education and training providers may not discriminate against disabled students. There are learning support units in mainstream colleges that can help you. There are also more training courses on a part-time or full-time basis, as well as five levels of competency in the system of National Vocational Qualifications. However, the curriculum is not designed with the specific needs of autism in mind, nor are the tutors particularly knowledgeable about ASDs.

Getting support

Many colleges now offer support for students with an ASD. You can ask at your local college, or look on the internet to find the ones that do. Here are some suggestions for making college a rewarding experience:

- Give information about the ASD and how it affects you, the challenges you face and what strategies can be used to help you.

- Find a sympathetic guidance counsellor or mentor. This person can help in many ways, for example by helping you find a group on campus that shares your special hobby or interest.

- Ask your guidance counsellor or mentor which teachers would be more accepting of your difficulties and willing to make you comfortable with learning in their class.

- The same kinds of support that helped in secondary school will be of benefit at college, and telling your guidance counsellor what those were is a good idea. For the visual learner, written schedules, lists, and visual aids for studying such as graphs, charts and videos are helpful. For the auditory learner, tape-recording lectures or having a note-taker works well. Textbooks on tape can be another useful tool.

- Tests or exams can be modified to take into consideration any difficulties you may have with test taking.

Finding a job or a career

Jerry Newport has a great philosophy about work. He feels that no matter what job you have, you should do it well. In *Your Life is Not a Label,* he gives many tips about work. He suggests that even low-entry-level jobs are important as they can teach you things that are necessary for all jobs, namely: how to follow instructions, how to be on time, how to dress appropriately and how to work independently.

FOOD FOR THOUGHT

'The bottom line is this: If you ever want the kind of job that buys you a house, a limo and anything close to that, you will have to do every job before that one as if it were the greatest job in the world. Just make believe, if you wind up cooking hamburgers, that every burger will have a photo of you on the wrapper, saying "cooked by . . ." Do every job to the best of your ability because you are proud of who you are and always do your best. If you do that, you will get the most out of your working days.'

Jerry Newport, *Your Life is Not a Label*

Temple Grandin suggests developing your special interest or obsession into an employable skill. Even though your social skills may be lacking, you can impress someone with your talents, strengths and abilities and be hired. People respect talent, and you can focus on selling your skills instead of your personality. Employers will have to understand your needs in order for a job or career to be successful, but having a special ability will convince someone you are worth employing. Employers should be reminded of the positive attributes that most people with ASDs have such as honesty and diligence, as well as the challenges you face.

Obviously, not everyone has the capabilities of Grandin or Newport; however, there are different ways of approaching the dilemma of employment. Alan Bicknell of the NAS Development and Outreach gives a clear overview of employment options and where you can get help in your search, in the booklet *Independent living for adults with autism and Asperger syndrome: A guide for families of people with autistic spectrum disorders*.

There is a Disability Employment Adviser on each Placing Assessment and Counselling Team (PACT). PACTs are part of the employment service, and the adviser will provide advice and specialist service to people with disabilities and their employers. You and the adviser will draw up an action plan once an assessment has been made of your abilities and the job market. The adviser may give information on many areas related to work.

Positive aspects of hiring someone with an ASD
Prospective employers should know that there are positive benefits to hiring someone with an ASD. Honesty, dependability, loyalty and diligence are traits that are can be found in abundance in the ASDs population.

Seeking employment
Basically there are three different paths to finding and keeping a job:

Open employment: These types of employment opportunities are usually good for people who can work at a job with some adjustments but who will not need support on a continual basis. People who have an employable skill will find it easier to find work. Networking through family members, friends, people from your church, mentors you have had can perhaps lead to employment. If you are attending college, you may find a job through contacts made there: people who admire your abilities who know people who can use your talents. Working as a freelancer in your area of interest is a possibility if you have the discipline that self-employment requires and someone who can refer work to you if the social aspect of marketing yourself is difficult. Local job centres are also a place to look for openings. There are employment service advisers who can help with advice on how to go about getting a job.

Supported employment: This provides assistance in areas where people with ASDs need help: job finding, job coaching, skills training, employment advice and guidance. These types of opportunities are much more established in the United States than anywhere else, but the UK is striving to develop more in this area. Some people with autism who also have learning difficulties may have used PATHWAY, an employment scheme run by Mencap.

Prospects, run by the NAS, is a successful employment scheme specifically created for people with ASDs. At time of writing it is limited to the London area, with plans for expansion to other parts of the UK, funds permitting.

Some voluntary charity groups, frustrated by the lack of

supported employment in their area, have made their own contacts with employers, local officials and job coaches. One such group is the Berkshire Autistic Society, a local chapter of the NAS (see p. 229). Although it is the Government's role to provide services, local groups are pushing the authorities into action.

Sheltered employment: This is an option for those who will need security in a work environment where people are knowledgeable about ASDs. These jobs tend to be repetitious, and those who like structure and repetition may do well in them.

FOOD FOR THOUGHT
Employment Tips from Temple Grandin

In her book *Thinking in Pictures*, Temple Grandin gives some useful information about how she was able to transition from college to work. Here are a few of the points she makes:

- It is important to make a gradual transition from an educational setting to the world of work. Starting a job or career part time while still attending a class or two can make this possible.

- The freelance route has been a way that many people with an ASD have been able to exploit their talent area.

- Sometimes it is possible to get in trouble at a job by being technically correct but socially wrong. This happens to people with autism because they have a hard time being diplomatic and tactful. Temple learned by reading about international negotiations and using them as models.

- Temple has had many mentors. These mentors, whether at college or at work, helped her by teaching her the social aspects she needed to be successful, such as how to dress and be groomed appropriately, how to put together a portfolio showing off her talents, explaining to her the social nuances she did not understand and helping others understand her behaviours and actions.

In her article on the web, 'Choosing the Right Job for People with Autism or Asperger's Syndrome' on www.autism.org Temple Grandin has made lists of different types of jobs appropriate for different types of ASD people. For visual thinkers she includes computer programming, commercial art, drafting, equipment design, small appliance and lawnmower repair, video game design and the building trade. For non-visual thinkers (who are good at maths, music or facts), Temple suggests jobs such as reference librarian, inventory control, accounting, taxi driver, computer programming, copyeditor, tuning pianos and other musical instruments, clerk and filing jobs and statistician. Those who are non-verbal or have poor verbal skills may do well at reshelving library books, copy shop, factory assembly jobs, restocking shelves, janitor jobs, cleaning and cooking in a fast-food restaurant, watering plants in large office buildings, data entry, and sorting at a recycling plant.

Helpful strategies for coping in the neurotypical world of college and work

Adults with ASDs face challenges in certain areas. For those who are not intellectually disabled, or who are on the mid to higher end of functioning ability, there are many strategies that can be put in place to help.

For challenges with social communication and contact: Getting and keeping a job or career, or signing up for and attending college can be very difficult for people with ASDs. The social skills that are necessary to network, ask questions and understand the true meaning (as opposed to the literal meaning) of what is being said, as well as interpreting non-verbal communication, are areas in which people with ASDs are lacking. However, there is much that can be done to overcome this obstacle:

● Much information can be accessed through the internet now without dealing directly with another person. This can be a good way also to make primary contact when trying to network for jobs.

- If possible, find mentors who admire your talent and know about your eccentricities and who can help you turn your talent into a career, or put you in touch with people who can help you find work or get through school.

- Decide who at work or college needs to know about your ASD and tell them how it affects you in the workplace. In his book *Beyond the Wall*, Stephen Shore has included a sample letter he helped develop for the Asperger's Association of New England. This letter, addressed to employers, explains the difficulties the person writing it has with reading non-verbal signs and understanding what it is like to be in someone else's shoes, and the situations that can result, as well as suggestions that would help the person.

- Practising areas that you are not comfortable with, such as job interviews, discussion with teachers, or going on a date or outing with a peer, can be very helpful in relieving some of the anxiety.

For problems with finding your way around: Many individuals with autism have difficulty going from one place to another at school, college, shopping malls and big buildings. This can be a problem for getting to classes on time or accomplishing your job. What you can do:

- **Go around the place** you will be needing to learn how to navigate a few times before starting school or your job. It helps if you can have someone with you who is already familiar with the building. In some areas you may need to ask permission for access. If possible, walk the route from one place to another that you will have to take.

- **Take pictures** or draw the different landmarks that are on the path from one place to another. List on a piece of paper or dictate into a mini-recorder the order of the landmarks, and where you need to turn or stop or take another direction.

- **Make a small guidebook** with the pictures and notes, including the times you leave one place and go to the next.

- **Draw a map** if you think it will be helpful to you, of all the corridors or alleyways or streets and landmarks.

- **Practise navigating** through the areas you have mapped out. Using a bicycle can be a viable means of getting round large campuses or small towns for some people with ASDs.

For sensory perception problems: Both Temple Grandin (*Thinking in Pictures*) and Liane Willey (*Pretending to be Normal*) have a lot of information to share about sensory difficulties. Getting an occupational therapist who has had sensory integration training to develop a programme to help you in this area can be very useful. Look at Chapter Five for therapies that address sensory issues. Meanwhile, there are a few things you can do:

- Auditory sensitivity can be minimised for some through auditory integration training. Meanwhile, wearing earplugs may be helpful in curtailing your sensitivity to sound. Make sure you can still hear people talking to you, and emergency vehicles and signals such as fire bells. If it doesn't distract you from your work or studies, wear headphones and listen at low volume to music you enjoy. Temple cautions against using these strategies all the time, as some exposure to noise can help desensitise a person, and there is a need to get used to some everyday noise.

- For visual sensitivity, try wearing sunglasses, a hat with a brim or a visor to minimise the amount of light reaching your eyes, making sure you can see well enough to continue with what you are doing in a safe manner.

- If you suffer from tactile sensitivity, tell those around you (at work, college, living environment) that you do not like to be touched. Wear only fabrics that you like the feel of. If you enjoy deep pressure, there are weighted vests available.

However, carrying a heavy backpack or shoulder bag or sewing pockets of little weights into your coat or sweater may work just as well and look better. Rub your skin with light or heavy pressure (depending on your preference) when you are alone, perhaps when getting dressed. If you feel the need to put things in your mouth, then chew gum.

● For those with olfactory sensitivity, put some of your favourite scent on a small piece of material, the inside of your elbow, or a cotton make-up-remover pad, so that you can smell this scent when others overwhelm you. If you can, tell those who are in close proximity to you all day long about your sensitivity and ask if they can refrain from wearing perfumes and other products with strong smells.

● If food sensitivity is an issue, think of the foods you *can* tolerate. Identify the restaurants or cafés that serve those foods. If invited to someone's home, you may wish to tell them you can eat only certain foods. If your food sensitivity is extreme and you are unlikely to find what you can eat in a restaurant or at someone's home, be prepared to make and carry your own foods when you are spending time outside your home.

Living arrangements

At some point in time, you may be leaving the family home. As Jerry Newport points out in his book, it is better to start that transition while your parents are still well. That way, you will still have the support of people who love and care for you and who you trust during the period of transition that you will be facing.

There are different options available, depending upon your skill level, your level of comfort of being on your own, and available funding from the Government or yourself and your family. Choices range from very sheltered to completely independent housing; from residential facilities, to group homes, to therapeutic communities, to residential colleges, to home ownership with support. Since the National Health and Community Care Act of 1990, the local authority is no longer the main provider of residential care, but has more of a responsibility to make it possible for people with ASDs to access services provided by others.

Housing services

To find out about available housing services in your area, you need to contact many different organisations, including the health authorities, social services, the Council for Voluntary Services (CVS), national organisations and the local council housing department. Your GP, as well as family, friends and colleagues, may be of help in finding pertinent information.

Keep in mind that the kind of strategies that help you with organising your school work or job will help you with your daily living skills. Perhaps you have already been using some of these when you were living at home. Some things that may be helpful are colour-coding for files of paperwork and bills, and schedules of your daily, weekly and monthly activities and chores. For example, some people find it helpful to do certain chores (laundry, hoovering, food shopping) on certain days and have them marked on the calendar. Other responsibilities with a home that crop up less often, such as paying the bills, can be noted on the calendar to remind you when they need to be done.

HAVING A SOCIAL LIFE

Leisure and recreation activities

Having a social life can sometimes be a challenge even for people who do not lack social skills. Some people are more gregarious than others, and those people tend to have more relationships and recreational activities. However, it must be remembered that it is not quantity but quality that counts.

For people with an ASD, building relationships and participating in recreational activities can be even more difficult because of the impairment of social interaction skills, and the lack of knowledge that most people in the leisure and community services have when it comes to ASDs. However, due to the increase in those being diagnosed with autism and Asperger's, people are at least becoming more aware of what they are. Rome was not built in a day, and even though laws protect your right to have access to leisure, recreational and cultural activities in the community just like every other citizen, in reality people out there still suffer from a lack of knowledge.

FOOD FOR THOUGHT

'Many young adults meet each other at places that cultivate a common interest. These should not be "negative" sites such as night-clubs, which are notoriously socially threatening environs for our people. Places like a bookstore that features poetry readings, health club, yoga club, running group, chess club, or any interest group are a good bet for our people, who have little problem expressing an interest in certain subjects. In these places, our extreme interest, which may not be appreciated ordinarily, might even come to be a social advantage.'

Jerry and Mary Newport, *Autism – Asperger's and Sexuality*

One way you can help in this area is by spreading knowledge of ASDs. Contact your local NAS chapter and tell them if you think an agency or organisation would benefit from training.

When looking for leisure activities, think about the talents, abilities and interests that you have and find out if there is a local group that meets pertaining to that subject. You may need to take any sensory-overload issues you have into consideration when looking at activities to join. Some activities may have more social pressure than you are ready to handle. Good places to start looking are local authority services such as leisure or sports centres, swimming pools, libraries, art galleries and adult education classes. Other places where you may find groups are bowling alleys and bowling greens, pubs, cinemas, ice and roller skating rinks, gyms and local sports clubs.

Depending on your ability level and the level of support needed there are different ways to access activities. You may be able to do it on your own, or with a parent or family member to start off with. If you need a high level of support and live in a residential facility, paid staff may accompany you. Sometimes there are autism-friendly volunteer organisations or befriending schemes in your area. Parents may already be providing a 'circle of support' of family friends and carers who can help you access recreational activities.

If funds are needed, make sure that you are getting all the financial support available to you, and that during the community care assessment this is an area that is addressed.

Social and internet groups

If you wish to socialise with other adults with ASDs, some local autism chapters have social meetings and outings. Contact the NAS or your local chapter to find out more. Other organisations provide social outings, but are not necessarily ASD-specific.

The internet has become a great resource for people with ASDs. Some people prefer to develop relationships this way and can communicate with others through the internet at any time that is convenient to them. There are electronic support groups. If you do not have access to a computer at home, perhaps you can use one at your local library.

TIPS FOR ALL WHO KNOW SOMEONE WITH AN ASD

Some people with ASDs manage well with little or no support. For others, social and communication issues, or perhaps learning disabilities, can get in the way of being as independent as possible.

The challenges and what can help

Parents can help their children by instilling values and a sense of self-esteem and pride, encouraging them to see their individuality as something to be respected and appreciated, eccentricities and all. Parents can also help by creating networks of people who can be available for different areas of need for their adult child. Friends of the family or church members who have certain professional skills can help in their area of expertise. This is one way that community members can be helpful. Whether you are a plumber or an accountant, it would give peace of mind to a friend to know that you are willing to help if the need arises. Parents can also educate their child about safety, police and emergency situations. (See Chapter Eight for more about establishing community ties.)

Depression in adults

Many adults with ASDs suffer at one time or another from depression or mental illness. This is not part and parcel of the ASD but can be exacerbated by the challenges they face in trying to find a place in our society. Friends and family members need to watch for signs that all is not well in order to get them the counselling or support they need.

Partners of adults with ASDs

As ASDs become more and more recognised and diagnosed, many adults are realising for the first time that they are autistic or have Asperger's. Sometimes this happens after the person is already married; it may even be that being married provoked getting the diagnosis. The spouse may have chosen her mate because he was calm and reliable, but after some years thought of her husband as cold, unemotional and unromantic, and realised that something was amiss.

FOOD FOR THOUGHT
Partners of Adults with ASDs

'If you are in an intimate relationship with someone who has Asperger Syndrome, you are one of the most important people in their lives. How you approach and cope with problems can make a difference to how he copes with many of the difficulties that having Asperger Syndrome can present him with. This is not to say that you will have to take responsibility for everything your partner does, but it is important that you are aware that there are some things that you will be naturally better at than he is.'

Maxine C. Aston, *The Other Half of Asperger Syndrome*

Finding out that a partner has an ASD can provoke different feelings. One of them is anger at missing out on aspects of a marriage that you were looking forward to. Another feeling is relief that your partner is not trying to shut you out, he is just unable to give you the emotional response you need. Other feelings can be acceptance and understanding, and letting go of the resentment you felt, because now you know he is not being thoughtless; he really does not get it.

The positive aspects of having a spouse with an ASD include the fact that he will most likely always be loyal and honest.

CHAPTER TEN

Closing Comments

I am a person who is autistic.

*What I want to say is that the hardest part of autism
is the communication.*

Music is helpful.

I like that I can see colours in everything.

Help us by encouraging us.

ANONYMOUS

*One's first step in wisdom is to question everything –
and one's last is to come to terms with everything.*

GEORG CHRISTOPH LICHTENBERG (1742–1799)

Emily Perl Kingsley wrote a wonderful story in 1987 entitled
'Welcome To Holland' in which she described how having a child
with a disability is like planning a trip to Italy, but then landing
unexpectedly in Holland. The point of the story was that Holland
may not be Italy, but it is still a nice place to be. Years later, Susan F.
Rzucidlo wrote 'Welcome to Beirut (Beginner's Guide to Autism)'
about having a child with an ASD being more like landing in Beirut
with bombs dropping everywhere, with occasional ceasefires, but
never knowing when the next enemy attack will begin, or where it
will come from, or who the enemy really is. I sympathise.

FINAL TIPS

As a person close to someone with an ASD, your role is extremely
important to him, even if he doesn't show it. Your main purpose will be
to explain or translate to him the complexities of the neurotypical

world and, in turn, to translate to the neurotypical world the eccentricities of the person with an ASD. You will be a sort of United Nations interpreter; a most important role to fill. Just as a stranger in a strange land needs to have customs explained to him, so will the individual with an ASD need explanations. And as the adopted country needs to have some understanding of the foreigner who has landed in their midst, so will the neurotypicals of our society need to learn from you about people with ASDs so as to be more accepting and tolerant of differences.

Parents need to do all they can to help their children, and as early as they can. Some will be 'cured' or 'recovered' and many will not be. The focus should be to teach them how to make sense of the world and give them the tools to function in it, so they can grow up to live independent, fulfilling lives.

As a parent you may have knowledge, but you will not always have control. You must learn to recognise that which you can change, and that which you cannot. And this advice holds true whether you are thinking about a behaviour your child has or a policy your Local Educational Authority is sticking to. In some instances, the only thing you may be able to change is your attitude.

Professionals should recognise that autism includes the family. You may spend a few hours a day or month with this person, but for his loved ones, it is 24/7. You need to respect the fact that you may be an expert in your area of expertise, but while the person is growing up at home, the parent is still the expert on their child. Together you offer strong support and assistance to the person with autism.

Friends and extended family can lend support by learning about ASDs, and be open-minded. Do not judge the person with an ASD or the carers; realise that they may all be a bit overloaded. Continue to extend invitations and keep the lines of communication open. If you can help in any way, offer to do so. The offer will be appreciated even if it is not taken up.

The general public can be instrumental in how a person with an ASD or the carers feel in the community. Acceptance and a non-judgemental attitude towards those who act differently will do wonders to ease the stress. We are all part of the same community, and it does take a village to raise a child and make the place we live into a neighbourhood.

LAST THOUGHTS

Some parents say that if it weren't for autism, they wouldn't have met the wonderful people they have come to know, that autism has given them a 'raison d'être', a reason for living. Perhaps I am much too cynical, but I tend to believe that even without autism in my life, I would have met some wonderful people and become committed to some worthy cause. This is not to speak disparagingly of all the fantastic autism-related friends my family has made over the years. It is more a comment about the fact that I could do fine without having to deal with the individuals who don't 'get it' or all the added stress of administrative paperwork, phone calls and resource-searching one needs to do in order to get any assistance. I could still have a wonderful, rewarding life without autism.

What is certain, however, is that I have learned much about what is truly essential in life. I have learned how fortunate I am that my body and mind work in synch, and how much inner strength I possess. I have also learned literally to stop and smell the roses and to take pleasure in the simple moments of daily living between the bombs falling. I have learned that heightened senses can bring both pain and pleasure, and that passing the time of day by staring at dust particles in the sunlight, feeling the sand sift through your fingers, or your body floating weightless in a pool, doesn't seem so crazy, after all. In fact, it's very relaxing. Try it sometime.

Glossary of Abbreviations

ABA – Applied Behaviour Analysis
ABC – Applied Behavior Consultants
ACE – Advisory Centre for Education
AIT – Auditory Integration Training
ANDI – Autism Network for Dietary Intervention
APMT – Association of Professional Music Therapists
APPGA – All Party Parliamentary Group on Autism
ARI – Autism Research Institute
AS – Asperger's Syndrome
ASA – Autism Society of America
ASDs – Autism Spectrum Disorders
BAS – Berkshire Autistic Society
CAN – Cure Aurism Now
CARD – Center for Autism and Related Disorders
CAT scan – Computer-Assisted Axial Tomography
CDC – Center for Disease Control and Prevention
CHAT – Checklist for Autism in Toddlers
CLASS – Cambridge Lifespan Asperger Syndrome Service
CSA – Center for the Study of Autism
CVS –Council for Voluntary Services
DAN! – Defeat Autism Now!
DfEE – Department for Education and Employment
DfES – Department for Education and Skills
DLA – Disability Living Allowance
DMG – Dimethylglycine
DSM-IV – Diagnostic and Statistical Manual of Mental Disorders, 4th edition
DT – Diphtheria and Tetanus vaccine
DTT – Discrete Trial Teaching
DTP vaccine – Diphtheria, Tetanus and Pertussis vaccine
EEG – Electroencephalogram
FC – Facilitated Communication

FEAT – Families for Early Autism Treatment
GFCF diet – Gluten Free / Casein Free diet
GP – General Practitioner
ICA – Invalid Care Allowance
IEP – Individual Education Plan
IOM – Institute of Medicine
IVIG therapy – Intravenous Immunoglobulin therapy
LEA – Local Educational Authority
LEAP – London Early Autism Project
MIND – Medical Investigation of Neurodevelopmental Disorders
MMR vaccine – Measles, Mumps and Rubella vaccine
MRC – Medical Research Council
MRI – Magnetic Resonance Imaging
MT – Music Therapy
NAAR – National Alliance for Autism Research
NAS – National Autistic Society
NHS – National Health Service
NIH – National Institute of Health
OASIS – On-line Asperger Syndrome Information and Support
OT – Occupational Therapy
PACE – Parents Autism Campaign for Education
PACT – Placement Assessment and Counselling Team
PDD – Pervasive Developmental Disorder
PDD-NOS – PDD Not Otherwise Specified
PEACH – Parents for the Early Intervention of Autism in Children
PECS – Picture Exchange Communication System
SEN – Special Educational Needs
SENCO – Special Educational Needs Coordinator
SENDA – Special Educational Needs and Disability Act
SENT – Special Educational Needs Tribunal
SI – Sensory Integration
SPELL – Structure, Positive, Empathetic, Low arousal and Links
TEACCH – Treatment and Education of Autistic and related Communication handicapped Children
TEN – The Education Network
YAP – Young Autism Project

Appendix

Since 1967, the Autism Research Institute has been collecting parent ratings of the usefulness of the many interventions tried on their autistic children. Page 250, *Parent Ratings of Behavioural Effects of Biomedical Interventions*, is a summary of the data from 21,500 parents who have completed questionnaires designed to collect such information. Page 255, *Autism Treatment Evaluation Checklist (ATEC)*, is a form intended to measure the effects of a treatment on your child. Parents can fill this out before beginning any treatment and after a treatment to help rate its effectiveness. The filled-out form may be returned to the Autism Research Institute for free scoring, and will be helpful in assessing the usefulness of interventions as perceived by parents.

Parent Ratings of Behavioural Effects of Biomedical Interventions

Autism Research Institute,
4182 Adams Avenue, San Diego, CA 92116

The parents of autistic children represent a vast and important reservoir of information on the benefits – and adverse effects – of the large variety of drugs and other interventions that have been tried with their children. Since 1967 the Autism Research Institute has been collecting parent ratings of the usefulness of the many interventions tried on their autistic children.

The following data have been collected from the more than 21,500 parents who have completed our questionnaires designed to collect such information. For the purposes of the present table, the parents' responses on a six-point scale have been combined into three categories: 'made worse' (ratings 1 and 2), 'no effect' (ratings 3 and 4), and 'made better' (ratings 5 and 6). The 'Better:Worse' column gives the number of children who 'Got Better' for each one who 'Got Worse'.

Note: For seizure drugs – the first line shows the drug's behavioural effects; the second line shows the drug's effects on seizures.

DRUGS	Parent Ratings				
	Got Worse[A]	No Effect	Got Better	Better: Worse	No. of Cases[B]
Aderall	39%	28%	34%	0.9:1	285
Amphetamine	47%	28%	25%	0.5:1	1174
Anafranil	31%	37%	31%	1.0:1	351
Antibiotics	30%	59%	11%	0.4:1	1617
Antifungals[C]					
Diflucan	7%	42%	51%	7.2:1	185
Nystatin	5%	48%	47%	10:1	727
Atarax	26%	53%	21%	0.8:1	443
Benadryl	24%	51%	25%	1.1:1	2512
Beta Blocker	18%	49%	33%	1.8:1	236
Buspar	26%	45%	30%	1.2:1	281
Chloral Hydrate	41%	37%	22%	0.5:1	375
Clonidine	21%	31%	48%	2.2:1	1090
Clozapine	44%	39%	16%	0.4:1	79
Cogentin	19%	53%	28%	1.4:1	149
Cylert	45%	35%	21%	0.5:1	580
Deanol	15%	55%	29%	1.9:1	195
Depakene					
Behaviour	25%	43%	32%	1.3:1	871
Seizures	12%	30%	57%	4.6:1	569
Desipramine	38%	25%	38%	1.0:1	61
Dilantin					
Behaviour	28%	48%	24%	0.9:1	1049
Seizures	14%	36%	51%	3.8:1	377
Felbatol	26%	45%	29%	1.1:1	38
Fenfluramine	21%	51%	28%	1.4:1	453
Halcion	37%	30%	33%	0.9:1	43
Haldol	37%	27%	35%	0.9:1	1119
IVIG	13%	45%	42%	3.2:1	31

DRUGS	Parent Ratings				
	Got Worse[A]	No Effect	Got Better	Better: Worse	No. of Cases[B]
Klonapin					
Behaviour	28%	33%	38%	1.4:1	156
Seizures	38%	50%	12%	0.3:1	26
Lithium	27%	42%	31%	1.1:1	384
Luvox	28%	36%	37%	1.3:1	120
Mellaril	28%	38%	33%	1.2:1	2023
Mysoline					
Behaviour	44%	40%	15%	0.3:1	131
Seizures	19%	58%	23%	1.2:1	57
Naltrexone	22%	46%	32%	1.5:1	200
Paxil	27%	28%	45%	1.7:1	192
Phenergan	30%	44%	26%	0.9:1	244
Phenobarb.					
Behaviour	47%	37%	16%	0.3:1	1052
Seizures	17%	43%	40%	2.4:1	458
Prolixin	34%	34%	33%	1.0:1	83
Prozac	31%	33%	36%	1.2:1	975
Risperidal	19%	28%	53%	2.8:1	401
Ritalin	44%	26%	29%	0.7:1	3540
Secretin					
Intravenous	8%	43%	49%	6.2:1	217
Transdermal	12%	47%	41%	3.6:1	78
Stelazine	28%	44%	27%	1.0:1	415
Tegretol					
Behaviour	24%	45%	31%	1.3:1	1345
Seizures	12%	33%	55%	4.5:1	721
Thorazine	36%	40%	24%	0.7:1	897
Tofranil	30%	37%	33%	1.1:1	698
Valium	36%	41%	23%	0.7:1	788

DRUGS	Parent Ratings				
	Got Worse[A]	No Effect	Got Better	Better: Worse	No. of Cases[B]
Zarontin					
Behaviour	34%	43%	22%	0.7:1	129
Seizures	21%	51%	29%	1.4:1	87
Zoloft	33%	31%	36%	1.1:1	212

BIOMEDICAL NON-DRUG SUPPLEMENTS	Parent Ratings				
	Got Worse[A]	No Effect	Got Better	Better: Worse	No. of Cases[B]
Vitamin A	2%	59%	39%	22:1	334
Calcium[D]	2%	62%	35%	14:1	988
Cod Liver oil	3%	51%	46%	14:1	411
Colostrum	6%	58%	37%	6.7:1	163
Detox. (Chelation)	3%	28%	70%	27:1	116
Digestive Enzymes	4%	44%	52%	14:1	314
DMG	7%	51%	42%	5.9:1	4547
Fatty Acids	4%	44%	51%	12:1	299
5 HTP	11%	55%	35%	3.3:1	66
Folic Acid	4%	55%	41%	11:1	1100
Food Allergy Treatment	4%	37%	59%	14:1	290
Magnesium	6%	65%	29%	5.2:1	288
Melatonin[E]	10%	33%	57%	5.9:1	302
Pepcid	9%	61%	30%	3.2:1	64
SAMe	25%	46%	29%	1.1:1	28
St. Johns Wort	11%	67%	22%	2.0:1	46
TMG	14%	42%	44%	3.1:1	182
Transfer Factor	18%	51%	31%	1.7	39
Vitamin B3	5%	55%	41%	9.0:1	487
Vit. B6 alone	7%	64%	29%	4.1:1	590
Vit. B6/Mag.	4%	49%	46%	11:1	5079
Vitamin C	2%	59%	39%	16:1	1306
Zinc	3%	55%	43%	17:1	835

BIOMEDICAL NON-DRUG SUPPLEMENTS	Parent Ratings				
	Got Worse[A]	No Effect	Got Better	Better: Worse	No. of Cases[B]
SPECIAL DIETS					
Candida Diet	3%	45%	52%	18:1	605
Feingold Diet	2%	47%	51%	23:1	645
Gluten-/Casein-Free Diet	4%	33%	64%	18:1	724
Removed Chocolate	1%	50%	49%	36:1	1491
Removed Eggs	2%	61%	37%	21:1	882
Removed Milk Products/Dairy	2%	51%	48%	30:1	4950
Removed Sugar	2%	51%	47%	24:1	3392
Removed Wheat	2%	53%	46%	26:1	2701
Rotation Diet	2%	50%	47%	20:1	678

[A] 'Worse' refers only to worse behaviour. Drugs, but not nutrients, typically also cause physical problems if used long-term.

[B] No. of cases is cumulative over several decades, so does not reflect current usage levels (e.g., Haldol is now seldom used).

[C] Antifungal drugs are used only if autism is thought to be yeast-related.

[D] Calcium effects not due to dairy-free diet; statistics are similar for milk drinkers and non-milk drinkers.

[E] Caution: While melatonin can benefit sleep and behaviour, its long-term effects on puberty are unknown.

Autism Treatment Evaluation Checklist (ATEC)

Bernard Rimland, PhD and Stephen M. Edelson, PhD
Autism Research Institute
4182 Adams Avenue, San Diego, CA 92116
fax: (619) 563-6840; www.autism.com/ari

This form is intended to measure the effects of treatment. Free scoring of this form is available by mailing or faxing this sheet to ARI or at our website at: www.autism.com/atec

---

Name of Child: Last .... First ....
Male/Female: .... Age .... Date of Birth ....
Form completed by: .... Relationship ....
Today's Date ....

Please circle the letters to indicate how true each phrase is

1. Speech/Language/Communication:

[N] Not true   [S] Somewhat true   [V] Very True

N	S	V	1. Knows own name
N	S	V	2. Responds to 'No' or 'Stop'
N	S	V	3. Can follow some commands
N	S	V	4. Can use one word at a time (No!, Eat, Water, etc.)
N	S	V	5. Can use 2 words at a time (Don't want, Go home)
N	S	V	6. Can use 3 words at a time (Want more milk)
N	S	V	7. Knows 10 or more words
N	S	V	8. Can use sentences with 4 or more words
N	S	V	9. Explains what he/she wants
N	S	V	10. Asks meaningful questions
N	S	V	11. Speech tends to be meaningful/relevant
N	S	V	12. Often uses several successive sentences
N	S	V	13. Carries on fairly good conversation
N	S	V	14. Has normal ability to communicate for his/her age

2. Sociability:

[N] Not descriptive   [S] Somewhat descriptive
[V] Very descriptive

N	S	V	1.	Seems to be in a shell – you cannot reach him/her
N	S	V	2.	Ignores other people
N	S	V	3.	Pays little or no attention when addressed
N	S	V	4.	Uncooperative and resistant
N	S	V	5.	No eye contact
N	S	V	6.	Prefers to be left alone
N	S	V	7.	Shows no affection
N	S	V	8.	Fails to greet parents
N	S	V	9.	Avoids contact with others
N	S	V	10.	Does not imitate
N	S	V	11.	Dislikes being held/cuddled
N	S	V	12.	Does not share or show
N	S	V	13.	Does not wave 'bye bye'
N	S	V	14.	Disagreeable/not compliant
N	S	V	15.	Temper tantrums
N	S	V	16.	Lacks friends/companions
N	S	V	17.	Rarely smiles
N	S	V	18.	Insensitive to other's feelings
N	S	V	19.	Indifferent to being liked
N	S	V	20.	Indifferent if parent(s) leave

3. Sensory/Cognitive Awareness:

[N] Not descriptive   [S] Somewhat descriptive
[V] Very descriptive

N	S	V	1.	Responds to own name
N	S	V	2.	Responds to praise
N	S	V	3.	Looks at people and animals
N	S	V	4.	Looks at pictures (and T.V.)
N	S	V	5.	Does drawing, colouring, art
N	S	V	6.	Plays with toys appropriately
N	S	V	7.	Appropriate facial expression
N	S	V	8.	Understands stories on T.V.
N	S	V	9.	Understands explanations
N	S	V	10.	Aware of environment
N	S	V	11.	Aware of danger

N   S   V   12. Shows imagination
N   S   V   13. Initiates activities
N   S   V   14. Dresses self
N   S   V   15. Curious, interested
N   S   V   16. Venturesome – explores
N   S   V   17. 'Tuned in' – Not spacey
N   S   V   18. Looks where others are looking

4. Health/Physical/Behaviour:
[N] Not a Problem   [MO] Moderate Problem
[MI] Minor Problem   [S] Serious Problem

N   MI   MO   S   1. Bed-wetting
N   MI   MO   S   2. Wets pants/nappies
N   MI   MO   S   3. Soils pants/nappies
N   MI   MO   S   4. Diarrhoea
N   MI   MO   S   5. Constipation
N   MI   MO   S   6. Sleep problems
N   MI   MO   S   7. Eats too much/too little
N   MI   MO   S   8. Extremely limited diet
N   MI   MO   S   9. Hyperactive
N   MI   MO   S   10. Lethargic
N   MI   MO   S   11. Hits or injures self
N   MI   MO   S   12. Hits or injures others
N   MI   MO   S   13. Destructive
N   MI   MO   S   14. Sound-sensitive
N   MI   MO   S   15. Anxious/fearful
N   MI   MO   S   16. Unhappy/crying
N   MI   MO   S   17. Seizures
N   MI   MO   S   18. Obsessive speech
N   MI   MO   S   19. Rigid routines
N   MI   MO   S   20. Shouts or screams
N   MI   MO   S   21. Demands sameness
N   MI   MO   S   22. Often agitated
N   MI   MO   S   23. Not sensitive to pain
N   MI   MO   S   24. 'Hooked' or fixated on certain
                       objects/topics
N   MI   MO   S   25. Repetitive movements (stimming,
                       rocking, etc.)

Resources

Autism Organisations and General Sources of Information

The National Autistic Society (NAS)
393 City Road
London EC1V 1NG
Tel: 020 7833 2299
Fax: 020 7833 9666
Website: http://www.nas.org.uk/

Great website for information for professionals, parents, and adults with ASDs. To find local chapters of the NAS look at http://www.nas.org.uk/groups.html

The Irish Society for Autism
Unity Building
16/17 Lower O'Connell Street
Dublin 1
Eire
Tel: (0) 71 744684
Fax: (0) 71 744224
Website: http://www.iol.ie/~dary/isa/

The Scottish Society for Autism
Head Office
Hilton House
Alloa Business Park
Whins Road
Alloa FK10 3SA
Tel: 01259 720044
Fax: 01259 720051
Website: http://www.autism-in-scotland.org.uk/

Autism Research Institute (ARI)
Bernard Rimland, Director
4182 Adams Avenue
San Diego
CA 92116
USA
Tel: (1) 619 281 7165
Fax: (1) 619 563 6840
Website: http://www.autismresearchinstitute.com

The ARI also publishes the quarterly *Autism Research Review International*, which reviews the latest autism research.

Autism Research Unit
School of Health Sciences
University of Sunderland
Sunderland SR2 7EE
Tel: 0191 510 8922 or 0191 515 2581
Fax: 0191 567 0420 .
Website: http://osiris.sunderland.ac.uk/autism/

The Schafer Autism Report
9629 Old Placerville Road
Sacramento
CA 95827
USA
Email: schafer@sprynet.com
Website: http://www.freewebz.com/schafer/SARHome.htm

Cure Autism Now! (CAN!)
5455 Wilshire Boulevard
Suite 715
Los Angeles
CA 90036
USA
Tel: (1) 323 549 0500, 1-888-8AUTISM
Fax: (1) 323 549 0547
Website: http://www.canfoundation.org/

Allergy Induced Autism
11 Larklands
Longthorpe
Peterborough
Cambridgeshire PE3 6LL
Website: www.autismmedical.com

Mencap
123 Golden Lane
London EC1Y 0RT
Tel: 020 7454 0454

Public Autism Awareness: www.paains.org.uk/
Very informative and thorough website run by parents with up-to-date autism news, general information about the world of ASDs and listing of other websites to go to for information.

Center for the Study of Autism (CSA): www.autism.org

Asperger Syndrome Educational Network (ASPEN): www.aspennj.org/
For professionals working with people with Asperger's.

Autismconnect aims to organise the wealth of autism-related websites currently available on the Internet.
Website: http://www.autismconnect.org/

AUTISM-EUROPE is a European network regrouping nearly 80 parent associations in over 30 countries (of which 14 are EU member states) whose main objective is to advance the rights of people with autism and their families and help improve their lives.

Avenue E. Van Becelaere 26B, bte 21
B-1170 Brussels, BELGIUM
Tel: +32(0)2.675.75.05
Fax: +32(0)2.675.72.70
Email: president@autismeurope.org
Website: http://www.autismeurope.org/

World Autism Organisation exists to help promote a better quality of life for autistic people and their families throughout the world through public awareness, through international conferences and contact with organisations such as UNESCO, WHO, United Nations, etc.
Website: http://worldautism.org

Books by Parents

Facing Autism: Giving Parents Reasons For Hope and Guidance For Help **by Lynn Hamilton**
This book is highly recommended as a well-written account by a parent of her search for treatment, the options she chose for her son, and how she did it. More and more families and professionals are turning to a combination of treatments to help children with ASDs, and Lynn explains how and why. Applied behaviour analysis, dietary and biomedical interventions, as well as education and communication needs are discussed. Her explanations about dietary and biomedical interventions are the easiest to read that I have seen anywhere. Lynn lists resources as well.

Breaking Autism's Barriers: A Father's Story **by Bill Davis**
Bill does not take any prisoners in his fight to get an appropriate education for his son. Bill's philosophy and positive attitude come through clearly in this book. He and his wife organised a home programme based on discrete trial teaching and left no stone unturned in their quest to get funding for it. Although the educational system is different in the UK from the USA, lessons can be learned from Bill's style and his questioning of professionals and authority figures, as well as his insistence on learning as much as he could about pertinent laws. This is the story of a couple who do all they can, but who are clearly accepting of who their son is. It is a very positive and uplifting read and is highly recommended.

Dangerous Encounters: Avoiding Perilous Situations with Autism **by Bill Davis and Wendy Goldband Schunick**
This excellent book is written with parents, shopkeepers and emergency responders in mind. Davis gives good suggestions on how to teach your child about safety, a concept that is difficult for these children to learn. Explanations for people who work in the community about how to approach someone with autism are helpful.

The Oasis Guide to Asperger Syndrome: Advice, Support, Insight and Inspiration **by Patricia Romanowski Bashe and Barbara L. Kirby**
Barbara Kirby founded the award-wining OASIS – Online Asperger Syndrome Information and Support. This is an excellent book on everything a parent who is bringing up a child with Asperger's should know, including informative chapters on medicines, the child in the social realm and in school, the different options and

interventions. Some of the information may not be valid for the UK, but there is a great section in the back entitled '54 Ways to make the World a Better Place for Persons with Asperger Syndrome'.

Autistic Spectrum Disorders: Understanding the Diagnosis and Getting Help by **Mitzi Waltz**
This book is very informative, with great appendixes in the back full of resources including information on medications and supplements. Mitzi's book covers education in all English-speaking countries. She is American and is currently completing a doctorate in health sciences at the University of Sunderland.

Let Me Hear Your Voice: A Family's Triumph Over Autism by **Catherine Maurice**
The first book written by a parent who used the Lovaas method with her two children and had great success, Catherine inspired many families to try ABA. Her description of all she endured on her search for help will come as no surprise to the parents who have been there. Her analysis of the treatments on offer at the time are very good.

The Siege and *Exiting Nirvana* by **Clara Claiborne Park**
Clara has written two detailed books about raising her daughter with autism. *The Siege* covers the first eight years, and *Exiting Nirvana* talks about her daughter as an adult. Clara raised her child when knowledge about and help for autism was relatively unavailable.

BOOKS BY PEOPLE WITH ASDs

Thinking in Pictures and Other Reports from My Life With Autism by **Temple Grandin**
In this book Temple shares with us how her thought processes work. She is a visual learner and thinker, and describes how that affected her growing up and even today. There is much valuable information about sensory processing, developing relationships and empathy, which is useful in understanding people with ASDs and how we can help them in their learning. Temple includes an informative chapter on traditional medications and how they have been helpful.

Freaks, Geeks and Asperger Syndrome by **Luke Jackson**
Here is a well-written account of an ASD teenager's experience and his recommendations to parents, professionals and other teens with ASDs. If you only give your more able child with an ASD one book, this is the one you should get.

Beyond the Silence: My Life, the World and Autism by **Tito Rajarshi Mukhopadhyay**
In this book published by the National Autistic Society (NAS), Tito allows us a rare glimpse into the mind of someone with severe autism. He writes beautiful prose and poetry. His mother read to him constantly when he was little, and developed a way to teach him to write and type by physically motoring him through the motions. Tito's descriptions of his feelings and what it is like to be trapped in a body that he cannot easily control help us to understand why some people with autism act as they do. Tito's book is a great reminder that you cannot assume what is going on inside the head of someone who is unable to communicate.

Pretending to be Normal: Living With Asperger's Syndrome by **Liane Holliday Willey**
This is a wonderfully written account of how the world is perceived by someone with Asperger's. Liane offers much insight into what she feels and what her senses tell her about the world. It is only when her daughter was diagnosed with Asperger's a few years ago that Liane recognised the traits in herself, although she had always known

she was a bit different from others. Liane includes useful appendixes in the back of her book that cover such topics as explaining about yourself to others, survivor skills for college students, coping strategies and employment options and responsibilities.

Your Life is Not a Label by Jerry Newport

Jerry has a wonderful sense of humour and his positive outlook can only inspire us. This is a guide book to help adults with ASDs handle the challenge of living in a neurotypical world, Newport's 'can do' attitude is apparent in every aspect of his life. Diagnosed at age 47, Jerry gives tips on everything from the small problems of everyday life to the big ones. This book has valuable information for all, including a great appendix section with resources, and lists such as 'Newport's Guide to Fast Money' and 'The Newport "Common Sense" Checklist for Autistic Personalities'.

Martian in the Playground by Clare Sainsbury

This is very interesting reading for parents and professionals and will help them understand what many students with ASDs go through on a daily basis during their school years. Includes many helpful suggestions.

Beyond the Wall: Personal Experiences With Autism and Asperger's Syndrome by Stephen Shore

Stephen shares much about himself now as an adult, and also as a child, talking about the bullying he was subjected to in school, sensory processing issues, dating and marriage among other subjects. He explains why college is heaven for him, and his experience now of working with children with autism and neurological impairments. He gives his thoughts on the world of work and university for people like him.

Nobody Nowhere by Donna Williams

This is Donna Williams' extraordinary first book that takes you through her painful childhood and on to when she discovers that she has autism. This book is emotionally wrenching, so I would not recommend reading it when you are feeling overwhelmed. However, the last chapter 'An Outline of Language in "My World"' is a very helpful analysis of the meanings of certain of her behaviours, which is interesting when trying to understand some of the behaviours of children with ASDs.

Autism: An Inside-Out Approach by Donna Williams

Donna explains what it feels like to have autism, how her senses are affected and what has been helpful to her in coping with some of the challenges. She describes useful strategies that may be helpful to others.

A Survival Guide for People with Asperger Syndrome by Marc Segar

Marc Segar passed away in 1997, but he left behind this wonderful guide, which covers many different areas including jobs and interviews, body language, boundaries, conversation, living with flatmates and finding the right friends. It is posted on this website: www.autismandcomputing.org.uk/marc2.htm

Through the Eyes of Aliens: A Book About Autistic People by Jasmine Lee O'Neill

Jasmine does not speak but writes with a positive attitude about what it means to be severely autistic.

EDUCATIONAL RESOURCES FOR SCHOOL AND HOME

Asperger syndrome – practical strategies for the classroom: a teacher's guide by the Leicester City Council and Leicestershire County Council, published by The National Autistic Society
Aimed at teachers but parents will also find it a great support.

Teaching young children with autistic spectrum disorders to learn: a practical guide for parents and staff in mainstream schools and nurseries by Liz Hannah, illustrations by Steve Lockett, published by the National Autistic Society
This wide-ranging, well-illustrated book offers all kinds of tried and tested strategies to help young people with autistic spectrum disorders develop and learn.

A Picture's Worth: PECS and Other Visual Communication Strategies in Autism by Andy Bondy and Lori Frost

Comic Strip Conversations: Colorful Illustrated Interactions with Students with Autism and Related Disorders by Carol Gray
The New Social Story Book by Carol Gray
The Original Social Story Book by Carol Gray

Asperger's Syndrome, A Guide for Parents and Professionals by Tony Attwood
This book outlines some of the strategies for communicating about emotions and learning about friendship.

Autism/Asperger's: Solving the Relationship Puzzle by Steven E. Gutstein

The Out-of-Synch Child by Carol Stock Kranowitz

Activity Schedules for Children with Autism: Teaching Independent Behavior by Lynn E. McClannahan and Patricia J. Krantz

I am Special by Peter Vermeulen

Life Beyond the Classroom: Transition Strategies for Young People with Disabilities by Paul Wehman
Community-Based Curriculum: Instructional Strategies for Students With Severe Handicaps by Mary A. Falvey

Steps to Independence by B. Baker and A. Brightman

Families: Applications of Social Learning to Family Life by Gerald R. Patterson

Parents Are Teachers: A Child Management Program by Wesley C. Becker

Teaching Developmentally Disabled Children: The ME Book by O. Ivar Lovaas

Behavioral Intervention for Young Children with Autism edited by Catherine Maurice, co-edited by Gina Green and Stephen C. Luce

A Work In Progress: Behavior Management Strategies and a Curriculum for Intensive Behavioral Treatment of Autism by Ron Leaf and John McEachin

My Friend with Autism by Beverly Bishop

Asperger Syndrome Employment Workbook by Roger N. Meyer
Written by someone with Asperger's, this practical workbook encourages the reader to engage in an exploration of their employment history, and to identify the work they are best suited for by analysing their needs, talents and strengths.

PEP: Parents, Educators, and children's software Publishers is an informational resource. This website has been developed in response to the interests and needs of these three audiences.
Website: http://www.microweb.com/pepsite/index/html

Autism – The Facts by Simon Baron-Cohen and Patrick Bolton

Asperger Syndrome, A Practical Guide for Teachers by Val Cumine, Julia Leach and Gil Stevenson

Children with Autism and Asperger Syndrome – A Guide for Practitioners and Carers by Patricia Howlin

A Mind of One's Own, A guide to the special difficulties and needs of the more able person with Autism or Asperger Syndrome by Digby Tantum

Autism, A social skills approach for children and adolescents by Maureen Aarons and Tess Gittens

Autism and ICT: A Guide for Teachers and Parents (ICT stands for Information and Communications Technology) by Colin Hardy, Jan Ogden, Julie Newman and Sally Cooper

Special Teaching in Higher Education: Successful Strategies for Access and Inclusion Editor: Stuart Powell

Social Use of Language Programme (SULP) by Wendy Rinaldi

Circles I: Intimacy and Relationships
Circles II: Stop Abuse
Circles III: AIDS: Safer Ways

Circles is a commonly used system for teaching appropriate social and sexual behaviours to people with developmental disabilities. It is an expensive video system and would be a good thing for a parent group or resource centre to buy. *Circles I* covers social and sexual distance, different levels of intimacy, understanding choice, appropriate behaviours and relationship boundaries. *Circles II* covers how to recognise and avoid threatening or abusive situations. *Circles III* explains about communicable diseases and the difference between casual and intimate contact. The *Circles* videos are published by James Stanfield Publishing and are devised by Marilyn P. Champagne and Leslie W. Walker-Hirsch. More information can be obtained from the website, http://www.stanfield.com/sexed.html

Primal Leadership: Realizing the Power of Emotional Intelligence by Daniel Goleman, Richard Boyatzis and Annie McKee

The University of Birmingham has developed a University Certificate of Higher Education ASDs web-based programme which should be of particular interest to those working with children and adults with ASDs in the home, classroom or residential environment. Learning Support Assistants, Residential Social Workers and parents will find this programme of study helpful. The Project Director is Dr. Rita Jordan.

Webautism, School of Education
THE UNIVERSITY OF BIRMINGHAM
Edgbaston, Birmingham B15 2TT
United Kingdom
Tel: +44 (0)121 414 7563
Fax: +44 (0)121 414 4865
Email: education@bham.ac.uk
Website: http://www.webautism.bham.ac.uk

RESOURCES ABOUT THE EDUCATIONAL SYSTEM

The Advisory Centre for Education (ACE)
1C Aberdeen Studios
22 Highbury Grove
London N5 2DQ
Tel: 0808 8005793 (advice line) or 020 7704 9822
Website: www.ace-ed.org.uk

ACE's *Special Education Handbook: The law on children with special needs* explains the law in simple terms and has a great resource section in the back with addresses and phone numbers for other helpful organizations. ACE also provides free independent advice to parents over the phone about the education system and legal rights.

The Education Network (TEN)
22 Upper Woburn Place
London WC1 0TB
Tel: 020 7554 2810
Fax: 020 7554 2801
Website: www.ten.info

TEN is an independent body that supports local educational authorities in their work of raising education standards. They have many useful publications available.

RESOURCES SPECIFIC TO FAMILIES

It can get better . . . dealing with common behaviour problems in young autistic children by Paul Dickinson and Liz Hannah, published by The National Autistic Society (1998)
Aimed specifically at parents and carers of young children, this book looks at common behaviour problems and offers tips on how to deal with them. It offers help with temper tantrums, toileting problems, sleep, feeding, self-help skills and learning to play, coping with obsessional and repetitive behaviour and self-injury.

Special Children, Challenged Parents: The Struggles and Rewards of Raising a Child with a Disability by Robert A. Naseef
From the Heart: On Being the Mother of a Child with Special Needs edited by Jayne D.B. Marsh
Uncommon Fathers: Reflections on Raising a Child with a Disability edited by Donald J. Meyer
Siblings of Children with Autism: A Guide for Families by Sandra L. Harris

Sexuality: Your Sons and Daughters with Intellectual Disabilities by Karin Melberg Schwier and Dave Hingsburger
This is a good resource for the parents of less able children, although some ideas could be incorporated for the more able. It covers a topic parents may have a difficult time addressing and therefore sometimes forget about, but it is a very necessary part of our teenagers and young adults that we would do well not to ignore. Even though this book is not written specifically with individuals with autism in mind, many concepts and strategies can be adapted.

The ABCs of Special Needs Planning Made Easy by Bart Stevens
A simple, step-by-step comprehensive guide to help families and professionals plan for the future care, supervision, security and quality of life of a person with special needs. It is an invaluable tool that you will reach for time after time. The current edition applies to laws and regulations in the United States. An edition for Canada, the United Kingdom and Australia is planned for early 2004. For more information, contact Bart Stevens Special Needs Planning at www.BSSNP.com

If you are travelling with an adolescent, or are helping an adult plan a trip, you may wish to read an article entitled 'Autism & Airport Travel Safety Tips' by Dennis Debbault on the NAS website at www.nas.org.uk/family/parents/airtravel.html

To find out more about discretionary trusts, go to http://www.housingoptions.org.uk/factsheets/19-discretionary.htm For specialist legal advice about discretionary trusts and will guardianship, contact Mencap (see p. 259). Information about guardianship can also be found at http://www.guardianship.org/whatis/index.htm

Lawyers for people with a learning disability
Anthony Quinn & Company
Tel: +44 (0) 207 242 3332

Disability Law Service
2nd Floor North
52–54 High Holborn
London WC1V 6RL
Tel: +44 (0) 207 831 8031

Resources Specifically for Siblings

My brother is different: a book for young children who have brothers and sisters with autism by Louise Gorrod, published by The National Autistic Society (1997)
This book is aimed at younger siblings aged 4–7.

Everything You Need to Know; When a Brother or Sister is Autistic by Marsha Rosenberg

Everybody is Different: A book for young people who have brothers or sisters with autism by Fiona Bleach

Sibshops: Workshops for Siblings of Children with Special Needs by Myer and Vadasy

Views from Our Shoes: Growing Up With a Brother or Sister With Special Needs by D. Meyer

www.autism.org/sibling/sibneeds.html
Website with a short article on what to discuss with different-aged siblings, as well as more information in regard to sibling issues.

www.siblingsofautism.com
This website was created by a sibling of a child with an ASD, and is for siblings of autistic children.

http://groups.yahoo.com/group/autism_sibs/
Another website for siblings of children with autism.

http://groups.yahoo.com/group/aspergers-teens/
A website for siblings of adolescents with Asperger's.

www.thearc.org/siblingsupport/
This website contains information on Sibshops, a support group for siblings of children with disabilities, as well as other resources geared towards siblings of children with special needs. There are two 'listservs', one geared towards child-age siblings (SibKids), another for adult siblings (SibNet).

RESOURCES SPECIFIC TO ADOLESCENTS WITH ASDs

Talking together about growing up – a workbook for parents of children with learning disabilities by Lorna Scott and Lesley Kerr-Edwards, published by The Family Planning Association (1999)
This book takes a very practical approach by suggesting a range of activities parents can do with their children to help them understand the changes in their body during puberty.

What is Asperger Syndrome, and How Will it Affect Me? A Guide for Young People by Martine Ives of the National Autistic Society. This is a very practical and useful booklet for adolescents, including more resources.

Autism – Asperger's and Sexuality: Puberty and Beyond by Jerry and Mary Newport
This book is a wonderful resource for the more able teenager and young adult, although parental guidance is recommended. The publishers suggest photocopying certain sections of the book to give to your child to read. In this way you can give him the information he is ready to handle. Jerry and Mary Newport are a married couple who both have Asperger's and share their experience and advice about puberty and sexuality.

Write Away (penpal network)
1 Thorpe Close
London W10 5XL
Tel: 020 8964 4225
Email: penfriends@writeaway.demon.co.uk

Asperger United is a quarterly magazine for adolescents with Asperger's written by people with Asperger's. It is free to those with a diagnosis of Asperger's who live in the UK. There is also a penpal section in *Asperger United*. You can contact *Asperger United* through the National Autistic Society or email asp.utd@nas.org.uk

Resources for Adults With ASDs and Carers

General

Community care: A guide for adults with autistic spectrum disorders and their carers
This can be found on the NAS website at www.nas.org.uk/pubs/faqs/qcare.html and explains how to request a community care assessment.

The Care Maze: the law and your rights to community care in Scotland by Patrick McKay

Independent living for adults with autism and Asperger syndrome: A guide for families of people with autistic spectrum disorders by Alan Bicknell

Autism: Preparing for Adulthood by Patricia Howlin

NAS Autism Helpline: 020 7903 3555; or autismhelpline@nas.org.uk

Citizens Advice Bureau: http://www.citizensadvice.org.uk/

Disability Benefits Enquiry Line: 0800 882200

Independent Living 93 Fund
P.O. Box 183
Nottingham NG8 3RD

National Centre for Independent Living
250 Kennington Lane
London SE11 5RD

Employment

Prospects
(NAS-supported employment service)
The National Autistic Society
393 City Road
London EC1V 1NG
Tel: 020 7903 3597
Email: prospects@nas.org.uk

The Association for Supported Employment
Pennine View
Gamblesby
Penrith CA10 1HR
Tel/fax: 01768 881225
Email: afse@onyxnet.co.uk

Placing Assessment and Counselling Teams (PACT): Various leaflets, audiotapes and videos are available from your local PACT office.

Housing
Specialist Information Training Resource Agency for Single Person Housing (SITRA)
3rd Floor, 55 Bandway
London SW8 1SJ
Tel: 020 793 4711
Email: post@sitra.org

Royal Association for Disability and Rehabilitation (RADAR)
12 City Forum
250 City Road
London EC1V 8AF
Tel: 020 7250 3222
Email: radar@radar.org.uk

Social
National Federation of 18-plus
8–10 Church St Chambers
Church St
Newent
Gloucestershire GL18 1PP
Tel: 01531 821210

Circles Network
Pamwell House
160 Pennywell Road
Upper Euston
Bristol BS5 0TX
Tel: 0117 939 3917

Outsiders
PO Box 4ZB
London W1A 4ZB
Tel: 020 7460 2244

Internet sites for adults with ASDs
http://www.paains.org.uk/aspergers/asplinks.htm

http://www.users.dircon.co.uk./~cns/index.html
Provides a forum for students to read first-person accounts, explore employment options and check out study tips.

http://www.udel.edu/bkirby/asperger/

http://www.ani.autistics.org

http://ani.autistics.org/

Websites for the more able individual
http://www.udel.edu/bkirby/asperger/
Online Asperger Syndrome Information & Support (OASIS) website.

http://www.inlv.demon.nl/
Independent Living on the Autism Spectrum website.

http://www.maapservices.org/
Maap Services Inc. is a nonprofit organisation dedicated to providing information and advice to families of more advanced individuals with autism, Asperger's syndrome and pervasive developmental disorder (PDD).

PUBLISHERS

National Autistic Society: Publications catalogue available online or by writing care of NAS Publications at the NAS main London office.

Jessica Kingsley Publishers
116 Pentonville Road
London N1 9JB
Tel: +44 (020) 7833 2307
Fax: +44 (020) 7837 2917
Email: post@jkp.com
Website: http://www.jkp.com/

Future Horizons, Inc.
721 West Abram Street
Arlington, TX 76013, USA
Tel: (1) 800 489 0727
Fax: (1) 817 277 2270
Email: info@futurehorizons-autism.com
Website: www.futurehorizons-autism.com/

PRO-ED, Inc.
700 Shoal Creek Boulevard
Austin
Texas TX 78757-6897, USA
Tel: (1) 800 897 3202
Fax: (1) 800 397 7633
Website: http://www.proedinc.com/

Woodbine House
6510 Bells Mill Rd.
Bethesda, MD 20817, USA
Tel: (1) 301 897 3570
(1) 800 843 7323
Fax: (1) 301 897 5838
Website: http://www.woodbinehouse.com/

Bibliography

Aarons, M., Gittens, T., *Autism, A Social Skills Approach for Children and Adolescents*.

Aarons, M., Gittens, T., *An Integrated Approach to Social Communication Problems*.

Advisory Centre for Education. (2002), *Special Education Handbook: The law on children with special educational needs*, 8th edition. London: Advisory Centre for Education.

Allison, H.G. (2001), *Support for the Bereaved and the Dying in Services for Adults with Autistic Spectrum Disorders – A guide for managers and service staff*. London: The National Autistic Society.

What's Next? Moving on from diagnosis. London: The National Autistic Society.

All-Party Parliamentary Group on Primary Care and Public Health (2000), *Conclusions on MMR vaccine safety*.

Allen, A., 'The Not So Crackpot Autism Theory'. *NY Times* 8 November 2002.

American Psychiatric Association (1994), 'Disorders Diagnosed in Childhood: Autism Disorder – DSM-IV Criteria'. Psychologynet Website: http://www.psychologynet. org/autism.html (28 January 2002).

Anderson, W., Chitwood, S., Hayden, D. (1997), *Negotiating the Special Education Maze: A Guide for Parents and Teachers*. Bethesda, MD: Woodbine House.

Aston, M. C. (2001), *The Other Half of Asperger Syndrome: A guide to living in an intimate relationship with a partner who has Asperger syndrome*. London: The National Autistic Society.

Attwood, T. (1998), *Asperger's Syndrome: a Guide for Parents and Professionals*. London: Jessica Kingsley Publishers Ltd.

Attwood, T. (2002), *Why Does Chris Do That?*. London: The National Autistic Society.

Autism Research Institute, 'Autism Research Review International'. Bernard Rimland, PhD (editor), vol 14, no 3. San Diego, CA: Autism Research Institute.

Autism Research Institute (2002), 'Defeat Autism Now! 2002, Conference Presentations Book'. San Diego, CA: Autism Research Institute.

Autism Research Institute (May 2001), 'Mercury Detoxification Consensus Group Position Paper'. Autism Research Institute Website: http://www.autism.com/ ari/mercury/consensus.html (14 January 2003).

Autism Research Unit, 'Descriptions of Common Vaccines Used'. Autism Research Unit Website: http://osiris.sunderland.ac.uk/autism/vaccine2.html (18 January 2003).

Autism Treatment Center of America, 'How Do the Son-Rise Program Profiles and Techniques Benefit Children with Special Needs?' Son-Rise Organization Website: http://www.son-rise.org/ (9 December 2002).

Baker, B., Brightman, A. (1997), *Steps to Independence: Teaching Everyday Skills to Children with Special Needs*. Baltimore, MD: Paul H. Brookes Publishing Co.

Barnard, J., Broach S., Potter, D., Prior, D. (2002), 'Survey: Autism in Schools, Crisis or Challenge?'. London: The National Autistic Society.

Barnard, J., Harvey, V., Potter, D., Prior, A. (2001), *Ignored or ineligible: The reality for adults with autism spectrum disorders –The National Autistic Society report for Autism Awareness Week 2001*. London: The National Autistic Society.

Barnard, J., Prior, A., Potter, D., (2000), *Inclusion and Autism: Is it Working? 1000 examples of inclusion in education and adult life from the National Autistic Society's members*. London: The National Autistic Society.

Baron-Cohen, S. (1995), 'Mindblindness'. Cambridge, Mass: MIT Press

Bashe, P.R., Kirby, B.L. (2001), *The Oasis Guide to Asperger Syndrome: Advice, Support, Insight, and Inspiration*. New York: Crown Publishers.

Becker, W.C. (1971), *Parents are Teachers: A Child Management Program*. Champaign, IL: Research Press.

Behavioral Intervention Associatio, 'Exploring Treatment Options'. Behavioral Intervention Association Website: http://bia4autism.org/ques3.php (7 December 2002).

Behavioral Intervention Association, 'Family Questions'. Behavioral Intervention Association Website: http://www.bia4autism.org/ques2.php (7 December 2002).

Behavioral Intervention Association, 'Questions to Ask Providers'. Behavioral Intervention Association Website: http://www.bia4autism.org/ques6.php (7 December 2002).

Berkshire Autistic Society, *Parents Supporting Parents*. October 2002, 1 – 14.

Berkshire Autistic Society (2002), *Fact File Two: Information on subjects including benefits, education, leisure and family support*. Berkshire: Berkshire Autistic Society.

Bernard, S., Enayati, A., Redwood, L., Roger, H., Binstock, T., 'Autism: A Novel Form of Mercury Poisoning'. Autism Research Institute Website: http://www.autism.com/ari/mercury.html (22 January 2003).

Bicknell, A. (1999), *Independent living for adults with autism and Asperger syndrome: A guide for families of people with autistic spectrum disorders*. London: The National Autistic Society.

Bishop, B. (2003), *My Friend With Autism*. Arlington, TX: Future Horizons.

Bleach, F. (2001), *Everybody is Different: A book for young people who have brothers or sisters with autism*. London: The National Autistic Society.

Bliss, E.V. (2000), *Recording Behavior*. London: The National Autistic Society.

Bliss, E.V. (2001), *Understanding Difficult Behavior*. London: The National Autistic Society.

Bolton, P., McGuire, M., Whitehead, S. (2001), *A Life in the Community . . . Supporting adults with autism and other developmental disorders whose needs are challenging*. University of Cambridge:

Bondy, A., Frost, L. (2002), *A Picture's Worth: PECS and other Visual Communication Strategies I Autism*. Bethesda, MD: Woodbine House.

Boyd, R.S. (2002), 'The Epidemiology of Autism In California'. UC Davis Mind Institute Study.

California Health and Human Services (1999), *Changes in the Population of Persons with Autism and Pervasive Developmental Disorders in California's Developmental Services System: 1987–1998*. Department of Developmental Services: Report to the Legislature.

Calman, K., 'MMR Vaccine is Not Linked to Crohn's Disease or Autism: conclusion of an expert scientific seminar; March 24, 1998'. Autism Research Unit Website: http://osiris.sunderland.ac.uk/autism/vaccine.html (18 January 2003).

CAN Consensus Group, 'Autism Screening and Diagnostic Evaluation: CAN Consensus Statement by the CAN Consensus Group'. Cure Autism Now Website: http://www.cureautismnow.org/aboutcan/consensu.cfm (30 October 2002).

Cave, S., Mitchell, D. *What Your Doctor may not Tell You about Children's Vaccinations*. Warner Books.

Chassman, M. (1999), *One on One: working with Low Functioning Children with Autism and Other Developmental Disabilites*.Verona, WI: IEP Resources Publication.

Claiborne Park, C. (1967), *The Siege: A Family's Journey into the World of an Autistic Child*. New York: Little, Brown and Company.

Claiborne Park, C. (2001), *Exiting Nirvana: A Daughter's Life with Autism*. New York: Little, Brown and Co.

Collier, V. (2002), 'Raising teenagers with autism'. Advocate: 35, 18–24.

Communication (the magazine of the National Autistic Society), Autumn 2002, 36: 3.

Crook, W. (1986), *The Yeast Connection*. Vintage Books.

Cure Autism Now! (2003), 'Cure Autism Now Science Watch'. Cure Autism Now! Website: http://www.canfoundation.org/sciwatch/sciwatch.cfm (24 January 2003).

Davies, J., *Able Autistic Children: Children with Asperger's Syndrome: A Booklet for Brothers and Sisters*. Child Development Research Unit University of Nottingham.

Davies, J., *Children with Autism: A Booklet for Brothers and Sisters*. Child Development Research Unit: University of Nottingham.

Davis, B. (2001), *Breaking Autism's Barriers: A Father's Story*. London: Jessica Kingsley Publishers Ltd. Reproduced with the permission of Jessica Kingsley Publishers.

Davis, B., Goldband Schunick, W. (2002), *Dangerous Encounters: Avoiding Perilous Situations with Autism*. London: Jessica Kingsley Publishers Ltd.

Defeat Autism Now! (DAN!) (2002), *Fall DAN! 2002 Conference: October 25-27*. San Diego, CA: Autism Research Institute.

Department for Education and Employment (2000), 'Quinquennial Review of the Special Needs Tribunal: Prior Options Report'. London: Crown copyright.

Department for Education and Skills: Autism Working Group (2002), *Autism Spectrum Disorders: Good Practice Guidance: Pointers to Good Guidance*. Nottingham: DfES Publications.

Department for Education and Skills: Autism Working Group (2002), *Autism Spectrum Disorders: Good Practice Guidance: Guidance on Autistic Spectrum Disorders*. Nottingham: DfES Publications.

Donaldson, L., Smith, J., Mullally, S. (15 October 2001), *Current Vaccine and Immunization Issues*. Department of Health: from the Chief Medical Officer, the Chief Nursing Officer and the Chief Pharmaceutical Officer.

Edelson, M. (23 March 2003), *Theory of Mind*. Center for the Study of Autism, Salem, Oregon http://www.autism.org/mind.html

Edelson, S., Rimland, B., *The efficacy of auditory integration training: Summaries and critiques of 28 report (January 1993 – May 2001)*. San Diego: Autism Research Institute.

Edgar, J. (1999), *Love, Hope and Autism*. London: The National Autistic Society.

Falvey M.A. (1989), *Community-Based Curriculum: Instructional Strategies for Students with Severe Handicaps*. Baltimore, MD: Paul H. Brookes Publishing Co.

'Famous people with Autistic Traits; Fictional, real, historical and contemporary celebrities', Geocities website: http://www.geocities.com/WestHollywood/Stonewall/4502/famousac.html (20 March 2002).

Fombonne, E. (2003), 'The Prevalence of Autism'. JAMA, 289,87–89.

Fowler, J., Evans, E. (2002), *A Guide to the Education Act 2002*. London: Advisory Centre for Education and the Education Network.

Friend, M. (1997), 'Educational Partnerships through Effective Communication: Workshop for North County CAC March 10'.

Frith, U. (1989), 'How Autism Was First Recognized'. AMA website: http://www.ama.org.br/autism-history.html (17 January 2002).

Goleman, D., Boyatzis, R., McKee, A. (2002), *Primal Leadership: Realizing the Power of Emotional Intelligence*. Boston: Harvard Business School Press.

Goleman, D. (1998), 'What Makes a Leader?' *Harvard Business Review*, November–December, 93-102.

Grandin, T. (1996), 'Making the Transition from the World of School into the World of Work'. Center for the Study of Autism website: http://www.autism.org/temple/transition.html (10 February 2003).

Grandin, T. (1995), *Thinking in Pictures and Other Reports from My Life with Autism*. New York: Bantam Doubleday Dell Publishing Group, Inc.

Grandin, T. (1998), 'An Inside View of Autism'. Center for the Study of Autism website: http://www.autism.org/temple/inside.html (14 November 2002).

Grandin, T. (1999), 'Choosing the Right Job for People with Autism or Asperger's Syndrome'. Center for the Study of Autism website: http://www.autism.org/temple/jobs.html (14 November 2002).

Grandin, T. (2000), 'My Experiences with Visual Thinking Sensory Problems and Communication Difficulties'. Center for the study of Autism website: http://www.autism.org/temple/visual.html (14 November 2002).

Grandin, T. (2002), 'Teaching Tips for Children and Adults with Autism'. Center for the Study of Autism website: http://www.autism.org/temple/tips.html (10 February 2003).

Grandin, T., 'Evaluating the Effects of Medication'. Center for the Study of Autism website: http://www.autism.org/temple/meds.html (13 February 2003).

Grandin, T., Scariano, M.M. (1986), *Emergence: Labeled Autistic*. Novato, CA: Arena Press.

Gray, C. (1993), *The Original Social Story Book*, Arlington, TX: Future Horizons.

Gray, C. (1994), *The New Social Story Book: Illustrated Edition*. Jenison, Michigan: Jenison High School.

Gray, C. *Comic Strip Conversations: Colorful Illustrated Interactions with Students with Autism and Related Disorders*.

Greenspan, S. I., Wieder, S. (1998), *The Child with Special Needs: Encouraging Intellectual and Emotional Growth*. Reading, Mass: Perseus Books.

Gutstein, S.E. (2001), *Autism/Asperger's: Solving the Relationship Puzzle*. Arlington, TX: Future Horizons.

Haines, G. 'Vladimir Nabokov'. Internet Obituary Network website: http://obits.com/nabakov.html (20 March 2002).

Hall, K. (1988), *Asperger Syndrome: The Universe and Everything*. London: Jessica Kingsley Publishers Ltd.

Hamilton, L.M. (2000), *Facing Autism: Giving Parents Reasons for Hope and Guidance for Help*. Colorado Springs, CO: Waterbrook Press.

Hammer, E. (1996), 'Anticipatory Guidance for Parents of Children with Disabilities: What happens to Families When a Child Has Chronic Problems?'. Website: http://www.winfssi.com/Anticipatory.html (8 September 2002).

Harris, S.L. (1994), *Topics in Autism: Siblings of Children with Autism: A Guide for Families*. Bethesda, MD: Woodbine House.

Harris, S. (1994), *Siblings of Children with Autism: A Guide for Families*. Woodbine House.

Health and Community Care Committee (2001), 'Report on Petition PE 145 calling for an inquiry into issues surrounding the alleged relationship between the combined Measles Mumps and Rubella Vaccine and Autism'. Health and Community Care Committee: 8th Report. Scottish Parliamentary Copyright material is reproduced with the permission of the Queen's Printer for Scotland on behalf of the Scottish Parliamentary Corporate Body.

Heflin, J., Simpson, R. (1998), 'Interventions for children and youth with autism: prudent choices in a world of exaggerated claims and empty promises. Part I: Intervention and Treatment Option Review'. *Focus on Autism and Other Developmental Disabilities*, 13,194–211.

Helps, S., Newsom-Davis, I.C., Callias, M. (1999), *Autism: The Teacher's View*. London: The National Autistic Society.

Hersey, J. (1998), *Why Can't my Child Behave? Why Can't She Cope? Why Can't He Learn?*. Jane Hersey.

Hesmondhalgh, M., Breakey, C. (2001), *Access and Inclusion for Children with Autistic Spectrum Disorders: Let Me In*. London: Jessica Kingsley Publishers Ltd.

High Performance/Organizational Effectiveness Unit, *Effective Meeting Guidelines*. San Diego: Office of the Deputy Superintendent San Diego City Schools.

Holmes, A. (2000), 'Autism Treatment: Chelation of Mercury for the Treatment of Autism'. Healing Arts website: http://www.healing-arts.org/children/holmes/html (22 January 2003).

Holmes, D.L. (1998), *Autism Through the Lifespan: The Eden Model*. Bethesda, MD: Woodbine House.

Hoopmann, K. (2001), *Of Mice and Aliens: An Asperger Adventure*. London: Jessica Kingsley Publishers Ltd.

Howlin, P. (1997), *Autism: Preparing for Adulthood*. London: Routledge.

Howlin, P., Baron-Cohen, S. (1998), *Teaching Children with Autism to Mindread: A Practical Guide for Teachers and Parents*. London: John Wiley and Son, Ltd.

Immunization Safety Review Committee (2001), 'Measles-Mumps-Rubella Vaccine and Autism'. *Institute of Medicine Review*. Washington, D.C.: the National Academy of Sciences, courtesy of the National Academies Press.

Ives, M. (1999), *What is Asperger Syndrome, and How Will it Affect Me? A Guide for Young People*. London: The National Autistic Society.

Jackson, Luke, Brenton, M. (2001), *A User Guide to the GF/CF Diet for Autism, Asperger Syndrome and AD/HD*. London: Jessica Kingsley Publishers Ltd.

Jackson, Luke (2002), *Freaks, Geeks and Asperger Syndrome: A User Guide to Adolescence*. London: Jessica Kingsley Publishers Ltd. Reproduced with the permission of Jessica Kingsley Publishers.

Kaufman, B.N. (1995), *Son-Rise and Son-Rise: the Miracle Continues*. Novato, CA: HJ Kramer.

Klein, F. (2001), 'Autistic Advocacy'. Frank Klein website: http://home.att.net/ ~ascaris1/index.html (8 September 2002).

Kranowitz, C.S. (1998), *The Out-of-Synch Child*. New York: Berkeley Publishing.

Kubler-Ross, E. (1997), *On Death and Dying: What the Dying Have to Teach Doctors, Nurses, Clergy and Their Own Families*. New York: Scribner Publishing.

Leaf, R., McEachin, J. (1999), *Behavioural Treatment of Autism*.

Lewis, L. (1998), *Special Diets for Special Kids*. Arlington, TX: Future Horizons.

Lovaas, O.I. (1981), *Teaching Developmentally Disabled Children: The ME Book*. Austin, TX: Pro-ed.

McCandless, J. (2003), *Children with Starving Brains: A Medical Treatment Guide for Autism Spectrum Disorder*. Bramble Co.

McGill-Smith, P. (1997), 'You are Not Alone: For Parents When They Learn That Their Child Has a Disability'. *News Digest*,20,1-53.

McKay, P. *The Care Maze: The law and your rights to community care in Scotland*. Enable Publishing.

MacDonald, L., 'Using SULP as an Intervention to Teach Social Skills to People with Autistic Spectrum Disorder'. Essay module 2, 1-6.

Marsh, D.B. (1995), *From the Heart: On Being the Mother of a Child with Special Needs*. Bethesda, MD: Woodbine House Publishing.

Maurice, C. (1993), *Let Me Hear Your Voice: A Family's Triumph Over Autism*. New York: Alfred A. Knopf, Inc.

Maurice, C., Green, G., Luce, S. (1996), *Behavioral Intervention for Young Children with Autism. A manual for parents and professionals*. Texas: Pro-ed.

Medical Research Council (December 2001), *MRC Review of Autism Research: Epidemiology and Causes*. London: Medical Research Council.

Mehl-Madrona, L. (2001), 'Origins of the Mercury Controversy'. Healing Arts website: http://www.healing-arts.org/children/vaccines/vaccines-mercury.html (22 January 2003).

Melberg Schwier, K., Hingsburger, D. (2000), *Sexuality: Your Sons and Daughters With Intellectual Disabilities*. Baltimore, MD: Paul H. Brookes Publishing Co.

Mesibov, G. 'What is TEACCH?'. TEACCH website: http://www.teacch.com/ aboutus.html (14 November 2002).

Meyer, D. (1995), *Uncommon Father: Reflections on Raising a Child with a Disability*. Bethesda, MD: Woodbine House Publishing.

Meyer, D. (1997), *Views from Our Shoes: Growing Up With a Brother or Sister With Special Needs*. Bethesda, MD: Woodbine House.

Meyer, R.N. (2001), *Asperger Syndrome Employment Workbook: An Employment Workbook for Adults with Asperger Syndrome*. London: Jessica Kingsley Publishers Ltd.

Mockler Casper, C., Timmons, K., Wagner Brust, B. (2001), *Emotional Intelligence Leader's Guide*. Carlsbad, CA: CRM Learning.

Moss, C.K. 'Ludwig Van Beethoven: A Musical Titan'. Classical Music website: http://classicalmus.hispeed.com/articles/beethoven.html (21 March 2002).

Mukhopadhyay, T.R. (2000), *Beyond the Silence: My Life, the World and Autism*. London: The National Autistic Society.

Myer, Vadassy (1994), *SibShops: Workshops for Siblings of Children with Special Needs.*

Nally, B. (1999), *Diagnosis: reactions in families*. London: The National Autistic Society.

Nally, B. (2000), *Experiences of the Whole Family*. London: The National Autistic Society.

Nally, B., Bliss, E.V. (2000), *Recognizing and Coping with Stress*. London: The National Autistic Society.

The National Autistic Society, The Special Educational Needs and Disability Act 2001 (SENDA), http://www.nas.org.uk/policy/parl/westminster/SENDA.html

Naseef, R.A. (2001), *Special Children Challenged Parents: The Struggles and Rewards of Raising a Child with a Disability*. Baltimore, MD: Paul H. Brookes Publishing Co.

The National Autistic Society (1991), *Approaches to Autism: An easy to use guide to many and varied approaches to autism*. London: The National Autistic Society.

The National Autistic Society (1999), *Opening the Door: a report on diagnosis and assessment of autism and Asperger syndrome based on personal experiences*. London: National Autistic Society.

The National Autistic Society. (1999) *Words Will Really Hurt Me: how to protect your child from bullying; A guide for parents and carers*. London: The National Autistic Society.

The National Autistic Society (2001), *The National Autistic Society: the Autistic Spectrum – A parent's guide*. London: The National Autistic Society.

The National Autistic Society (September 2001), 'Briefing on mercury and autism'. The National Autistic Society Fact Sheet.

The National Autistic Society (2002), *The Autism Handbook*. London: The National Autistic Society.

The National Autistic Society (2002), What is the SPELL approach?'. National Autistic Society Fact Sheets website: http://www.autismni.org/spell.html.

'Neal Halsey Reaffirms Vaccines Do Not Cause Autism'. *NY Times* 14 November 2002.

Newport, J., Newport, M. (2002), *Autism – Asperger's and Sexuality: Puberty and Beyond*. Arlington, TX: Future Horizons Inc.

Newport, J., *Your Life is Not a Label*. Arlington, TX: Future Horizons Inc.

Ogaz, N. (2002), *Buster and the Amazing Daisy: Adventures with Asperger Syndrome*. London: Jessica Kingsley Publishers Ltd.

O'Hare, A. (2002), 'Severing the Link Between MMR and Autism'. The Journal of the Royal College of Physicians of Edinburg, 32,167-169.

O'Neill, J. L. (1999), *Through the Eyes of Aliens: A Book About Autistic People*. London: Jessica Kingsley Publishers Ltd.

Opening The Door: A report on diagnosis and assessment of autism and Asperger syndrome based on personal experience. London: The National Autistic Society (1999).

O'Toole, M., 'Boston Higashi School: Daily Life Therapy'. Parents and Professionals autism website: http: www.autismni.org/bostonhig.html (15 January 2003).

Ott, J. *Health and Light*.

Pangborn, J.B., Baker, S. (2002), *Biomedical Assessment Options for Children with Autism and Related Problems: A Consensus Report of the Defeat Autism Now! (DAN!) Scientific Report*. San Diego, CA: Autism Research Institute.

Parents Helping Parents of Wyoming Inc., 'You are not alone on the emotional roller coaster – when you learn that your child has a disability or special health need'. Parent Information Center Brochure.

Patterson, G.R. (1971), *Families: Applications of Social Learning to Family Life*. Champaign, IL: Research Press.

Pollack, R. (1997), *The Creation of Dr. B: A Biography of Bruno Bettelheim*. New York: Simon and Schuster.

Powell, A. (2002), *Taking responsibility: Good practice guidelines for services – adults with Asperger syndrome*. London: The National Autistic Society.

Powers, M.D. (1989), *Children with Autism: A Parent's Guide*. Bethesda, MD: Woodbine House Inc.

'Questions and Considerations Concerning Services for Young Children with Autism Spectrum Disorder'. Behavioral Intervention Association website: http://www.bia-4autism.org/questions.php (7 December 2002).

Rapp, D. (1996), *Is This Your Child's World? How you can fix the schools and homes that are making your child sick*. New York: Bantam Books.

Rimland, B. (1964), *Infantile Autism: The syndrome and its implications for a Neural Theory of Behavior*. Prentice Hall.

Rimland, B. (1993), 'Plain Talk about PDD and the Diagnosis of Autism'. *Autism Research Review International*, 7, 3.

Rimland, B. (2000), 'The most airtight study in psychiatry? Vitamin B6 in autism'. *Autism Research Review International*, 14, 3-5.

Rimland, B., 'The MMR/Autism Controversy: Should We Believe the IOM?'. Autism Research Institute website: http://www.autism.com/ari/editorials/iom.html (24 January 2003).

Rollens, R. (2003), 'Increases in Autism Diagnosis in California Keep Rising'. FEATNEWS website: http://www.feat.org (21 January 2003).

Rosenberg, M. S. (2000), *Everything You Need to Know; When a Brother or Sister is Autistic*. New York: The Rosen Publishing Group, Inc.

Sacks, O. (1995), *An Anthropologist on Mars: Seven Paradoxical Tales*. New York: Alfred A. Knopf, Inc.

Sainsbury, C. (2000), *Martian in the Playground*. London: The Book Factory.

Satkiewicz-Gayhardt, V., Peerenboom, B., Campbell, R., Belliveau, K. (1997), *Crossing Bridges: A Parent's Perspective on Coping After a Child is Diagnosed with Autism/PDD*. Stratham, NH: Potential Unlimited Publishing.

Schafer, L. (2002), 'Autism – A Hit and Run Epidemic'. California: The Schafer Autism Report.

Schools, Units and Classes: For children with autism and Asperger syndrome. London: The National Autistic Society (1992).

Secretary of State for Health (2001), 'Valuing People: A New Strategy for Learning Disability for the 21st Century', White paper presented to Parliament (March 2001). London: the Stationery Office.

Segar, M. (1997), 'A Survival Guide for People with Asperger Syndrome'. Autism and Computing Organization website: http://www.autismandcomputing.org.uk/marc2.html (18 January 2003).

Semon, B., Kornblum, L. (2002), *Feast Without Yeast*. Wisconsin: Wisconsin Institute of Nutrition.

Seroussi, K. (2002), *Unraveling the Mystery of Pervasive Developmental Disability*. Broadway Books.

Shattock, P., Whiteley, P. (2000), 'The Sunderland Protocol: A logical sequencing of biomedical interventions for the treatment of autism and related disorders'. Autism Research Unit School of Science, University of Sunderland website: http://osiris.sunderland.ac.uk/autism/durham2.html (13 January 2003).

Shattock, P., Whiteley, P., Savery, D. (2002), *Autism as a Metabolic Disorder: Guidelines for Gluten and Casein-free Dietary Intervention*. Autism Research Unit. University of Sunderland.

Shaw, W. (2002), 'Biological Treatment for Autism and PDD': http://www.noamalgam.com/biological treatments.html (18 January 2002).

Shellenberger, S., Williams, M. (1992), *An Introduction to "How Does Your Engine Run": The Alert Program and Self-Regulation*. Albuquerque, NM: Therapy Works, Inc.

Shore, S. (1961), *Beyond the Wall: Personal Experiences with Autism and Asperger's Syndrome*. Shawnee Mission, KS: Autism Asperger Publishing Co.

Shore, S. (2002), 'Dating, Marriage and Autism'. *Advocate*, 35, 24-28.

278 | A<small>UTISM</small> S<small>PECTRUM</small> D<small>ISORDERS</small>

Siegel, B. (1996), *The World of the Autistic Child: Understanding and Treating Autistic Spectrum Disorder.* Oxford: Oxford University Press.

Sinclair, J. 'Don't Mourn For Us'. *Our Voice* newsletter (Autism Network International) 1993, 1, 3.

Slater-Walker, G., Slater-Walker, C. (1988), *An Asperger Marriage.* London: Jessica Kingsley Publishers Ltd.

'Special Educational Needs and Disability Act' (2001). London: Queens Printer of Acts of Parliament. (Crown Copyright 2001).

Stehli, A. (1991), *The Sound of a Miracle.* New York: Avon Books.

Stengle, L. J. (1996), *Laying Community Foundations for Your Child With a Disability: How to Establish Relationships That will Support Your Child after You're Gone.* Bethesda, MD: Woodbine House.

Summer, Donna, *Autism: An Inside Out Approach.* London: Jessica Kingsley Publishers Ltd. Reproduced with the permission of Jessica Kingsley Publishers.

Szatmari, P. (2003), 'The Causes of Autism Spectrum Disorders: Multiple factors have been identified, but a unifying cascade of events is still elusive'. *BMJ*, 326,173-174.

Tantam, D., Prestwood, S. (1999), *A Mind's of One's Own: A guide to the special difficulties and needs of the more able person with autism or Asperger syndrome.* London: The National Autistic Society.

Timetable for Autism: An overview of educating children and young people with autistic spectrum disorders. London: The National Autistic Society (1999).

UK Joint Committee for Vaccination and Immunization, 'The British National Vaccination Schedule'. Fit for Travel website: http://www.fitfortravel.scot. nhs.uk/General/british_national_vaccination.html (22 January 2003).

University of Sunderland, 'Autism and Vaccination'. Autism Research Unit website: http://osiris/sunderland.ac.uk/autism/vaccine.html (18 January 2003).

Vermeulen, P. (2000), *I am Special: Introducing Children and Young People to their Autism Spectrum Disorder.* London: Jessica Kingsley Publishers Ltd.

Wakefield, A. (1998), 'Ileo-colonic Lymponodular Hyperplasia, Non-specific Colitis and Autistic Spectrum Disorder in Children: A New Syndrome?'. Autism Research Unit website: http://osiris.sunderland.ac.uk/autism/vaccine.html (18 January 2003).

Waller, E. (2001), 'Gerontology 130 Working with the Frail: Lesson Twelve Understanding Grief'. Coastline Community College website: http://www.cvc3.org/modelcvc3courses/elliswaller/lesson12.htm (8 September 2002).

Waltz, M. (2002), *Autistic Spectrum Disorders: Understanding the Diagnosis and Getting Help.* Sebastopol, CA: O'Reilly and Associates.

Wehman, P. (2001), *Life Beyond the Classroom: Transition Strategies for Young People with Disabilities.* Baltimore: Paul H. Brookes Publishing Co.

'What is Autism? Genetic Conditions Associated with Autistic Disorder'. Exploring Autism website: http://www.exploringautism.org/autism/evaluation/html (4 November 2002).

Willey, L.H. (1999), *Pretending to be Normal: Living with Asperger's Syndrome.* London: Jessica Kingsley Publishers Ltd. Reproduced with the permission of Jessica Kingsley Publishers.

Willey, L.H. (2001), *Asperger Syndrome in the family: Redefining Normal.* London: Jessica Kingsley Publishers Ltd.

Williams, D. (1988), *Autism: An Inside-Out Approach.* London: Jessica Kingsley Publishers Ltd.

Williams, D. (1992), *Nobody Nowhere.* New York: Times Books.

Williams, D. (1994), *Somebody Somewhere.* London: Transworld Publishers Ltd.

Wing, L., *Asperger Syndrome: A Clinical Account.* London: The National Autistic Society.

Wing, L. (2001), *The Autistic Spectrum.* London: Ulysses Press.

Yeargin-Allsopp, M., Rice, C., Karapurkan, T., Doernberg, N., Boyle, C., Murphy, C. (2003), 'Prevalence of autism in a US metropolitan area'. *JAMA*, 289,49–55.

Index